REFLECTIONS

Preparing for Your Practicum
and Internship

REFLECTIONS
Preparing for Your Practicum and Internship

Mary Bold Ph.D., CFLE
Texas Women's University

Lillian Chenoweth Ph.D.
Texas Women's University

THOMSON

DELMAR LEARNING™   Australia Brazil Canada Mexico Singapore Spain United Kingdom United States

THOMSON

✦

DELMAR LEARNING

Reflections: Preparing for Your Practicum and Internship
Mary Bold, Ph.D., CFLE and Lillian Chenoweth, Ph.D.

Vice President, Career Education Strategic Business Unit:
Dawn Gerrain

Director of Learning Solutions:
John Fedor

Managing Editor:
Robert L. Serenka, Jr.

Acquisitions Editor:
Christopher Shortt

Product Manager:
Philip Mandl

Editorial Assistant:
Alison Archambault

Director of Production:
Wendy A. Troeger

Production Manager:
Mark Bernard

Content Project Manager:
Jeffrey Varecka

Technology Project Manager:
Sandy Charette

Director of Marketing:
Wendy E. Mapstone

Channel Manager:
Kristin McNary

Marketing Coordinator:
Scott A. Chrysler

Marketing Specialist:
Erica S. Conley

Art Director:
Joy Kocsis

Cover Design:
Dan Masucci

Interior Design:
Judi Orozco

Library of Congress Cataloging-in-Publication Data

Bold, Mary, 1952-
  Reflections : preparing for your practicum and internship / Mary Bold, Lillian Chenoweth.
      p. cm.
  Includes bibliographical references and index.
  ISBN-13: 978-1-4180-4083-3
  ISBN-10: 1-4180-4083-5
  1. Internship programs. 2. Practicums. 3. College students—Employment. I. Chenoweth, Lillian Cochran, 1949- II. Title.
  LC1072.I58B65 2008
  378'.013—dc22
                                2007026471

NOTICE TO THE READER

Contents

v

Preface

This book focuses on the student approach to the internship, with strategies intended to maximize the benefits of the field experience for the intern. This purpose is clear and paramount. But this preface permits us to acknowledge the tremendous sharing of the professionals who make the internships happen. We invite the student intern to join us in applauding the patience and cooperation of the mentors who will support their entry into the field: the internship site supervisors and the campus advisors.

Site supervisors benefit pragmatically from the seasonal influx of preprofessionals, through the addition of energy and enthusiasm to their organizations. The benefit that may be more important to the continuance of an intern program is the site professional's intrinsic reward for mentoring preprofessionals and new professionals. Such a reward sustains the site supervisor as each new internship season makes a demand on time and resources of the organization. As professionals in the field, site supervisors see the long-term gain in helping interns learn about practice and begin to develop their own professional identity. Site supervisors appreciate the gain in terms of the intern's need for a first exposure to the field, the organization's interest in developing new professionals, and the profession's need to continue to expand with the next generation of practitioners. The supervisor's own interest in serving as a mentor includes the intrinsic reward of sharing knowledge and modeling professionalism.

Campus advisors serve in roles such as an internship course instructor, academic counselor, and liaisons between the college or university and the community. These campus-based professionals strive to ensure that the intern candidate is well prepared for the move into the community and, often, the employment that follows soon after. Supporting interns does not always mean making the intern's task easier. Indeed, the campus professionals maintain high expectations for intern readiness and for intern performance on the job. When the internship experience is based on rigorous standards, the quality of programs is assured. The authors' support for academic rigor arises from our experience in teaching internship courses and our collaboration with higher education programs demonstrating institutional effectiveness through field placements.

This book's attention to site supervisors and campus advisors is placed in the context of the intern's perspective, which may appear to slight the value of the professionals. It is a context that is apt: just as this book casts the professionals in a supporting role in the background, so do the real professionals reside in that background space. Their patience with preprofessionals and their willingness to serve as mentors is invaluable. In our own institution, these traits are exemplified by the faculty and staff who support our interns.

✳ SUPPLEMENTAL MATERIALS

The CD-ROM that accompanies *Reflections: Preparing for Your Practicum & Internship* contains all of the guided practice forms found in each chapter. Users of the text can print out and complete the guided practice forms as needed.

There is a student Online Companion Website that contains additional material and resources that complement this text, such as the following:

- personal experience stories from graduates and current practicum students
- Webliography for internship/practicum assistance sites
- group interaction projects about becoming a professional
- tips for approaching potential internship/practicum sites
- quiz questions

The Online Companion Website can be accessed at http://www.earlychilded.delmar.com.

✳ ACKNOWLEDGMENTS

We are especially grateful to our colleagues Dr. Karen Petty and Dr. Joyce Armstrong for their encouragement to create a text to assist interns, instructors, and mentors. These master teachers devoted time and energy in outlining what they would like to see in a textbook for the field experience. Their optimism for a book that could serve our own students, as well as others, was instrumental in committing to the long months of writing and editing.

As all manuscripts must, this one relied on good friends for the close reading and critical thinking that finally allows authors to have confidence that the book is finished. Erin Maurer shared with us her talent as a writer and editor, as well as her professional expertise as an advisor to undergraduate students. Holding a master's in family studies, Erin also served as a critical reader of text directed at child and family preprofessionals. We regularly benefit from Erin's talent in organization and presentation, and we treasure her as an esteemed colleague.

Our extended network of friends included Carol Small, often working virtually to prepare files for the manuscript and to interpret our requests for graphics that would illustrate the internship experience. Carol's willingness to make herself available for projects, often with little notice, has been a source of comfort to us many times. Help in composing discussion questions and tailoring language to engage student readers came from Katy Bold and Ellen Chenoweth. Their wisdom as educators belies their short years of experience and their élan inspires us.

Our efforts were guided by an editorial team that saw the value of the book even through its shifts in focus and chapter organization, and even a change in title. Our editors provided feedback through the several drafts of the manuscript, as did the following reviewers with experience in supervising internships. We appreciate all of their support and guidance.

Professor Ruth M. Sasso, Naugatuck Valley Community-Technical College, Waterbury, Connecticut

Dr. Pamela Davis, Henderson State University, Arkadelphia, Arkansas

Judith Lindman, Rochester Community and Technical College, Rochester, Minnesota

Jorja Davis, Blinn College, Bryan, Texas

Dr. Lynn Baynum, Shippensburg University of Pennsylvania, Shippensburg, Pennsylvania

J. Christine Catalani, San Antonio College, San Antonio, Texas

Jill E. Fox, University of Texas at Arlington, Arlington, Texas

Julie Bakerlis, Becker College, Worcester, Massachusetts

~ Mary Bold and Lillian Chenoweth

About the Authors

Mary Bold and Lillian Chenoweth are frequent collaborators in teaching, writing, and presenting. As faculty members at Texas Woman's University, they coordinate programs in family studies for undergraduate and graduate students, as well as contribute to the university's initiatives in distance learning and institutional effectiveness.

Dr. Chenoweth has taught thousands of students in the internship courses that are called Practicum in TWU's Family Studies program, and she also directed the university lab preschool. In her third decade of university service, she continues to develop programs for family field professionals, including a new graduate practicum for working professionals earning the master of science in a wholly on-line program. Dr. Chenoweth holds a Ph.D. in sociology and has developed courses in Family Change and Diversity, Family Financial Counseling, and Qualitative Research Methods.

Dr. Bold has also taught the internship course at TWU (though numbers decidedly fewer than thousands) and bases her interest in experiential education on her background as a parenting educator in the field. Through curriculum writing and collaboration with a community parenting center and a local community college's Child Development program, Dr. Bold works to identify how partnerships strengthen a college program. Through the assessment of students' learning, program outcomes can be continuously improved, to the benefit of the student, institution, community, and society. Dr. Bold holds a Ph.D. in family studies and the Certified Family Life Educator (CFLE) credential. She has developed courses in Academic Life & Scholarship and Effective On-line Education, as well as translated traditional campus family studies classes to an on-line format for delivery over the Internet.

As cofacilitators, Drs. Bold and Chenoweth conduct workshops nationally on assessment and distance learning. They are frequent presenters at national technology conferences as well as state and national family field conferences. Their recognition in distance learning includes an award from the Blackboard online learning management system for excellence in on-line course design.

CHAPTER 1

Becoming a Professional

Major Points in This Chapter:

Introduction
Approaching the Internship
Defining Internship
Who Benefits from This Opportunity?
What Are the Benefits of an Internship?
When Is the Optimum Time?
Are You Ready for the Internship?
How to Use This Book

CASE STUDY: Marta is enjoying an end-of-semester party with her friends and family. It seems to Marta that everyone is bombarding her with questions about next semester. What is this course she will be taking off campus? Where will she be? Why is she working for free? While Marta has some apprehension about approaching the internship (she isn't even sure whether to call it an internship or practicum or field experience), she tries to explain to her friends. "I'll get to have hands-on experience instead of just listening to my teacher talk about what happens." She patiently describes the observation process she has gone through for site selection, choosing a site that will match her interests and further her career goals. Her friend, Elena, is curious about how much Marta will be making. "Well, I won't really get a salary; I'll just get the experience and get my foot in the door. Maybe meeting people there will help me get a job later. I'm also hoping that I'll learn whether or not I would want to work there." Marta thinks this is the right time for her to have this capstone experience.

✳ INTRODUCTION

The internship is unlike any other course in your degree plan. It is the course that moves you out of the classroom and into the community. In other classes you might have been assigned a short field experience that was essentially an observation assignment. The internship takes you to the field not only as an observer but also as a participant. It is this activity that sets the internship apart and earns the usual description of **capstone** course.

> ✳ **capstone**
>
> Culminating event or decisive moment; the internship or practicum is often described as a capstone course, typically meaning it is a concluding course or represents the final stage of undergraduate education.

The internship is also the most diverse course in that it reflects as many field locations and purposes as there are students in the class. It is the class that honors *your* goal as its own course objective. It may even permit you to earn money (in a paid internship) or gain experience that may lead directly to employment or a higher starting salary because you participated in an internship. In a diverse class, internships could range from pre-K teaching assignments to juvenile detention centers to museum docent training. A class could reflect paid internships at businesses, educational stipends for a research experience, and nonpaid assignments. The mix of purposes and types of internships allows peers to compare notes about their experiences and, especially if a degree program requires two semesters of internship, make informed choices about the future.

Ideally, the internship launches you in your chosen profession. What does it mean to become a professional? (See Table 1-1.) Certainly one way to answer that is to describe the core role of the person, such as *teaches children*, or *supervises family life educators*, or *counsels youth offenders*. Another way to answer is to cite the person's credentials, such as *Montessori-trained*, or *certified family life educator*, or *state-certified teacher*. All of these terms indicate that a person has a professional identity, and it is likely that you will adopt such titles early in your career. But does the gaining of the titles and certifications make you a professional? While they may describe your qualifications, they do not ensure the professional identity. Becoming a professional means assuming a self-identity that is different from your current identity of student. It's a process that is as individual as personality. No two people progress in the same way, and even if they share professional credentials, they have their own professional identities.

Becoming a professional, then, implies development (change across time) and self-awareness (because the process affects self-identity). Your internship experience is a starting point and sometimes a prod: you will be in an environment that requires thinking like a professional, and so a cognitive change will begin. You may recognize turning points in your thinking and abilities, but much of the change will be gradual. At some point—perhaps during the internship or perhaps later—you will identify yourself as a professional.

✳ APPROACHING THE INTERNSHIP

How you approach the internship will be unique. Your dreams about learning, fun, work, and family are different from anyone else's. Differences among people are often described in terms of perception, and you can make an analogy to how people perceive shapes in clouds. One person sees a face outlined

Table 1-1 What Distinguishes a Professional from a Student?

A professional . . . works independently much of the time, without oversight or direct supervision.

A professional . . . is informed about current research and its relevance.

A professional . . . is caring and committed, placing priority on providing service.

A professional . . . practices ethical treatment of families and children.

A professional . . . accepts responsibility for decisions and actions.

A professional . . . separates personal beliefs from agency practices.

A professional . . . distinguishes between personal experience and research findings.

A professional . . . models and mentors.

A professional . . . advocates for families.

A professional . . . is committed to ongoing personal growth and development.

in a cloud, while the next person interprets the same shape as a ship. A cloud shape of a mountain range may be obvious to one viewer, but another person sees ocean waves. And if the clouds are watched for a span of time—even just a few minutes—perception by a single viewer will change. Thus, one's perception of clouds is unique (different from anyone else's perception) and always evolving (changing due to movement of the clouds). Viewing the future can be described the same way: unique and evolving.

Perception may be driven by your recent experiences but also may reflect things you want to do or want to see. For one student entering the internship, thinking about the future is exciting and exhilarating. For another student, the future is scary. To be sure, most people are somewhere in between, but that space is very wide. That's why your perception of the future is likely to be different from your peer's or friend's or family member's perception. For some people, the future is unimaginable—unknown and unknowable. Just as clouds may appear without recognizable shape, the future may loom as a strange and distant unknown.

The unknown future may not be so daunting if you consider that in many environments not everything is visible at all times. You have been in this situation before: when you entered college, you likely did not have an overview of your entire course of study. You had to focus on the immediate tasks at hand: getting registered, adjusting to campus life, learning how to interact with professors, and (sometimes) just surviving the semester. With time, you were able to see more of the whole: you understood the context for the individual courses, and you could literally take in more information about the campus. The campus setting may have been stable, but your perception changed as you came to know the environment. Your perception of yourself as part of the environment also changed. In effect, your role as student developed, and you probably took on more roles: as member of a student government, as staffer on a publication, or as officer in an organization.

The internship can help you visualize yourself in different settings as well as different roles. The internship allows you to think in terms of potential. The context of your current daily life impacts what you can see of the future. In the college classroom, you may have taken the safe route, knowing what the teacher wanted and not going beyond that. In the internship, you will not necessarily know what route is safe and what route is risky. While your objective as a student may have been to avoid risk, the field experience is the setting in which people are willing to take a risk because there is much to be gained. The process of risk taking is vital to making an investment in yourself.

Risk taking involves testing what you and others have assumed to be true about you. The people around you may have frequently commented, "You're so good with children." You cannot know the validity of that until you actually work directly with children day after day. Parents, professors, advisors, and trusted friends have provided guidance, but self-knowledge is the critical assessment at this point in your career path. Self-knowledge involves recognizing your own traits and knowing what is right for you. Gaining self-knowledge is a lifelong process; frequently, it occurs indirectly, as you focus on tasks and your relationships with other people. The internship experience offers the opportunity to explore directly, with focus on self.

Immersed in that exploration, you are engaged in experiential learning, which is the hallmark of the internship or practicum. The intern must shift from being told what to do and how to do it to a new philosophy: expecting yourself to know or figure out what to do. In the classroom, seeking information or guidance was usually straightforward: ask the teacher. In the field, seeking information may mean first figuring out all potential sources of information, then evaluating them, and then collecting data that may lead to starting the

---

Famous Interns

What do Sigourney Weaver, Oprah Winfrey, Spike Lee, and Steven Bochco have in common? They were all interns. These celebrities' intern titles turned up in a search of biographies on the Internet. Your own search may uncover more!

Madeleine Albright at *The Denver Post*

Carl Bernstein at *The Washington Star*

Steven Bochco at Universal Studios

Dick Clark at WRUN-AM radio mailroom in Utica, New York

Patrick Ewing, summer at U.S. Senate Finance Committee

Jodie Foster, summer intern at *Esquire* magazine

Bill Gates, before going to college, as a U.S. Congressional page

Donna Karan with designer Anne Klein

Matt Lauer at WOWK-TV in West Virginia

Spike Lee at Columbia Pictures

Rob Reiner at regional theatre on the East Coast

Brooke Shields at the San Diego Zoo as a high school intern

Kiefer Sutherland at Williamstown Theatre Festival

Mike Wallace at *Brookline Citizen*

Sigourney Weaver at Williamstown Theatre Festival

Oprah Winfrey, during sophomore year, at WTVF-TV in Nashville, Tennessee

process all over again. The student approaching the internship is capable of making this transition from classroom to field, but may feel uneasy about the differences between the two settings.

✳ DEFINING INTERNSHIP

The **internship** represents a bridge across theory, research, and practice (see Table 1-2). Each of these elements may have been learned separately, but the intern experience brings them together. The internship synthesizes lessons from academic subject matter, student background and experiences, and client contact in the field. The synthesis is not an immediate convergence of these areas. In fact, a single semester of an internship may produce only a partial synthesis. But the intern will see enough change in his or her own thinking to be able to imagine the effect over a longer time. Professors on campus and supervisors at the sites have the benefit of seeing the big picture that develops from interaction over years. The synthesis is most obvious when a school and site have cooperated for several years and have worked together to supervise many students. The professionals at both ends of the bridge benefit just as much as the student interns. Maintenance of the campus-community partnerships encourages continuous improvement of academic programs and the appropriate preparation of students for the workplace.

> **internship**
> Structured and hands-on student activities across weeks or months, synthesizing content knowledge, observation, and field experience; also known as practicum or field experience.

The internship also represents service learning—meaningful contribution to the community as learning takes place. Following the Hurricane Katrina disaster in New Orleans, hundreds of college students found new meaning in citizenship as they volunteered in rebuilding the city and its human services. Service learning involves giving back to the community to mutual benefit of students and residents. In service learning, service and learning are equal goals. For child and family professionals, this pairing is not unusual. Internships frequently center on the organizations whose missions focus on improving the quality of life for families. Especially nonprofit organizations attract interns who want to work directly with children and families in need of help.

The joint benefits for intern and the site are an example of the social context of learning. The scaffolding concept based on the work of Vygotsky describes the process of individual problem solving, but emphasizes that individual cognition advances with consultation and concomitant learning with other people. Scaffolding refers to a learner having the assistance (or even just availability) of higher skilled people in the vicinity or near environment. Easily accessible resources may include an expert available by texting or instant messaging as well as an expert down the hall. Some related concepts are mentoring, tutoring, and learning through social interaction. Joint learning is at the heart of collaborative group work or learning pods in schools. Even the most independent learner at some time benefits from collaborative

Table 1-2 **Practicum Bridges All Three**		
Theory *Why*	**Research** *What, How*	**Practice** *How-to*
The why behind human behavior	How humans behave	How to address human behavior

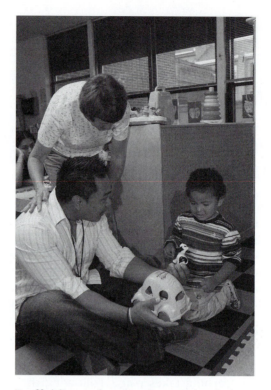

Scaffolding refers to a learner having the assistance or availability of higher skilled people in the vicinity or near environment.

learning environments. Shared tasks, both in school and on the job, reflect the interaction that promotes sound problem solving. In fact, tasks directly tied to problem solving have been shown to produce highest learning.

The internship experience provides the combination of individual reflection and shared learning, as well as mentoring, as extra benefits that on-the-job training by itself does not provide. As you undergo site training, you will likely experience many of the same activities that a new employee does. But you will have help in processing the new information, and you will not be expected to master it immediately. By contrast, the regular employee has less room for error and is expected to adopt all the new standards at once. As the intern enters the worksite, there's plenty of support for the bridging of classroom to workplace.

In some programs, the internship is intended to be a hands-on experiential education. In another field, it may be an observation of practice. (Especially in health-related internships, observation may be the primary activity.) The pre-professional experience of the internship features a protective environment that promotes exposure and learning. This book explores all these features of the field experience, with special attention to selecting the site and making adjustments to a workplace. Potential sites range from close community to international opportunities. This range of geography requires coordination of actions and expectations of students and schools as site approvals are made and logistics are negotiated for establishing internship agreements.

The advancement through levels of field experience is often described as culminating in an internship. A first level, for example, may be a class or

Table 1-3 **Variations in Field Experience Schedules**	
Prepracticum semester Practicum semester	Practicum 1 semester Practicum 2 semester
Pre-internship Internship I Internship II	Courses with lab hours (or observation hours) Internship

assignment called **prepracticum**. Not all programs divide the experience into levels, however. Across schools, the opportunity is known variously as field experience, practicum, and internship. Too, some programs distinguish between Semester 1 and Semester 2 (see Table 1-3). Add to this variety the many ways that placement sites organize internships, and we can conclude that there is no single best way to conduct the experience.

There is one common feature to internships and practica: the field experience is structured across time. Intern work is typically reflected in a log of hours, ideally over a dozen or more weeks. A span of months is ideal because we humans learn about an environment slowly. Perhaps an internship requirement of 120 hours (for example) could be accomplished in twelve 10-hour days or four weeks of five-hour days. But the span of time of a dozen days or even several weeks would not allow learning of the culture of the site and probably wouldn't permit a range of activities. Rather, the span of months (even though the number of hours of interning might be the same 120) permits observation over time and change (by the intern) over time. Change over time is the primary definition of development, and a high-quality internship permits development by the intern. Development will occur in terms of

- skills, either building a new skill set or refining skills introduced in the college classroom.
- attitude, which may include self-awareness of one's readiness for employment.
- thinking, which may include new understanding of a profession that was not possible from the vantage point of college classroom.

From the perspective of what occurs at the internship site, a longer span of time for the experience permits exposure to and involvement in not only more activities but also tracking of clients' experience. For example, following the course of treatment for a child in early childhood intervention (ECI) typically requires months in order to see change. In a school setting, a semester's view (about four months) allows observation of not just a single child's development but also the classroom dynamic changing from the first day of school to more routine days as the children become a cohesive group. Both of these internship experiences would be diminished if the span of intern hours were accomplished in four weeks instead of four months.

Just as we do not assume there is a single best way to conduct the experience, we do not assume a single best number of hours. Whether 120 or 240 or 400, the hours should be spent in high-quality activities. Some internships resemble full-time jobs (for example, 10 weeks in summer with a time commitment of 40 hours per week). Depending on the setting, the experience may be literally "on the job," such as an internship at *Parenting* magazine in New York

✳ **prepracticum**

The preparatory work prior to a practicum placement that facilitates exploring sites and placement options. In some academic programs, prepracticum is a semester course.

In a school setting, a semester's view allows observation of not just a single child's development but the classroom dynamic changing as the children become a cohesive group.

City. Or it may be a mix of study and research with dorm living on a campus, such as a stipend-supported REU (research experience for undergraduates). An internship with an education focus may combine college course work with observation in a public school classroom. Some college courses provide a glimpse of such internships through shorter field observation requirements such as a 15-hour field requirement. Whether short and introductory or long and in-depth, the field experience or internship can be valuable in meeting student objectives. As Table 1-4 shows, the number of hours may be related to the end result. The spread of hours over time is as important as the total number of hours.

Characteristics of Internship

Because of the wide variety of field experiences, there is not a list of characteristics common to all internships. Still, general characteristics can be assumed; most internships will feature at least some of these traits to some degree.

The internship is *self-directed*. Within the boundaries of the organization or agency, the intern has an opportunity to decide how to get the job done and even how to approach problems. For example, the intern in a preschool classroom does not expect a script for conversations with young children. Rather, the intern

Table 1-4 **Development over a Field Experience of 120 Hours**	
Quality of Development of Skills and Professionalism	**Schedule of 120 hours**
High quality	10 hours/week for 12 weeks
Moderate quality	15 hours/week for 8 weeks
Low quality	40 hours/week for 3 weeks

expects to listen to the children and respond appropriately. Problem solving in the preschool classroom is a dynamic process that may involve action and reaction between children, the intern, the teacher, the preschool director, and the parents. Creative solutions can emerge from any combination of those people interacting. By contrast, problem solving for the same situation in the college classroom depends on discussion and solutions that are largely prescribed, often with expectation of just one or two correct ways to reach a solution. Self-direction does not begin on the first day of the internship, of course. The intern has the support and guidance of mentors to become self-directed, and the process is expected to take weeks or months.

The internship is *self-initiated*. Even from the start, when the choice of internship location is made, the process is initiated by the student. Throughout the internship, there are many opportunities to demonstrate that you are a self-starter. In the college classroom, self-initiative may be less valued and sometimes even prohibited. Many interns hold back at first in their new work environments. With time, and especially through observing professionals on the job, the intern can determine if taking the initiative is acceptable. Offering an idea is a good start, and the most cautious intern may choose to do that privately with a mentor in the workplace (instead of in a large staff meeting). The mentor's reaction to the idea will encourage the intern to look for other ways to contribute. A further example of being self-initiated would be seeking tasks at the worksite rather than waiting to be instructed. After a little time onsite, you will become familiar with what needs to be done and be able to start tasks on your own or to see things that need to be done without being told. For example, an intern who knows that tables and chairs need to be arranged for the regular weekly staff meeting may show initiative by arriving at the meeting space 10 minutes early to make that rearrangement. At a more complex level, self-initiation might be reflected by the intern's ability to respond to a client's question without asking for a mentor's guidance.

The internship is *experiential*. Real-world activity at the site produces understanding through the intern's own perspective; learning is highly individual. By contrast, understanding in the college classroom comes primarily through a planned curriculum that is meant to be standardized for all learners. Experiential learning is necessarily tied to a real-world environment and little standardization exists. Even for two interns at the same site, trained in the same way, the experiential learning will differ.

The internship involves students' *self-developed objectives.* Goal setting is a feature of the internship and may be a required part of the internship class. The student is the author of the goals and objectives. By contrast, instructors and administrators write the objectives of traditional courses. In the case of the practicum or internship class, the official course objectives may actually specify that students will develop their own objectives (or goals). Instructors expect to guide students in writing objectives, and the instructors may approve and grade the objectives, but the focus of the assignment is on students' expectations for their own learning. For a first-time intern, this focus is challenging. The instructor provides guidance so that realistic expectations are expressed in the objectives.

The internship features students' *individual and self-chosen outcomes.* In college courses, learning outcomes are typically outlined by instructors and administrators and may serve to measure institutional effectiveness. An outcome is the actual result of a course (as opposed to a course goal or objective, which is more likely to describe the learning expected to take place). For the internship, an outcome may be that the student is prepared for success in the workplace. Because of the wide variety of settings and professions represented in an internship class, the outcomes are individual and self-chosen. One way that a sponsoring college may measure its own effectiveness is by how prepared students are for employment; internships demonstrate that preparation very effectively. Some examples of outcomes are

- parent educator—prepared to write a curriculum for new parents
- pre-K teacher—prepared to design developmentally appropriate centers
- youth director—prepared to organize educational programs and trips

Outcomes are assessed by measures such as the site supervisors' evaluations of interns, instructors' observations of interns, and employment rates after graduation.

The internship is *process oriented*. Most internships center on activity, not products. The process orientation values experimentation and does not make an assumption that a skill or practice will necessarily be mastered in the course of the internship. By contrast, the college classroom is more likely to be product oriented. The production of assignments implies an expectation of improvement from start of semester to end of semester. In fact, some classroom products are evaluated on the basis of corrections from first draft to final submission. There is an end product that can be judged (graded). The end product could be a research paper or a unit plan or even a skill in leading a group. For the student who is accustomed to the product-oriented style of learning, the shift to a process orientation may require an adjustment in thinking. For example, an internship of child advocacy in the courts may follow cases for months with little progress. The intern's learning will be through the processing of those cases, not necessarily the products or conclusions of the work (the court's verdict). The intern may not have a tangible product to submit for a grade other than reflective writing about the process.

The internship is *student-centric*. Being at the center of the activity, of the learning, and of the course purpose is a big change for most college students. They are accustomed to the traditional classroom, which is instructor-centric. By nature of being an authority figure, a teacher cannot help but be the center of students' attention in class. For the intern who experiences the shift from instructor-centric to student-centric, this focus on self is usually rewarding, but it does dictate changes in student work. For example, if an internship journal or log is required, the student will usually write in first person ("I, me, my, mine"), a departure from most academic writing. Internship journals also require a change in content from academic writing: documenting the internship includes not only some objective, fact-based writing ("The Head Start staff meets weekly to discuss curriculum") but also much more subjective, opinion-based writing ("I have been hesitant to speak in the weekly staff meetings"). Sharing personal thoughts, feelings, and fears with an instructor may take practice, but the reward is having a mentor's support and, if necessary, guidance in interpreting internship activities. The intense focus on the intern (student-centric) may make the intern feel scrutinized and even criticized. Part of the learning experience is to tolerate the feeling of self-consciousness and trust that mentors and instructors work in the interns' best interest.

The internship is *adaptable*. While most interns must conform to certain conditions at their temporary workplaces, they nevertheless enjoy some freedom in how they adapt their experience. Either through choice of assignment or through adjustments to time and setting, interns can shape the internship to meet their own needs. This could mean an intern in a child care center adjusts the hours of work to have teaching opportunities with a variety of age groups. Coordinating with the site supervisor, the intern could increase the opportunities of exposure to different pre-K classes, and the resulting experiences could even help the intern decide on a professional goal of working with a particular age group. In some internships, the environment is large enough that interns are routinely given a choice in assignment. For example, a large adoption agency can offer the intern a choice of populations to observe and work with: families being matched with infants, families being matched with siblings, families being matched with children with special needs. Further, the agency may have specialized caseworkers who can offer access to different stages of the adoptive process. Thus, the intern may be able to select a mix of assignments that best suits his or her career goals.

The internship offers a *wide range of options*. While classroom learning on campus necessarily limits the number of directions for learning, field experiences can be arranged in virtually any geographic location and virtually any discipline. This range is especially attractive for the intern whose curriculum requires more than one field experience. For example, the student who needs to compare experiences in the K-3 classroom with career options in corporate child care will find internships appropriate for assessing the two environments. In terms of geography, the flexibility of internships permits travel to parts of the globe the intern has never visited—or to a new type of community contrasting with the one the intern grew up in. Thus, an intern considering a career in youth programs may apply for an internship aboard a cruise ship or at a YMCA halfway across the country.

The *hands-on emphasis* of the internship may contrast sharply with many campus offerings, where cognitive activity is emphasized. Hands-on, or experiential, education is credited with the highest retention of learning. Confucius said long ago, "Tell me and I will forget; show me and I may remember; involve me, and I will understand." For a college student seeking a career, book learning and campus simulations can only go so far. A sports analogy puts this in perspective: how much preparation for playing basketball can come from book work? Learning the history of basketball may be stimulating but probably won't inform your technique on the court. Studying theory and mechanics of

Hands-on, or experiential, education is credited with the highest retention of learning.

basketball similarly will take you only so far. If your goal in playing basketball is to compete to win a championship (or even a single game), the book study is not directly relevant. The topic of basketball is not the same as the playing of basketball. Watching other people play—observing—similarly has limitation. Even solitary practice on a court is limited; you may become a very good dribbler, but you won't have learned to play the game. Only the game environment will provide all the information necessary.

Joint evaluation, by student and instructor or student and supervisor, distinguishes the internship from the classroom. Colleges must carry the responsibility of assessment in order to meet external accreditation standards; therefore, instructors assess student performance and assign grades. In the internship, performance is evaluated by multiple people: student, instructor, site supervisor, and potentially other personnel at the site. The intern may find it difficult, at first, to self-evaluate; this book provides numerous opportunities for self-assessment through Discussion Questions and Guided Practices. Making self-assessments during and after the internship prompts interns to (a) explore personal growth, (b) document changes in thinking, (c) consult with mentors and instructors, (d) self-monitor behavior according to professional standards and ethics, and (e) articulate evaluation of that behavior. Joint evaluation during the internship supports the transition between being graded (through instructors' assessment of preprofessionals) and making self-evaluation (an expected skill of working professionals).

The internship provides the opportunity for *role-taking and active participation*. While experience in college may include simulations such as role-playing, the context of classroom is inherently limiting. The internship's potential for practical application in the field—the K–12 classroom, the community organization, the state agency, the hospital—sets the stage for active participation and a process called *role-taking*. Based on the study of roles and identity, role-taking refers to the process of assuming a new role or stepping into another person's experience. Through role-taking, the intern can assume a professional's perspective, gaining an insider view of an environment, even if the intern has not yet begun a shift in self-identity from student to professional.

The internship allows *real-world problem solving,* moving from the theoretical to the practical. Real-world pressures and schedules are experienced and understood. The intern uses real-time management skills to match resources to needs and sometimes faces failure. In community settings, problems are not always solved within short time frames and resources are not always obtainable. By contrast, in college educational settings, the consideration of problems must be accomplished in the space of the semester; even problem-based learning (PBL) techniques may be time-bound. The intern in the field also learns to acknowledge that some problems persist despite all efforts. Long-standing problems are not necessarily unsolvable, but they may require commitment of a variety of resources and professionals—interns in the field are more likely to understand the needed coordination for such solutions than are students in the classroom.

Real-world problem solving does fail sometimes, of course. Interns learn about such failures and have the opportunity to discuss with professionals what comes next. In an elementary school classroom, the unsolved problem may be the school's inability to meet every child's needs. In a hospital, the unsolved problem may be the institution's inability to control the spread of infection. In a nonprofit agency, the unsolved problem may be the lack of funding for a follow-up program. Whether the lack of solution produces a minor irritation or a major crisis, new professionals feel the disappointments sharply. Working professionals' perspective on and strategies to manage unsolved problems can be shared during internships.

Working professionals' perspective on and strategies to manage unsolved problems can be shared during internships.

Paid Internships

Internships may be paid at some organizations because of the way the U.S. Department of Labor requires that employees be classified. For example, some for-profit sites pay interns as temporary employees because the internship consists of activities that regular employees would be paid to perform. If the intern is in a training capacity and not substituting for a regular employee, it is more likely that the internship will not be paid. Another criterion for deciding paid or unpaid status is whether the internship is tied to employment at the end of the period. While paid internships are popular among students, they are not common in the helping professions. Some colleges stipulate that all internships be voluntary rather than paid.

Internships that provide a stipend for living expenses may be referred to informally as *paid internships,* although for purposes of income tax, the stipend may not be a salary. In such a case, the internship sponsor must clarify whether the payment is taxable income, an educational grant, or some other category of stipend. Stipends are more common for research internships, especially those held on college campuses where stipends can cover the cost of dorm and cafeteria fees. Some internships that require travel provide an allowance for moving to the site (sometimes as a stipend and sometimes as a travel per diem, or monetary allowance per day). While technically not a paid internship in terms of salary, these allowances may be called paid.

An apprenticeship, usually thought of as learning a trade, is similar to an internship. An apprentice learns on the job—earning a salary—and is supervised by a master in that specialization. Through schooling or working alongside a professional, the apprentice is allowed to learn under less pressure. The expectation is that time is needed to develop the skill or practice of the profession. Gradually, the apprentice takes on responsibility for performing work, and a mentor directs and assesses the progress. Some trades, such as electricians, use the apprenticeship model to structure several years of learning for the new employee. In many industries, the model is used for shorter spans of time for training programs. A management trainee may spend three to six months in a graduated program that ends with the employee being named a manager.

Similarly, cooperative programs (co-ops) blend employment and learning, with learning still taking place in the campus setting. A co-op student benefits from support and mentorship in both locations. Co-op programs typically represent long-term relationships between a community employer and the college; procedures are well known and well tested.

In the broad category of internships, we expect to see a mix of paid and unpaid positions. Sometimes students set a goal to work only in a paid internship. When such a position cannot be found, the student may feel disappointed in taking an unpaid internship. While the child and family professions honor volunteerism (and frequently rely on volunteers), the student may not have envisioned accomplishing the internship in the mode of volunteer work. An alternative view is to consider the worth of the experience the student will gain through the internship, paid or not. The short list of gains would be job skills, supervision by professional mentors, and a close-up view of a workplace. Imagine what you would have to pay to gain access to an environment that provided all that experience and exposure. That is what the internship is worth in pay, and so even an unpaid position is worth a lot.

✳ WHO BENEFITS FROM THIS OPPORTUNITY?

The most direct beneficiary of the internship is you. You are at the center of the experience as you synthesize classroom knowledge and try out a new role in the workplace. But there are other beneficiaries: the community organization and its clients or the school and its students, the professionals in that organization, the community, and the profession represented in the work you accomplish.

The organization invests in you as a temporary contributor; its reward may be short term (having your help with particular tasks) or long term (assisting in your training as a future professional). Clients, whether they are children or adults, benefit from your efforts, and some may not even be aware of your novice status. In some communities, the presence of interns means that a service can be provided when none was possible before. Especially in the helping professions, small measures and temporary relief are appreciated even if it is known that the

In elementary and early childhood schools, the presence of an intern directly impacts children in their daily lives.

relief will end when the intern leaves. In elementary and early childhood schools, the presence of an intern directly impacts children in their daily lives.

Professionals in the organization benefit by having the help of the intern (even temporarily) and also by interacting with preprofessionals. The interaction is stimulating to the professional and may include transfer of new knowledge—in both directions. The professional provides guidance in learning about the job, and the student provides current research-based information. In addition, the student often brings up-to-date technical expertise that is needed. For many professionals, the mentor role is rewarding because of their awareness of the need to bridge classroom and workplace. Their own training may have included field experience of a similar nature, and so mentoring an intern is opportunity to give back to the community of professionals. Classroom teachers have a special affinity for the role of mentor because almost without exception they entered their profession as either a student teacher or a beginning teacher working under a mentor. In internships, the supervising classroom teacher may be called a *cooperating teacher* (referring to cooperation between college and school district), master teacher, or mentoring teacher. Depending on the style of program, an intern in the classroom may be referred to as *intern, student teacher, precertified teacher,* or *new teacher.*

The community benefits from your internship by your application of new knowledge and new theory, not just by the hours you commit. Your energy and new approaches in problem solving provide fresh perspective. Interns and new professionals typically bring idealism and optimism that generates new enthusiasm by everyone. In some communities, internships permit attention to be paid to long-standing issues and this attention, in itself, prompts action.

The profession represented by your internship benefits through the expansion of knowledge and relationships. Partnering between new professionals and seasoned mentors generates best practices and ensures that standards are maintained. Continuous improvement and growth of the profession become the goals of the new generation and frequently engage new professionals in the work of organizations such as the National Association for the Education of Young Children (NAEYC) and the National Council on Family Relations (NCFR). The entry level for such work may be in the organizations' state and local chapters; more extensive involvement includes attending and presenting at national conferences as well as holding national offices. National organizations provide extra support to and representation of new professionals; this may include special sessions at annual conferences.

Reciprocity among stakeholders may be seen in the relationship between campus and community. Your training and curriculum in college have been planned in light of workforce needs. Colleges seek input through advisory boards composed of community leaders to ensure that students are being adequately prepared for employment. Surveys of employers also help to align in-school preparation with workplace requirements. During an internship, interaction between university and community may include a survey assessing the effectiveness of your particular program. Communication between site supervisors or cooperating teachers with the college instructors and coordinators not only supports future internship relations but also assures that the internship or practicum meets the mission of the organization. Through such collaborative practices, strong partnerships are formed and maintained.

Study of published mission statements of organizations, school districts, agencies, and colleges or universities brings focus to the purposes of institutions. Look for key words and themes in the published mission statements of these examples. Mission statements usually appear on the Web sites and brochures of organizations. The aim of your content analysis is to become aware of the match of purposes between the organization and you. In an exercise such as this, your aim is not to select an internship. Much more analysis is needed to ensure that a site is the right fit for you. The analysis of mission statements is preliminary to the search for an internship. This first exercise in awareness serves to highlight the general statements of purpose of potential sites.

✳ WHAT ARE THE BENEFITS OF AN INTERNSHIP?

Becoming a professional is the purpose of the internship and therefore is the primary benefit to you. Your overall goal is to move from student to professional. Articulating your professional identity is a daunting task, and one that requires the hands-on involvement provided by the internship. The process is not accomplished in a single class or internship. It is ongoing and continues throughout your career. As you take on different roles and interact with different people, that professional identity changes. Your role may shift from leader to contributor, from initiator to interpreter, from researcher to facilitator. Depending on the situation and your coworkers, as well as your level of training, the professional identity evolves.

Beyond the purpose of becoming a professional, the most commonly named benefit of the internship is securing a job or employment. Many internships do not produce job offers, of course. And many students expect to seek employment in a different location, anyway (not the town in which they have interned). Nevertheless, the internship provides valuable generalized learning to support a job search. You will learn more about one specific setting for employment and know whether it is a good match for you. You will acquire the skills and terminology to enable you to work in a similar setting. This exposure to a work setting allows you to learn an industry position, such as the growth areas or the declining areas. In the internship, you learn these aspects from an insider's perspective, meaning the mentor or professionals you work with at the site. This sort of knowledge is quite possibly not knowable (at all) from the outside. The insider view, therefore, is accessible only to those people who spend time on the inside, including interns.

Similarly, the intern setting allows learning about the *hidden job market*. That's not a code for work in espionage; *hidden* refers to the unpublished nature of job market information. The internship can provide you with inside contacts, references to be used in making employment applications, and networking opportunities. Some jobs are never publicly advertised because professionals networking together leads to placement of "my colleague's ex-intern" or even "my colleague's former assistant's ex-intern." Even among agencies or school districts that are required to advertise all vacancies, the hidden resources may produce the person who is hired because the networking occurs so quickly that a colleague's recommendation may arrive sooner than the applications from a job posting.

An advantage of the internship that is not commonly discussed is the opportunity to realize and appreciate what you already know or have already learned in college. This self-knowledge helps you to focus on other skills you want to develop, extending your skill set. For example, a student may have thoroughly developed presentation skills, and the internship affords the opportunity to practice those skills in the K–3 classroom. The extended skill set, to be accomplished during the internship, would include learning how to work with parents and interact with professionals. In the workforce, all of these abilities form a marketable skill set. Appreciation of your existing knowledge and skills is more difficult to articulate. Interns may come to recognize their preexisting skill set on their own (by making comparisons in the workplace) or through conversation with a mentor or site supervisor. An intern may be surprised to find that his or her writing skill is equal to that of a professional's in the field— of course, that would reflect the intern's schooling and very likely a college's determination to graduate seniors who are prepared for the workforce. Similarly, you may discover through conversation with the site supervisor that your understanding of technology is superior to the existing staff's. These realizations will build the intern's confidence in feeling ready for the workplace.

We do not learn a new set of skills for every environment, of course. The transferability of skills helps us adapt to new environments. The K–3 classroom intern described above may not find employment as a teacher in a school district where the intern wants to live. Fortunately, the intern's skills are transferable to other settings. New skills in interaction could lead to a position as an educator in a parenting center or a parent liaison for a school district.

Besides thinking about how to transfer skills to other work settings, the intern benefits in meta-learning: learning about learning. As an intern, you have the opportunity to learn about yourself and *how* you learn. You will be able to observe your reactions to chaos, to challenges, to workplace routines. Such observation allows you to step back and learn about yourself, discovering strengths you may not have known you had or realizing preferences for settings and styles. For the intern who can conclude, "I found out that I was happiest when I spent my time working directly with children," or "I couldn't learn the software until I took the manual back to the solitude of my work cubicle," meta-learning has transpired. These realizations will lead to successfully transferring skills to other environments.

For the intern who can conclude, "I found out that I was happiest when I spent my time working directly with children," meta-learning has transpired.

✳ WHEN IS THE OPTIMUM TIME?

Researching different fields or career areas for an internship can begin as early as the first semester of college. Students can initially rely upon their interests and then augment those as they become informed through classroom instruction or through professional activity, such as conferences. Although the internship is most often completed toward the end of the student's tenure in an academic program, sometimes students find it necessary to spread the internships over a couple of years. To make the best use of this situation, internships can be aligned with ongoing course work. For example, a course in aging or lifespan development can be followed by an internship at a senior center. After another year of course work, perhaps in which several courses focus on communication and family development, an internship at a parenting center would be a good choice. Course work in **developmentally appropriate practice (DAP)** stimulates interest in any number of settings with children: pre-K classrooms, kindergarten and elementary school classrooms, pediatric hospitals, community youth programs, and so forth.

Most internships are scheduled near the end of the academic program, not only to take advantage of knowledge gained in completed course work, but also to permit workplace experience close to the expected time of graduation. Job opportunities may emerge from internships as may the transferable skills of interviewing for employment.

Your own stage of adult development may also be pertinent to the timing of the internship. While we expect any college student to be mature enough to meet the responsibilities of an internship, there are surely better times than others to begin this activity. Most students try to plan for the internship semester so that it will not be at risk of an interruption. This may mean scheduling courses so that other study will be at a minimum during the internship. The time of year may also be a factor: if a college's calendar of semester breaks will impact the internship hours, then the choice of semester may need to take break times, spring break, holiday weekends, etc., into consideration. For the college student who has family responsibilities, timing of the internship may mean choosing a semester when family members can tolerate the student's change in hours and activity.

You can think of the choice of timing in terms of clearing the decks, a reference to clearing loose objects from a ship's deck before stormy weather hits. The expression is now used to describe preparing for any major event, usually with the idea of uncluttering your life or your environment so that you are ready for the next event or activity.

For certain types of internship, the optimum time for the site must also be considered. An obvious time-sensitive site is a summer camp. Other internships may have seasonal advantages and disadvantages worth weighing. An elementary school setting has different features in fall, winter, and spring. An after-school program can be viewed only when school is in session, of course. Youth programs in general follow a community's school calendar, and so even an internship in program administration varies in activities several times during the year. An intern interested in parenting education finds little opportunity for working with parents during holiday months, but an intern interested in aging and working with elders is likely to find much programmatic activity during holidays. Working with the homeless population changes according to season, with cold weather bringing extra challenges. Similarly, weather dictates activity for interns at nature reserves and parks. For the intern who seeks to travel, planning for weather is a pragmatic requirement.

developmentally appropriate practice

Developed by the National Association for the Education of Young Children, guidelines for early childhood programs to provide for the respectful and supportive treatment of children based on knowledge of children's development; abbreviated as DAP.

✳ ARE YOU READY FOR THE INTERNSHIP?

Readiness can be assessed through both objective and subjective measures. Objective measures may be in place on your campus. Whether an internship is a voluntary choice or an assigned degree requirement, you probably must meet certain prerequisites or follow application procedures. These standards serve to regulate entry times to internship courses and set parameters for the field experiences. From the college or university's perspective, the standards assure that interns are prepared for the experience and that campus resources are adequate to provide supervision and support to interns. Internship sites also establish standards to regulate the entry of preprofessionals to their facilities and programs. Prerequisite experience may be specified or screening interviews may be utilized to assure that prospective interns are suited to the work of the internship.

Subjective measures of readiness refer to the intern's own assessment of knowledge, skill, and values appropriate for entry to an internship. Content knowledge, gained in the college classroom, prepares preprofessionals for interaction with various populations and working from a knowledge base of theory and research. Skill in communication and critical thinking permits the preprofessional to work with confidence in addressing challenges. Values are expressed in the desire for advancing to the internship with an appreciation for the opportunity to work in the field alongside professionals. The intern candidate assesses his or her own knowledge, skill, and values through internal dialogue, conversation with peers, and consultation with instructors.

Articulation of Values

Values refer to knowing what is important to you. As a student, your values may have been expressed through selecting a major, earning good grades, and persisting toward your educational goal. In the internship, your values may be expressed through your choice of a site, your demeanor on the job (whether it be at a hospital, in a children's classroom, or in a community program), as well as your treatment of the children or clients you work with. Articulating your values will help to focus your entry into the internship. There are no right or wrong answers in completing an exercise of identifying and stating your values. But your effort in such an exercise will give you a chance to state clearly what you think is important—or to identify those areas about which you do not have a clear picture yet. Values clarification is a process that supports articulation of values but does not create values. The creation stage begins much earlier in your life and was influenced by family, friends, peers, and the larger society. You may already have a sense of your core set of values, the guiding principles that help you make decisions. As you step into the internship, you will find new situations that require reflecting on those guiding principles—or a need to clarify your values in light of new needs.

Acting on your values does not come without challenge and the internship almost always generates new questions that require values clarification. While eager to serve a population you have studied, you may need some reassurance about your ability. Readiness does not come automatically simply because the internship comes next in your program. You may feel a strong commitment to the community you have been trained to serve but doubt your ability to help. This challenge may come in the form of **fraud syndrome**, a nonclinical description of a common response to an unfamiliar situation (see Table 1-5). This frequent reaction to uncertainty or unknowns includes anxiety and feelings

✳ **fraud syndrome**

Common response to stress or a new situation due to inability to internalize success, making the individual doubt his or her ability to perform at a task; aka imposter syndrome.

Table 1-5

Signs of Fraud Syndrome	Responses to Defuse Fraud Syndrome
I'm not ready . . .	I have years of preparation for this experience.
I do not know enough . . .	My study will now include application.
The children will see through me . . .	My students will grow to trust me.
The boss will find out I'm not good enough . . .	I have been good enough in the past.
I'm not good enough yet . . .	I have been complimented on my classroom performance.
I don't know what to do . . .	I have had to learn "from scratch" before.
I've been lucky up to now . . .	My accomplishments are not all due to luck.
I don't belong here . . .	My comfort will have to grow over time.
I'll mess up on the important stuff . . .	My record is one of care and completion.
No one knows if I can do this . . .	Many teachers and advisors have encouraged me.
I'm an imposter . . .	Real imposters never think to say such a thing.

of inadequacy. Although you are trained and up to the task of the internship, you may doubt your readiness or worry about what may happen if you do not know everything you need to know.

Work Ethic

work ethic

A person's attitude toward work exemplified by pragmatics such as attendance and meeting deadlines as well as intrinsic characteristics such as loyalty and commitment.

Another challenge that may emerge in readying for the internship is creating or committing to a **work ethic**. Your work ethic may reflect a deeper value about making commitments, or it may generate a new value for you, one specific to your professional life. Work ethic is commonly displayed in everyday activity, but its reach goes beyond the daily routines to your attitude of commitment to the profession or job. Day-to-day displays of work ethic include arriving at the workplace on time and dependably, meaning that you arrive on time (or early) *every* day, not just usually or with exceptions. Perhaps less noticed is your attention to the clock during the day: taking breaks but getting right back to work after breaks, and doing the same at lunch time. While an occasional delay in returning to work after lunch is tolerated in some workplaces, in other settings it is not. For example, an intern working in a Head Start classroom may discover that promptness following a lunch break is just as important as arrival at the start of day. Many people (both adults and children) rely on every worker to keep to a schedule. The classroom teacher with a strong work ethic realizes this in a first day of observation and immediately adopts the discipline necessary to maintain the schedule.

In an office setting, the work ethic of maintaining schedules is likely to include meeting deadlines. Your natural tendency to work ahead of schedule will hold you in good stead—or your natural tendency to work at the last minute will work against you. Self-knowledge about your own pace of work obviously helps in adopting an ethic of meeting deadlines in the workplace. Studies in time management acknowledge that humans do not always make good estimates of time needed for tasks, even when they have experience in the tasks. Thus, for the intern seeking to display a positive work ethic, the best strategy is caution in pacing work before a deadline. The local culture of the workplace also plays a part in how deadlines are approached. One community program may use deadlines as goal dates, to be met when possible. Another community program may use deadlines as absolute, certain end points because an external funding agency needs the information to continue a grant. For the intern whose project impacts report writing (even if the intern's impact is indirect, such as freeing up a staff member's time to work on the report), knowing the local culture's attitude about deadlines will help in matching the pace of the organization.

The more intrinsic characteristics of work ethic are loyalty and commitment. While they may be displayed every day (often indirectly), they are rarely assessed every day. In fact, evaluation of an employee's commitment may be very occasional or just in an annual review. A site supervisor's mention of an intern's loyalty and commitment may be made because the intern has sought to make these characteristics of work ethic visible. For example, an intern who responds to a workplace pressure by volunteering more hours or a shift in hours impresses the supervisor. If half the workforce is home sick due to flu, the intern who can step into a receptionist's position or take over the mail run will help keep the program running because it is these public interface functions that serve as infrastructure for the rest of the operations. Being committed to the workplace does not always involve personal sacrifice, but it does reflect a worker's ability to discern what is needed and focus energies effectively to meet that need.

✳ HOW TO USE THIS BOOK

No amount of reading and study can replace the experiential learning of the internship, of course. This book can take you only so far in preparing for a field experience, but it can serve as a guide to skills and strategies to enhance the experience. Through explanations of common internship processes and challenges, the text provides pragmatic information that you can put to use in investigating and accomplishing a variety of field experiences in the child and family professions. Special features of the book are the Guided Practices and Discussion Questions at the ends of chapters. They may be used as independent work or in an internship class to assist in processing the experience of moving from campus to professional setting.

To address the many variations in academic programs and internships, the language in this book relies on general terms. Sometimes the vocabulary may match your campus terminology, but often you will find it necessary to translate a word or phrase to a more familiar term to reflect your experience. The wide variation of terms is indicated in Table 1-6.

The scope of this book is intentionally broad in order to serve students who are just beginning to contemplate a field experience as well as students who are graduating and facing the challenge of a job search. Chapter contents are arranged in the presumed order of needs for most students; however, the wise student will access whatever information is relevant, regardless of its location in the text. For example, a student nearing graduation may be simultaneously enrolled in an internship semester and also engaged in a search for a permanent job. For that student, reading Chapter 8, "After the Internship," may be a priority! The following guide to chapter contents will help you identify sections that you may have immediate interest in.

Table 1-6

Words Used in This Book	Equivalent Terms in Some Settings
Internship, field experience	Practicum, community placement, field placement, preservice experience, experiential learning placement, service learning assignment, co-op, external learning experience
Intern, intern student, intern candidate	Preservice candidate, preservice teacher, practicum student, student
Academic instructor, college/university instructor, academic advisor, campus instructor, mentor	Course instructor, campus advisor, campus mentor, college/university supervisor, professor, college advisor
Site supervisor, professional in the field, mentor	Internship supervisor, internship director, field supervisor
Intern coordinator	Field placement office/coordinator

Chapter 1—Becoming a Professional. The internship moves you out of the classroom and into the community, often serving as a capstone course in your academic program and simultaneously as the beginning of your professional identity development. In **Approaching the Internship,** your perception is key to how you proceed in this endeavor. Your approach will be unique, just as your perception is like no other person's. **Defining Internship,** as a bridge across theory, research, and practice presents the experience as a process of synthesis that features hands-on activities across weeks or months. Characteristics of internships are not universal, but most are self-directed, self-initiated, experiential, and adaptable to some degree. A highly desired characteristic is a salary or other compensation. Technically, a paid internship is one that supplies a taxable salary for work accomplished, but the term is often used informally to include internships that provide stipends, grants, or travel allowances. When stakeholders ask, **Who Benefits from this Opportunity?**, the intern acknowledges that he or she is the primary beneficiary of the field experience. But others benefit, too: the community organization and its clients or the school and its students, the professionals in that organization, the community, and the profession represented in the work accomplished. Common **Benefits of an Internship** are the intern's launch to becoming a professional, preparation for employment, self-knowledge, and skill-building. **When Is the Optimum Time?** Internships scheduled near the end of the academic program take advantage of knowledge gained in completed course work and permit workplace experience close to the expected time of graduation. Questioning if you are **Ready for the Internship** may lead to use of objective measures controlled by the campus or internship site and also by subjective measures such as your own self-assessment of your knowledge, skill, and values. By articulating your values, you can identify your core set of values or guiding principles, which may inform your readiness for an internship. Similarly, you may asses your work ethic, often expressed as your attitude of commitment to the profession or job.

Chapter 2—Placement. Although highly individual in meeting interns' needs, **Typical Purposes of Field Experience** can be identified as common functions for most college students. The selection of an internship site is facilitated by students taking time for **Self-Assessing** of strengths and weaknesses. In **Searching for Sites,** the wise intern candidate looks beyond preexisting lists of internships, putting electronic, print, and people resources to best use. **Previewing and Interviewing** sites, though, may require obtaining permission from the college or university. **Evaluating Sites** includes researching the size of the applicant pool and a site's selectivity rating. The personal match includes consideration of long-term career goals, as well as site conditions. Multiple steps lead up to **Finalizing the Site Selection:** approvals, applications and references, and required background checks.

Chapter 3—On the Job as an Intern. The intern's **First Day and First Impressions** set the tone for the experience. A range of activities will compose **What Interns Do on the Job.** Adjusting to the workplace includes being aware of role boundaries. While individual students may identify site-specific **Internship Goals,** a common universal goal is to apply knowledge and theory while learning new skills in a workplace. Assimilation and acculturation are major processes of **Understanding the Culture.** A key component is developing **Observation Skill and Technique** from the level of novice to expert. The intern focuses on observing internal dynamics, which includes processes of group formation and teaming. A new challenge for the college student may be **Processing Feelings and Personal Reaction,** in order to manage emotions in a professional manner.

Chapter 4—Knowledge to Practice. The **Transition from Preparation to Application** is essentially a shift from preparatory studies to application of content knowledge in the real world. Much of the work in the helping professions can be classified as with the terms **Intervention and Prevention.** Overlap occurs, and professionals may be trained in both types of service. **Theory and Perspective** describe and predict behavior. Professionals draw from theoretical models such as family strengths model, resilience, ecological theory, systems thinking, biosocial perspective, stress theory, feminist perspective, conflict theory, solution-focused intervention, and the broken window thesis. Professionals also focus on **Understanding Audiences through Theory.**

Chapter 5—Communication and Networking. **Communication Skills of a Professional** are developed intentionally to communicate with children, clients, and audiences in multiple ways. Through **Self-Presentation,** interns send intentional and unintentional messages through written, verbal, and non-verbal communication. Professional communication encompasses **Communicating with Diverse Audiences,** such as adults, adolescents, and children. Through **Journaling,** interns maintain a record of activities and also create a reflexive account of experiences. **Electronic Communication in the Workplace** involves learning about formal policies and informal practices regarding equipment, Internet access, e-mail, voice mail, and cell phones. An intern's electronic image and identity may enhance or destroy reputation in the workplace and deserves scrutiny. A common theme of internships is the opportunity for **Mentoring and Networking.**

Chapter 6—Ethics and Public Policy. **Introduction to Ethics** guides behavior, conduct, and decision making. Across professions, rules of conduct may have similar **Themes of Professional Standards. Elements of Ethical Codes** include legal requirements, confidentiality, conflict of interest, accountability, conduct, responsibility to the profession, collegiality, cultural competence,

A common theme of internships is the opportunity for mentoring and networking.

assumptions, and plagiarism. **Articulating a Personal Code of Ethics** is a key feature of the internship. The intern may observe **Workplace Ethics** that influence development as a professional. Verbal and nonverbal communication has **Impact on Clients, Children, and Families.** The four steps of the C^4 model of **Ethics and Decision Making** are clarify, collaborate, consider, and choose. In conducting research, professionals employ **Research Ethics,** providing for protections such as informed consent, confidentiality, and honest presentation of results. In the **Application of Ethical Thinking to Public Policy,** professionals model advocacy and personal agency. Through acknowledgment of **Ethical Dilemmas,** professionals accept that there is no single, correct answer for many situations encountered in working with people.

Chapter 7—Assessment and Evaluation. Why Evaluate? Reasons to evaluate include tracking changes or differences, determining mastery of skills or concepts, and comparing with other programs, techniques, or attempts. **Measuring the Intern** may involve multiple measures or multiple evaluators, both formally and informally, with focus on the intern's competencies and performance areas. Self-evaluation by the intern is also encouraged. Some interns have the opportunity to assist with **Measuring the Program** they are assigned to. Programs are evaluated to demonstrate that they are effective and that activity is appropriate to the purpose of the organization or agency. For example, NAEYC accreditation standards include provisions for evaluation to assess quality. Safeguards for promoting effective evaluation include a systematic plan, needs assessment, benchmarks, a pilot test, appropriate model of evaluation, choice of evaluators, permission to collect data, multiple measures and methods, adequate sample size, appropriate analyses, and publication of results.

Chapter 8—After the Internship. Following the internship, taking time for **Self-Assessment and Reflection** can ease the pressure of employment decisions. Then, the intern can begin taking actions to initiate the job search. Those actions may include taking interest inventories and assessing likes and dislikes. While selection of a job may be a first consideration, selection of a community is also important and may encompass decisions about climate, cost of living, commuting distance, access to public transportation, landscape and scenery, and so forth. **The Job Search** may include contacting headhunters and company

recruiters, visiting campus resources such as offices of career services, and attending career fairs on and off campus. A large proportion of job offers are produced by off-campus networking. The strength of weak ties refers to the highly productive networking between systems of family, friends, and acquaintances.

The Resume is the job applicant's main tool for articulating strengths and abilities and deserves careful planning and proofreading. Selecting and recruiting references also requires planning. **The Portfolio** is another presentation tool. Selective works are compiled in a portfolio to illustrate qualifications and skills for employment. The job search advances quickly when applicants begin to hear back from recruiters. **The Interview,** whether in person or by telephone, is the opportunity for a conversation that answers the applicant's questions, too. **Ethics of the Job Search** includes accepting travel for interviews, commenting on other applicants, and committing to a period of employment. **The Job Offer** typically includes information about salary and start date, which may be negotiable. **On the Job Challenges** may include new clothing costs, unexpected bills, and a period of adjustment to the new environment. Continued growth on the job and as a lifelong learner is recommended through **Professional Affiliations and Professional Development.**

⊙ SUMMARY OF CHAPTER CONTENTS

Introduction: The internship moves you out of the classroom and into the community, often serving as a capstone course in your academic program and simultaneously as the beginning of your professional identity development.

Approaching the Internship: Perception is individual and so, too, is the approach that a preprofessional takes to the internship.

Defining Internship: As a bridge across theory, research, and practice, the internship is a process of synthesis that features hands-on activities across weeks or months.

> *Characteristics of Internship:* To some degree, most field experiences are self-directed, self-initiated, experiential, adaptable.

> *Paid Internships:* Technically, a paid internship is one that supplies a salary for work accomplished. The term may be used informally to include internships that provide stipends, grants, travel allowances, and so forth.

Who Benefits from this Opportunity? The intern is the primary beneficiary of the field experience, but these stakeholders also benefit: the community organization and its clients or the school and its students, the professionals in that organization, the community, and the profession represented in the work accomplished.

What Are the Benefits of an Internship? Becoming a professional is the primary purpose of field experience; other benefits include preparation for employment, self-knowledge, and skill building.

When Is the Optimum Time? Internships scheduled near the end of the academic program take advantage of knowledge gained in completed course work and permit workplace experience close to the expected time of graduation.

Are You Ready for the Internship? Readiness may be indicated by objective measures controlled by the campus or internship site and also by subjective measures such as the intern candidate's self-assessment of knowledge, skill, and values.

> *Articulation of Values:* Identifying a core set of values or guiding principles is one of the processes that lead to readiness for an internship.

Work Ethic: Work ethic is commonly displayed in everyday activity, but its reach goes beyond the daily routines to your attitude of commitment to the profession or job.

How to Use this Book: Reading and studying cannot replace the experiential learning of the internship, but books such as this one can assist the intern in focusing on skills and strategies to enhance the field experience.

◉ DISCUSSION QUESTIONS

1. Referring to the opening case study of this chapter, how would you describe your own approach to the internship?

2. Perhaps you spent time as a child watching clouds changing shape as they drifted overhead. Do you make similar observations today, of clouds or anything else?

3. What images come to mind when you concentrate on these terms: hands-on, bridge, capstone?

4. Identify examples of paid internships and nonpaid internships.

5. For a preservice teacher entering an internship, what are the likely costs and benefits of the field experience?

6. What are the optimum conditions in your life for gaining the most benefit from an internship? What is the likelihood that you will experience those optimum conditions?

7. Do you think that objective measures of readiness or subjective measures of readiness are more important in scheduling a field experience?

8. What role does maturity play in deciding if a college student is ready to undertake an internship?

9. Describe your work ethic in one or two paragraphs.

10. Use your own words to describe the benefits you hope to realize through an internship.

◉ GUIDED PRACTICES

Guided Practices offer structured exercises in critical thinking, observation (including self-observation), synthesis, and self-expression. The title of Guided Practice sums up the purpose of providing a guide: an opportunity that permits practice and does not require a final, ultimate effort.

All of the guided practices can be used by one person or by a group of people. The practices are designed as self-report instruments, meaning that answers are reported by the respondent and not collected by an interviewer or by another person who may speak with or observe the respondent.

There is not a standard amount of time to spend on the exercises. One person may use a guided practice for making a quick check while the next person may choose to spend hours on the same practice. Individual interest in a topic makes a difference in use, as does current need for the topic.

The greatest value is derived when the guided practice is completed with honest answers and observations. Any instrument may generate socially desirable answers, the kind of responses that a person thinks will be acceptable or expected. Especially when related to academic study, an instrument that calls for self-disclosure or self-evaluation risks being answered this way.

Guided Practice:
Anticipating the Field Experience

As you anticipate your field experience, reflect on the following questions:

What do I hope to gain from this experience?

_____

_____

_____

How have I changed during my academic career so far?

_____

_____

_____

How do I hope to change or grow during an internship or field experience?

_____

_____

_____

Am I ready for an experience that is self-initiated and self-directed? Why?

_____

_____

_____

Has my previous course work been more process oriented or product oriented?

_____

_____

_____

What characteristics of an internship seem most problematic for my own work preferences? Why?

_____

_____

_____

How will the internship differ from other work experiences I have had?

_____

_____

_____

Guided Practice:
Work Ethic

Assess elements of the work ethic you see clearly in yourself and in peers.

	Self?	Peers?
Punctual		
Dependable		
Focused on tasks		
Loyal		
Goal oriented		
Purposeful		
Persevering		
Does not quit		
Motivated		
Ambitious		
Follows the rules		
Honest		
Appreciative		
Team player		
Courteous		
Hardworking		
Persistent		

Guided Practice:
Interview with Former Intern

Arrange an interview (in person, telephone, or e-mail) with someone who has recently completed an internship in a position similar to one that matches your career objective. Prior to the interview, develop a list of 10 questions to ask. Some sample questions are shown to get you started.

1. What are you proudest of accomplishing during your field experience?

2. What was the hardest task?

3. What do you wish you had known before you began the experience?

4. _____

5. _____

6. _____

7. _____

8. _____

9. _____

10. _____

 Guided Practice forms are also included on the accompanying CD-ROM.

⬤ ADDITIONAL RESOURCES

Search Terms: Your own exploration of internships should begin with a general Internet search to see the scope of resources available to you—both for planning the internship and also selecting actual internships. Recommended terms for searching: internship, field experience, intern blog, paid internship, co-op education.

Recommended Reading: The leading author in career exploration is Richard Bolles, whose classic text, *What Color Is Your Parachute?*, generated new methods of career counseling and many self-help manuals for job applicants.

For additional material and resources to complement this chapter, the Online Companion Web site can be accessed at http://www.earlychilded.delmar.com.

Placement

CASE STUDY: By midterm in the fall semester, Stephen had decided on the site for his internship in the spring. He was able to complete the required background check, submit his letters of reference, and complete the interview well in advance of all deadlines. Stephen explained to his friends and family that this internship would be the culminating experience of his undergraduate years, providing him with the opportunity to work with different kinds of people in new environments. While Stephen had started college as a criminal justice major, he had since changed to family studies. His internship would be a blend of his interests and allow him to apply his skills. That letter from his professor in the family law class, combined with the letter from his teacher in the family economics class, had moved him to the top of the applicants for this choice position.

Stephen had carefully researched county programs, and he observed and interviewed at several levels. His internship with the county probation services would focus on educational programs designed to prevent repeat legal offenses. Stephen planned to shadow the probation officer in charge of training, helping to teach financial management classes for hot check writers and other budgeting programs for low-income offenders.

This segment of the population and this unique environment would be a great challenge for him but also a good match for his talents and expertise. He was looking forward to hands-on work and the opportunity to teach, without being in a public school setting or working with young children. Stephen described himself as a novice at teaching, but he was passionate about working with the population of adult probationers and their family members. Making a difference in the lives of the families and populations discussed in his classes was important to him, maybe even more important than a large salary at this point in his life.

When Stephen's family expressed some doubts about his internship choice, he was able to describe the future job prospects and demand for persons in this field. He was glad a teacher had given an assignment on job trends where he learned the best sources for employment outlook. He was also pleased to be able to report to his mother that if this internship led to being hired, the county had generous benefits and would even help pay his tuition for a graduate degree.

✳ TYPICAL PURPOSES OF FIELD EXPERIENCE

Your purpose in pursuing an internship may range from the very specific (for example, observe methods of intake at a crisis center) to the very broad (for example, learn more about the education profession). After selecting or being assigned to a site, your purpose will be related to goals and objectives that you, with advice from professionals, will tailor to your experience.

The intern's previous experience and readiness for fieldwork will determine how advanced or how exploratory the internship should be. It is possible for an internship to satisfy more than one purpose, of course, and a single purpose can be expanded to include multiple goals and activities.

One way to clarify your personal purposes is to use the list of typical purposes shown in Table 2-1 and reorder them, ranking from highest priority to lowest priority. For a student new to the field, exposure to diverse community

Table 2-1 Typical Purposes of Field Experience

1. Awareness of professional organizations and credentials
2. Development of skills and professional attributes appropriate to the workplace
3. Integration of content knowledge from the student's academic program
4. Observation of and interaction with professionals in work environments
5. Exposure to diverse community populations and programs
6. Service in a mutually beneficial experience for student and community agency
7. Application of communication skills
8. Development of framework for ethical conduct
9. Understanding of evaluation and assessment principles
10. Acquisition of career credentials to enhance employability

populations and programs may be the top priority in order to see the broad array of professional settings available. This student may seek a field experience that includes interaction with several agencies. For a student who is nearing graduation, acquisition of **career credentials** to enhance employability may be the top priority. This student may well apply to intern settings that include training or certification, realizing that any extra investment of time and energy during the internship could pay off in the job search. (Even short trainings such as CPR add value to job applications.)

✳ SELF-ASSESSING

> **career credentials**
>
> Certifications or documented training that enhance employability. Examples: First Aid, CPR, hotline response training, outdoor physical encounters, conflict resolution training.

Selecting an internship site requires preparation and self-evaluation. When you have completed a self-assessment of your personal traits and identified what you hope to gain, the narrowing of choices for an internship begins. Questioning can begin at the global and general level, which will lead to more specific self-assessments.

What are my abilities?

What do I hope to gain from the experience?

Where am I most interested in spending time?

What kind of work do I want to do?

Which population or sector do I want to serve or work with?

Where can I best display my talents and abilities?

At the end of this chapter, you can use a Guided Practice, "Self-Assessment of Strengths and Expectations," to begin. When you can describe the type of environment in which you want to work as well as your goals (short and long term), you move closer to identifying your priorities for selecting an internship. At this stage, goals are described in general terms; specific goals and objectives in an internship are addressed later in the process.

Another self-assessment should be focused on your work style. For example, knowing that you would prefer to work alone and develop curriculum rather than coach a sports team outdoors is important self-knowledge. A Guided Practice at the end of the chapter, "Self-Assessment of Work Style," suggests some points to consider about yourself. From the agency's perspective, the ideal candidate might enjoy a blend of individual and collective experiences. Because internships often offer a rotation of assignments, the ability to work in multiple styles may be important. For example, the intern may rotate through a public relations office, an education office, and a business office; each requires a different style of work. The intern does not have to be an expert in each style (for example, greeting the public in the first capacity, working with adult learners in the second, and reviewing administrative reports in the third). But the intern must be willing to attempt the work of multiple styles. Knowing one's own preference or strength helps to plan for work in a style that is unfamiliar.

Self-assessments are, by definition, subjective descriptions. To begin thinking more analytically about your strengths, you may find a readiness scale helpful in gauging your readiness for an internship. Although the acceptance into an internship provides one objective view of your readiness, you should embrace the opportunity to scrutinize yourself as others see you. Although a self-evaluation at this planning stage is still a subjective view, you can use a rating scale to identify your level of readiness. The third Guided Practice at the end of the chapter, "Self-Analysis of Readiness for Internship," will help you distinguish between levels of readiness. The rating scale of expert, developing, and novice requires categorizing your abilities. *Expert* implies high proficiency and the level of readiness appropriate for beginning a professional position. *Developing* indicates some experience and comfort level in interacting with people or delivering services. *Novice* indicates no experience or low confidence in your current skills.

You should feel comfortable in using the rating of novice. At this stage of your preprofessional career, the novice level is not only expected, but also respected. By selecting novice or developing, you acknowledge your areas for growth. This demonstrates maturity in "knowing what you don't know." Internship sites are aware that most interns arrive with novice ratings on many dimensions.

These Guided Practices launch you on a path of self-evaluation. The intern experience is often a time of self-reflection and learning about yourself in the context of a career. Most internship courses include journal writing requirements and reflective thinking. Another issue that may arise during an internship semester is the compatibility of your personal **values** with the institutional or corporate values of the site. If your values place importance on how a company invests its assets, you would want to be aware of and investigate the company's annual report. Another example of investigation would be to ask how employees' retirement contributions are invested. Environmental standards may be important to you, or the political affiliations of board members. You might want to work only in a facility with a diverse workforce, where many ethnicities and ages are represented. For some, it is important to know if the workplace benefits are extended to domestic partners.

Personal freedom on and off the job may be important to you: keeping a blog on the Internet is forbidden by some companies. Even where policies are not written, blogging might be discouraged or lead to dismissal. Even the keeping of an intern blog (as a temporary worker at the site) must be considered carefully. If the site you are considering disallows blogs of all kinds, you will need to make a decision about pursuing an internship there.

If you are choosing among several internship possibilities, how might you rank the sites with contrasting values? Depending on how close you are to employment decisions, or if you anticipate a long-term commitment to an internship site, a comparison of values may or may not be a worthwhile activity.

values

Beliefs that are held as true and important; can be defined by the individual or by a group or a larger entity such as a business or government.

✳ SEARCHING FOR SITES

A list of potential internships can be constructed through the Internet and published guides. If your personal situation and academic policies allow travel or an extended time span for an internship, you can screen possibilities for a distant internship through the Internet and telephone. View the internship as an opportunity to learn about environments beyond your own familiar neighborhood or community (and that does not have to involve great distance, of course). Some interns intentionally select sites that are very different from anything they have seen before. This may be the time in your life that you experience an environment different from your upbringing: stretching and going beyond your comfort zone for a finite period of time. Risks are limited and the protective environment of an internship makes the internship an ideal time for such exploration.

The intern is allowed to try on a role for a predetermined time period. This opportunity is very different from professional employment, where the expectation is frequently a commitment of a year or more. It may also be a time to try a field that is related to, but not exactly, the career goal. Broadening your thinking from the *probable* to the *possible* may produce a new career path and will at least allow you to see how many areas are interconnected. Table 2-2 demonstrates

Table 2-2 Expanding from the Probable to the Possible

The Probable Common Sites	The Possible Related Uncommon Sites
Child care	Children's museum
Women's shelter	Office of the State Attorney General
AIDS advocacy/support	Centers for Disease Control and Prevention (CDC)
Local Head Start center	National Head Start Association

how a common internship site or population can be related to a different internship experience. You can make a similar chart on your own to expand your thinking beyond the most obvious sites. Another approach is to select a population you want to work with and then list all the places that you would find that population. (Young children: preschool, library storytime, Mom & Me exercise classes, children's museum, recreation center swim lessons, Sunday school classes, Mothers' Day Out programs, foster care programs, Ronald McDonald House, WIC nutrition classes, shopping mall play areas.) Through these exercises you can make the internship a self-initiated process, reflecting your own creative thinking.

The intern is allowed "to try on a role" for a pre-determined time period.

Shifting your focus will also encourage thinking beyond your near borders. Not every student is able to travel for an internship, but when time and circumstances allow, the change in geography can be valuable. Living in a different region (or even country) for several months introduces you to a new culture and new understanding about human development (including your own). The challenge of the internship away from home is that you must adjust to many new environments simultaneously. Learning a job at the internship site plus adjusting to a new home and climate (and even language) is stressful. Considerable planning is involved in such an internship, but the rewards can be great.

```
Starter List of Regional, National, International Sites
(URLs provided in the Helpful Web Sites section at the end
                  of the chapter.)
```

U.S. Congress

U.S. Federal Reserve Banks

U.S. Centers for Disease Control and Prevention

National Head Start Association

Families and Work Institute

Smithsonian Institution and Museums

Habitat for Humanity (worldwide)

British National Health Service

U.K. House of Commons

National Park Service

Education Regional Service Centers

World Health Organization

American Cancer Society

Ronald McDonald House

Gilda's Club (cancer support organization)

Make a Wish Foundation

Resources for Site Selection

Utilizing multiple resources can turn your search for an internship site into an organized campaign. This means that you put multiple strategies to work for you. Launch several inquiries at the same time, tracking the sources or Web sites you have accessed as well as all the Web sites you have logged onto or where you have created a profile. Electronic job listings, which permit simultaneous searches, can be included, and your campus career center and its Web site can also be part of the campaign.

Popular Web resources include MonsterTrak.com (affiliated with Monster .com, the large employment Web site) and WetFeet.com (a Web-based recruitment-management system that hosts Web sites for colleges, universities, and companies). Such commercial resources provide interactive tools for students to search for internships or jobs. Like most on-line databases, they allow searches by geographic area and other criteria, including salary (or, in the case of internships, scholarships and stipends). On-line newspapers for a desired location can be accessed, typically at no cost. On-line classified ads as well as community and job market information also provide needed details at this stage.

Table 2-3 provides an overview of key search engine terminology. If you've never performed an on-line search, it will be helpful to review this list before starting out. Once you've done so, you can use basic terms such as *internship, paid internship, government internship, experiential education,* and *field experience* to narrow your search. As you become more selective, you can add descriptive qualifiers such as *health services, outdoor, nonprofit sector*. Use more than one search engine to expand your results. And also expand the search by including

Table 2-3 **Search Engine Terminology**

Boolean search	Keyword searching with logic parameters, typically using words such as *and, or, not*. Different search engines recognize full or modified Boolean methods.
Browse	Scan listings or hyperlink choices on a Web page, index, or site map (akin to window shopping to become aware of available options).
Domain name	International Internet address system by which a reserved name loads a Web site or Web page. Extensions include .com (commercial), .org (organization), .edu (education), .gov (government), .mil (military), .us (United States), .ca (Canada), .cn (China).
Google	Popular search engine whose name is sometimes used as a verb to mean "to make an Internet search."
IP address	Numerical Internet Protocol address of a Web site.
Keyword search	Text search that queries multiple databases and retrieves Web pages on which the text appears; depending on the type of search engine, results may be based on relevance to topic, ranking of Web sites according to frequency of use, or other criteria (such as paid commercial listings).
Multiple keyword search	Use of multiple terms to filter results; may slow the rate of response. Can also be used to broaden the search to more possibilities.
Multiple window search	See remote window below.
Remote window	Search feature on some Web sites that opens a new window for every site clicked. You can apply the same strategy yourself: either right-click a hyperlink to select Open in New Window or preset your browser to open search results in either a new window or new tab.
Search engine	Software program that searches and retrieves across the Internet using algorithms to customize results for each query or keyword search.
Search-engine-sponsored site	An employment site (like http://www.HotJobs.com by Yahoo) of a search engine that utilizes the company's searching technology to provide customized results.
URL	Uniform Resource Locator, or the words that describe a domain and Web site (e.g., http://www.google.com). The URL is similar to a physical street address.

job listings, especially if a paid internship is important to you. To locate employment sites, use search terms such as *job listings* and *employment agency*.

Thorough on-line searches can be organized by location, keyword, job category, part- or full-time hours, salary range, and even **pay grade**. Series codes published by the Office of Personnel Management (also known as OPM in the federal government) can guide searches. You may also want to record your path as you search the Internet: create a folder of Bookmarks or Favorites in your browser. As your sources build, you will find an organizing scheme like this helpful.

pay grade

Job level that typically restricts pay to a specific dollar range, based on experience, training, years of service. Many government entities use standard categories of pay grades, 1 through 15. These are further delineated by numbered steps within each grade.

On-line placement services (such as employment Web sites) may offer to list your resume or match you to a company. Most such services charge a fee; investigate total cost before committing. You may also receive advertisements as a result of logging in to a service site. Evaluate the trade-off of being on a list that may or may not provide new information for you. A drawback to on-line listings and storage of your resume is that they become dated, and you must return to update them regularly. Another drawback is that your name or e-mail address may be widely distributed to marketers. One strategy to try out a service is to enter an e-mail address that you can abandon if you find that the service generates unhelpful e-mail.

On-line databases for employment can generate lists of job titles and even relate college majors to common jobs. A sampling of job titles for popular college majors is shown in Table 2-4. You will find considerable crossover between the lists, and you can look for similar common ground among other college majors. The job titles can be used as search terms, broadening the number of resources you can research.

Systematic note-taking at the start of your search will pay off later as you compare and evaluate possible sites. A spreadsheet maintained on your computer or an on-line file storage (or even a table in a word processing program) could include information such as name of organization, contact information, mailing address, telephone numbers, fax number, e-mail address, Web site URL, types of majors, brief description of responsibilities, how to apply, and a hyperlink to an on-line application. You can create codes for variables or characteristics most important to you. Sample codes might include "H" for housing provided, "F" for food provided, "T" for access to public transportation, "$" for stipend provided.

Table 2-4

Majors: Early Childhood Education/Child Development	
Camp director	Cooperative extension agent
Head Start teacher	Child care provider/director
Recreation leader	Preschool teacher
Child life specialist	Youth probation officer
Case manager	Volunteer coordinator
Youth services worker	School-community-family liaison

Majors: Family Studies/Family & Consumer Sciences	
4-H agent	Family advocate
Family financial advocate	Parenting educator
Family services coordinator	Housing project manager
Customer services coordinator	Victim services coordinator
Wellness director	Overnight shelter staff
Community educator	Family and consumer sciences teacher

Table 2-5 **Types of Resources for Aid in Site Selection**	
Electronic	On-line commercial registries, Listservs (such as https://listserv@list.nih.gov), professional associations' Web sites
Print	Listings for co-op jobs, employment ads, want ads, yellow pages, community directories
People	Former high school teachers or university instructors, university alumni association, placement center on campus, special interest camp directors, former employers, executive directors of state and national professional organizations

Access a variety of sources, including electronic, print, and personal, by phone, e-mail, or visit (see Table 2-5). The same resource may be found in print in the library as well as online. Currency is important, but you should not reject all print materials that appear dated. The listing for a past internship can guide you as you update the information on the Web or through a phone call. For example, a print directory of internships may be organized is such a way that you can learn about whole categories of opportunities. Similarly, a print source may suggest a list of key terms that you can then use in an on-line search.

A reference librarian can help you identify mainstream guides, like *Peterson's,* as well as more focused directories for a specific occupation. Specialty guides are published by level (for example, undergraduates only), by discipline (for example, humanities or social services), by industry sector (for example, non-profit only), and location (geographic region or size of community). Descriptions may also specify the time or length intended. For example, a placement may be for summer or academic year, or for full- or part-time hours.

How to Interpret Site Characteristics

In searching the Internet for internship and field experience directories, you may come across words that are unfamiliar. Like most areas of interest, a vocabulary or unique jargon develops that is specific to that field. Acronyms may also initially be confusing. As you review more listings, you will become familiar with the meanings.

Accredited Site: Meets guidelines set by an external professional organization. Accreditation is generally equated with high quality.

Capstone Experience: Suggests that the agency is offering an internship for students nearing graduation or at the culmination of their course work.

Credentialing: Professional expertise recognized through a certification or credential. Examples include teaching credentials, child life specialist certification, licensed social worker, licensed professional counselor (LPC), Certified Family Life Educator (CFLE). At internship sites, credentialing may determine job assignments.

For-profit: Corporate or business organization. In the human service field, internships at these entities are often overlooked in listings, but they may be excellent choices especially for paid internships. Examples include corporate child care, private medical practices, and human resource departments in large corporations.

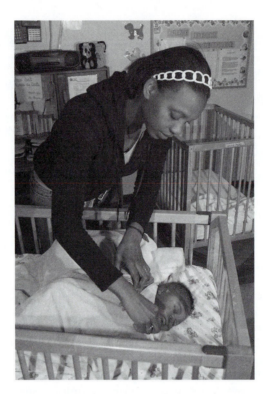

A corporate day care setting may be an excellent choice for a paid internship.

In-kind Payment: Nonmonetary payment such as company products, eligibility for employee discounts toward products or services, and similar benefits.

NAEYC-accredited: Child care facility that has been inspected and approved by the National Association for Education of Young Children. This designation is recognized in the U.S. as the highest quality rating of a facility for child care. The rigorous process of internal and external assessment is achieved by few centers.

Nonprofit: Private or government entity that operates without profit as its central motive. Often the term *nonprofits* is used in conversation to refer to community-supported agencies or foundations, excluding governmental agencies.

NGO: Nongovernmental organization comparable to a nonprofit agency.

PACs: Political action committees typically based at state and national levels. Often involved in lobbying or advocacy activities.

Paid: See Stipend below.

REU: research experience for undergraduates. This research experience is a sponsored scholarship-style program located on college campuses. Its purpose is to allow students to explore a discipline, prepare for a graduate school choice, or participate as a novice researcher. REUs frequently provide housing support, a travel allowance, and a stipend. Many offer the opportunity to serve on a research team led by university faculty members.

Stipend: Monetary support but not necessarily at the level of a salaried position. Often, a stipend is a flat amount that approximates the cost of housing and food, for example. Stipends vary depending on sponsors and even on geography, and may range between $500 and $3,000. Paid interns assume the responsibility for any tax liability; sometimes the stipend is offered as a *grant,* and this language may be important in reporting to the IRS.

Study Abroad: Study in a country outside the U.S. Some opportunities are tied to service learning and may also constitute an internship.

Travel Allowance: Monetary support for travel to and/or from the internship site. Sometimes the allowance is for one-way travel only. Travel allowance may be provided as *mileage reimbursement* based on a federal or state formula of X cents per mile, or as *per diem,* meaning "payment per day." Typically, per diem is limited to a flat dollar amount. For all such allowances, it is important to ask if receipts are required for reimbursement. Interns may be asked to keep and later submit an expense log in addition to original receipts.

Tuition Reimbursement: In lieu of a salary or stipend, some internships make a tuition reimbursement or offer a grant for the next semester's tuition at the student's home institution.

How to Interpret Job Listings

On-line job listings can provide leads on internships and even produce paid internships. These listings are different from the sites that advertise only internships. Known as employment sites, they range from the large on-line clearinghouses of Monster.com and USAJOBS.gov to a single agency's Web site with a list of available positions. A company or nonprofit entity may organize its job openings under a Department of Human Resources. Personnel or job descriptions also have distinct vocabulary and many acronyms. The following phrases are common to many disciplines.

Ability to lift weight of 35 pounds/Requires light lifting: References to physical requirements are closely tied to federal and state regulations about employee safety. Applicants may have to sign agreements that they understand the physical demands of a job.

Alcohol and drug testing: Initial drug screening at application may be required. Some jobs will include random testing on a continual basis. Applicants and employees are typically asked to sign an acknowledgment of the agency's right to require drug tests or make searches.

Background check: Different levels of background checks may be specified. Common ones are criminal history, security level clearance, fingerprint check, and credit history. Checks may also be made on histories you write on the application, such as employment dates or supervisors; similarly, reference checks can be made with the people you list as personal or professional references. For some jobs, the results of security checks must be available before an interview can be scheduled. Interns are often included in security checks but may be granted a low-level clearance that does not take very long to complete.

Bilingual skills: Level of skill may be specified in writing or determined at an interview. Typical levels are fluency (oral and written), conversational (oral), and ability to translate. Tests of oral fluency may include an in-person or telephone interview with a native speaker of the language. Sign language may be tested in person or through a videotape submission.

CFLE Preferred/Required: Certified Family Life Educator credential of the National Council on Family Relations. If the job description says "preferred," an applicant with the credential may be rated higher than other applicants, but the credential is not required for hiring.

Close date: Date that a job listing will close, whether the job is filled or not. After that date, an applicant should query to see if applications are still welcomed, rather than submit a resume without asking.

Contingent upon funding: Position depends on receipt of outside funding such as a grant. If funding is not received, the position may be cancelled.

Driver's license required: Valid and current license in the state of employment is required; there may be a requirement of use of personal transportation to conduct agency business.

Familiarity with software: The word *familiarity* carries with it an expectation of a working knowledge of and a certain level of skill with the software. Skill level should be clarified to determine expectations of the employer.

For immediate placement: A vacant position needs to be filled right away; suggests there is no room to negotiate a start date.

Internal candidates only: Position is open only to current employees.

Montessori-trained: When a specified training is mentioned, the expectation is that the training or certification can be proven and has already been accomplished.

Open until filled: The position listing will continue until a qualified applicant is hired.

Proof of compliance with Selective Service: The legal responsibility of males in the U.S. is to register for selective service (for armed forces) upon turning 18 years old. Proof of compliance would typically require written documentation.

Required versus Preferred: Required refers to a credential or certification that serves as a screening for the position; applications without that requirement may be discarded. *Preferred* refers to a credential or certification that is desired for the job, but lack of the credential does not exclude the candidate for consideration.

Salary commensurate with experience: Base salary for the position will be set according to the experience the employee brings; typically, a salary range begins with entry level (no experience) to higher levels (based on years of experience).

Salary negotiable: No salary range is published; employer may be willing to consider alternate experience or credentials as reason for a salary above entry level.

Security clearance required: Position is rated for access to confidential records or other security or sensitive information. Thorough background check will be required prior to employment.

Teacher certification required: Based upon state regulations or licensure for classroom teachers; may include alternative certification approaches.

How to Interpret Professional Credentials and Qualifications

Professionals' credentials, as shown in Table 2-6, can be a major clue as to the scope of work at a site, as well as a valuable primer for the preprofessional who is not sure of what certifications or further educational degrees to seek (see Table 2-7). A good strategy for exploring careers is to visit the Web site of a workplace and take note of the credentials behind staff members' names. Credentials may vary from state to state, but some standards are recognized nationally.

Table 2-6 **Professional Credentials**

CDA	Child Development Associate: entry-level credential honored in many states; requires renewal every three years; reflects minimum age of 18, high school diploma or GED, as well as specific number of hours in work experience and formal training; administered by the Council for Professional Recognition.
CCP	Certified Childcare Professional: entry-level credential reflecting approximately double the number of experience and training hours of the CDA; administered by the National Child Care Association.
CFCS	Certified in Family and Consumer Sciences through the American Association of Family and Consumer Sciences; the credential is typed as an acronym following the professional's name.
CFLE	Certified Family Life Educator: credential of the National Council on Family Relations; the credential is typed as an acronym following the professional's name.
CPA	Certified Public Accountant: designation that reflects licensing or testing in the professional's state.
CFP	Certified Financial Planner: credential reflecting training and testing by the Certified Financial Planner Board of Standards.
CPR/Child CPR	Cardiopulmonary resuscitation for adults or children: rescue technique required at some job sites; requires retraining and recertification at regular intervals.
LCDC	Licensed Chemical Dependency Counselor: credential reflecting training in the specialty areas of chemical dependency, alcoholism, addictions.
LMFT	Licensed Marriage and Family Therapist: designation of counselor or therapist who has passed examinations and met requirements stipulating hours of supervised therapy sessions of the American Association of Marriage and Family Therapy.
LMSW	Licensed Master of Social Work: credential reflecting both education level (master's degree) and licensure, requiring accomplishment of supervised casework.
LPC	Licensed Professional Counselor: credential awarded by a state Board of Examiners, resulting from testing and meeting education and fieldwork requirements.
NAC	National Administrator Credential: specialized training for directors and administrators of child care centers and programs; must be regularly updated with continuing education; administered by the National Child Care Association.

Table 2-7 **Educational Credentials**

AS/AA	— Associate in Science/Arts, two-year degree
AAS	— Associate of Applied Science, two-year degree
BA	—Bachelor of Arts, four-year degree
BS	— Bachelor of Science, four-year degree
BSW	— Bachelor of Social Work, four-year degree
DO	— Doctor of Osteopathic Medicine, professional medical degree
EdD	— Doctorate of Education, graduate degree
GED	— General Equivalency Diploma, substitute for high school diploma
IB	— International Baccalaureate, two-year pre-university program and international degree
JD	— Juris Doctor, professional graduate degree in law
MA	— Master of Arts, graduate degree
MAT	— Master of Arts in Teaching, graduate degree
MBA	— Master of Business Administration, graduate degree
MD	— Medical Doctor, professional degree
MDiv	— Master of Divinity, graduate degree
MEd	— Master of Education, graduate degree
MS	— Master of Science, graduate degree
MSW	— Master of Social Work, graduate degree
PhD	— Doctor of Philosophy, graduate degree

Local Sites for the Field Experience

Internship possibilities number in the hundreds in metropolitan areas. Even in rural areas, many so-called metropolitan agencies are represented in outreach or satellite programs. And, of course, local programs exist in all counties and towns. Your own research can uncover new opportunities. The telephone book *Yellow Pages* and the Internet are good starting points. On the Internet, visit Web sites such as United Way and county governments, which list social service agencies and schools, many of which welcome interns.

If your internship requirement is for two semesters, you may be encouraged by your academic program or advisor to select two different sites. Exposure to two agencies and, ideally, two populations broadens the student view of professions as well as the view of the community. The two semesters of

List of Local Sites That May Offer Internships

Salvation Army

Habitat for Humanity

Friends of the Family Shelter

Curriculum and Research Center

Public Library

Family Resource Center

Big Brothers/Big Sisters

CASA: Court-Appointed Special Advocates

CPS: Child Protective Services

ECI: Early Childhood Intervention

Retired Senior Volunteer Program

Parenting and Family Center

Child Advocacy Centers

County Probation

County Youth Probation

Independent School Districts

Charter Schools

Museum and Zoo

Camp for Diabetic Children

Red Cross

YMCA

Senior Centers

Cooperative Extension Service

4-H Program

Head Start

internships may be logically paired or intentionally very different. Examples are as follows:

Semester 1: Court advocate

Semester 2: County Youth Probation

Semester 1: NAEYC-accredited preschool

Semester 2: Hospice care

Semester 1: Parenting education

Semester 2: Community Senior Center

✳ PREVIEWING AND INTERVIEWING

Ideally, at least a semester before your internship, you can visit several sites that you are considering for the field experience. Visits can be accomplished in person, on-line, or through phone or e-mail. A site preview may include an interview or tour to see typical activity and scope of the agency. An interview may be scheduled with a volunteer coordinator or intern supervisor. Your academic program or instructor may require that you interview at a site only after securing the instructor's permission or "clearing" the site as an acceptable internship setting. Even if your instructor does not require notification first, the instructor may be a good first interview! The instructor may have important background information about the site or may refer you to the best person to interview.

Ideally, an intern should visit several sites being considered for the field experience.

Planning the Interview

In a site interview, you will want to discuss the role of an intern at that site, along with possible tasks and activities (see Table 2-8). Common opportunities include observing professionals working with clients, joining a project team, conducting a study or participating in research, and learning to facilitate an on-site program or conduct an educational program. Obviously, the range of opportunities varies according to type of site. As you learn more about the site, you will consider the practical issues of hours, transportation, energy required, familiarity of tasks, amount of supervision or autonomy, level of hands-on or observation activity, and so forth. You may want to make notes during the interview, especially if you intend to interview at other sites and make a comparison of opportunities.

Whenever possible, tour the internship site when you visit it for an interview. Ideally, view areas where interns work and ask to see typical work stations for interns. If such a visit is not possible, ask specific questions that will permit you to have an image of what everyday life would be like. Sometimes, interns are surprised to find themselves in settings that have little or no interaction with other people. Such a circumstance can be distressing, especially if the internship is structured for full eight-hour workdays. Good questions to ask are the following:

Do interns work together, or are they assigned to different areas?

Will I have use of a desk and computer? Located where?

Will I be paired with a professional to observe?

Table 2-8 **Opportunities to Ask about in an Interview**

Possible role of intern	Assistant Trainee Observer Aide
Possible tasks	Note-taking Interviewing Analyzing Report-writing Researching Teaching Interpreting
Possible activities	Staff meetings Trainings Networking Client meetings Conferences
Rules or expectations	Hours, overtime hours Dress code Personal phone calls, etc.

How much time will I work completely alone?

How much time each day will I be interacting with other people?

Research each possible site by talking with peers who are already working there or who have interned there in the past. Check on-line for intern blogs that relate to your site or others like it. Take time to talk with instructors, family, and friends. Interviewing several people about a site will enable you to avoid making a snap decision or a last minute selection.

Interviewing also helps in learning important details about sites that look similar. For instance, several hospitals offer child life internships, but not all child life internships are structured the same. While the best way to find out if the site will meet your needs is to visit and conduct the interview in person, other methods are possible. Using the hospital example, consider who you could interview to learn more (see Table 2-9). If you were to ask only about child life internship, you might find few opportunities. By asking more questions, of more people, you may find several opportunities to choose between. The core goal is to work with children in a medical setting. That may be accomplished in a hospital or in related facilities. Hospital services that revolve around children include the pediatrics department, social work support, and physical therapy department. A division of hospital life that has access to all of those areas is Volunteer Services. After discharge from the hospital, children still access medical services, and you may find your internship with one of those services. Possibilities are the hospital's outpatient department, clinics offering physical therapy and occupational therapy, and outreach programs such as early childhood intervention. By looking beyond the first idea of a child life internship, you will find multiple opportunities for internships that match your core goal of working with children in a medical setting.

Table 2-9 **Interviewing to Learn about Working with Children**	
Internship Goal	**Hospital Personnel to Interview**
Child life internship	Child life specialist
Work with hospitalized children	Pediatrics dept. Social work dept. Physical therapy dept. Volunteer services
Work with discharged children	Outpatient dept. Physical therapy dept. Occupational therapy dept. Early childhood interventionist

Ethical Considerations for the Interview

Just as a job applicant must strive to be honest about background and abilities, an intern applicant must also make an ethical representation of himself or herself. Site supervisors are aware that most students have limited professional experience. They do not expect a lengthy resume. Just being a student speaks well of you.

Resist the impulse to oversell yourself. A misrepresentation can back-fire if later, during the internship, you are not able to perform as you claimed earlier. But don't hesitate to include information on hobbies and interests. Experiences such as a camp counseling job or cross-country hiking might interest a site supervisor and lead to an internship. Frequently, the student underestimates the value of such informal qualifications. But to the site supervisor, these student experiences (even the recreational ones) represent qualities that are highly valued in the workplace. The short list of those qualities are initiative-taking, adventurous, able to be alone, energetic.

Another point of interviewing ethics is your determination of the likelihood of accepting an internship, if offered. When you engage in an interview, you are commanding the time of at least one professional at the intern site. To honor that time commitment, schedule an interview only for internships that you are seriously considering.

✳ EVALUATING SITES

Site selection should follow an evaluation process. Preparation up front in the selection can help prevent disappointment later, when placement decisions are made by the site or even later when the internship is under way. Internship programs at some sites are highly competitive with many applicants. The **applicant pool** may build many months in advance, and some applicants will not even know this. Applicants may imagine that they are the only people thinking about that site. In actuality, the same site may attract many students. Local sites, as well as national sites, routinely receive applications from multiple universities in the region. Thorough research will include knowing about the **selectivity** and deadlines of the program. Your instructor may know the traditions of selectivity for sites and give advice on timing of applications.

● **applicant pool**

Total number of applicants for set number of positions in a program with a known deadline or start date.

● **selectivity**

Commonly a ratio or formula by which the applicant pool is compared to the number of selected interns. A program with a small number of interns selected from a large number of applicants would be referred to as highly selective.

A risk in researching internship possibilities is extending the search beyond the point of being productive. Such overpreparation can be called *analysis paralysis*. In short, there is a risk that a search will become circular and have no end. It is possible to overanalyze both your goals and the available sites. For some people, this may end in frustration and indecision. For others, the search simply continues and no decision is even attempted. When academic pressures require a site selection, the student who cannot take action may have a site selected by a professor, and rarely is the intern experience satisfactory in such a scenario.

Matching Personal Characteristics with a Site

When choosing a site, think about a place where you would like to be employed. Does this site offer a professional experience that will add to your employability? Will you acquire skills that will make you more marketable? Choose a site that is compatible with your **long-term career goals**. If you are not certain about your career goals, think of the site as a place to explore possibilities.

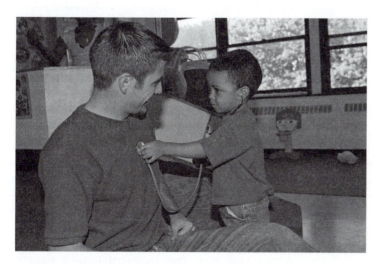

An intern should choose a site compatible with his or her long-term career goals.

As well as considering long-term career goals, you may want to reflect on your long-term personal goals. Some sites are known for their family-friendly policies such as flextime, on-site dependent care, and leave time. At other sites, arrangements around family responsibilities may be more difficult and a matter for the personnel office. Although American society is more aware of work-home balance, growth of family-friendly policy has been slow and not widespread. Federal regulations, such as the Family and Medical Leave Act, affect some workplaces and some workers, but not all.

Quality of experience is another consideration in selecting an internship (see Table 2-10). After visiting some sites (in person or virtually), you will no doubt be able to generate a list of quality issues that influence your selection. For many interns' purposes, a high-quality field experience centers on the opportunity to work with professionals, which may include a professional as a **mentor** to the intern. Other quality indicators may be professional accreditation, work with multiple populations, and opportunity to undergo training.

long-term career goal
Eventual professional position or desired career path, frequently described in a 10-year plan or similar long view.

mentor
Model, supervising professional, guide, advisor, facilitator, friend, experienced worker, manager, teacher. (Terms may be field-specific.)

Table 2-10 **Characteristics of High-Quality Internships**
Opportunities for interaction with clients
Experience working with real clients in diverse situations
Experience working with different needs or different age populations
Professionally accredited site
Child care centers accredited by NAEYC
Qualified site supervisor
Supervisor with appropriate degree/training to oversee students
Supervisor with professional experience
Supervisor willing to mentor students
Site different from current place of employment
Site different from previous intern assignment
Site with new opportunities beyond previous work experience
Site with a planned intern training or orientation
Protective screening by site and by academic program

Other internship characteristics may have high value to some individuals but are not crucial to the question of quality. In other words, these issues have more to do with preferences (see Table 2-11). The intern's preference may be a deciding factor about a site, but so might an instructor's recommendation. When the intern is inexperienced and does not have a basis for preferences, the instructor's guidance becomes more important. Ultimately, you hope to match your interests and preferences for type of relationship to the best site for you. The last Guided Practice in this chapter, "Self-Assessment of Ecological Fit," introduces the word *ecological*. The idea of a fit between you and your environment makes your choice an ecological one (see Table 2-12). A special example of personal preference arises in the helping professions because of the large number of opportunities in **faith-based settings**. In addition to institutions such as church and temple, you will find facilities such as homeless shelters, abuse shelters, adoption agencies, schools, and child care centers that are sponsored and staffed by religious organizations.

faith-based setting

Agency or program affiliated with or sponsored by a religious organization.

Special Considerations Regarding Safety. In all modern workplaces, emphasis on employee safety reflects government regulations and policies as well as site policies. Regardless of the assumption that other people have provided a safe environment and are looking out for employees' well-being, interns should demonstrate self-care in assessing risks and taking measures to ensure personal safety.

A site will likely provide specific instructions about safety considerations such as exposure to potentially infectious materials. Some sites will provide protective gear such as gloves, equipment, or clothing. Discuss, in advance, procedures for handling emergencies and hazardous products, which may include calling on designated people for first aid measures. Such procedures or situations, especially pertaining to ill children, must be treated confidentially.

Table 2-11 **Site Characteristics That May Be Preferred**

Paid internship; salary paid for hours worked

Stipend; payment that covers transportation or expenses

Site mission aligned with personal philosophy

Convenient site location (near home or with access to mass transit or major airport)

Geographic preference (South America, Central America, Europe, Pacific Northwest U.S.)

Climate (hot and humid, desert dry, multiple seasons, cool, days of sunshine)

Convenient schedule or assigned hours (may include weekends)

Proximity to natural resources (mountains, beach, parks, rivers, caves)

Recreation and cultural facilities (concerts, theatre, rock climbing, diving)

Faith-based setting

Table 2-12 **Conditions That Bother One Worker but Appeal to Another**

Controlled environment (windows for viewing but not opening)

Open classroom (no walls or doors)

Close oversight by management

Raises based on cost of living rather than merit

Large amount of paperwork

Routine work

Frequent change of focus on projects

Dress code or required uniforms

Regular travel

Independent, solo work

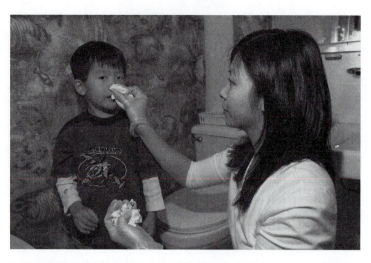

A site will likely provide specific instructions about safety considerations, and some sites will provide protective gear such as gloves, equipment, or clothing.

Your own health professional can advise about the myriad of vaccinations today, such as TB, Hepatitis B, tetanus, flu shots, HPV vaccine. Personal safety decisions—thinking through your own level of risk and exposure—may influence where you apply for an internship. You'll want to take into account your tolerance for infections and illnesses, as well as your comfort level.

Expectations and Responsibilities of Stakeholders

Stakeholders in the internship are the student, the college or university, and the community (which may be the internship program itself or the agency sponsoring it). Student expectations of the internship are usually optimistic. Sometimes the selection interview process takes longer than students anticipate or desire, but the end result of being accepted to the internship is almost always considered well worth the wait. Meeting expectations involves matching student needs with site opportunities. Thus, two things must come together to make the match. The student responsibility in this process is to assess personal career objectives and then research more than just one site that could meet those needs.

The college or university's expectation is often based on years of experience in assisting students with placement. This may mean the campus stakeholders' expectation is more realistic than the student's because it includes more knowledge about a range of sites. The value of experience with many sites thus allows guidance to the student new to the selection process. The campus responsibility is to approve a match that serves both student and community. Protection of students is paramount. For example, if a site requires a contract with the student, the university will evaluate or review that contract and is usually in the position of approving/disapproving the contract.

Community expectations range from accepting the intern as an observer to providing preprofessional training. Thus, an agency may expect little prior knowledge or experience on the part of the student or may expect (and require) a number of pre-internship competencies. The community responsibility is usually described in terms of their own program purpose and responsibility to their clients or participants. Additional responsibility is to provide a structured environment for assisting students and new professionals in their growth and helping to prepare and develop the workforce. In the best internships, students have opportunity to shadow the supervisor, be mentored, do interesting and engaging work, *and* help with the site's more mundane or routine tasks.

✳ FINALIZING THE SITE SELECTION

While many students approach the final steps of site selection expecting immediate approval, most sites require application, formal interview, or even a contract. Some selections require preapproval from your campus, especially if you have designed your own unique site search. Multiple steps may be involved just to get to the application stage, and some steps will be conditional on completion of others. A timeline, with anticipated deadlines, can be constructed to track all the requisite procedures. This chapter ends with timeline examples that work backward from the first day on the internship to identify how much lead time is typically needed for a successful application.

Approvals

Approval for your internship may be simultaneous from the campus and the site, but you may also have an academic requirement of preapproval by your instructor. An advising session with an academic instructor as much as a year ahead of time is not unusual. If you are in the position of making a search more independently, you should still check in with your department or internship placement office before making an application to an internship. With approval to make the formal application, you can then plan how to secure a successful placement.

Some colleges have internship agreements with school districts and agencies. If this is the case, there may be a separate office or person on your campus who reviews all applications and especially the prescreening for placement in schools. If an internship requires signing a contract, your university may require review by the legal officer. The preapproved or commonly used sites for students from your university have appeal of expedited application and acceptance. The drawback may be that multiple students are assuming those positions will be available. Thus, even students who propose internships at sites with an existing agreement will need to start early: the process may be just as competitive at existing sites as in the case of new sites.

Your university may require proof of **liability insurance** before your placement is approved. Some universities structure fees so that insurance for you during the internship will be covered. The policies will be well known to your instructor. Research the dates for such coverage, as it may not be year-round. If tied to the semester, your internship start date will need to be scheduled to coincide with the start of coverage. The site may also require proof of coverage or want to confirm that you do not have to be added to their insurance during your internship. If neither institution requires or provides liability insurance, you may want to check with professional organizations or even a homeowner's insurance company to secure insurance on your own.

✳ **liability insurance**

Protection against damage caused unintentionally in the conduct of your duty. In some fields, this is called *malpractice insurance*.

Applications and References

Beginning the paperwork of the application represents a commitment of time and energy toward the internship. By some sites' standards, it may constitute a commitment on the part of the student and implied promise of availability. Your instructor may provide insight about which internships can be applied for simultaneously or if you should limit yourself to one application.

Applications are found online for many opportunities, but some sites continue to require forms submitted on paper with original signatures. A good strategy is to download the application form and print it out to plan how you will answer each question. Even if the official application is completed online, a practice form will help you with accuracy. (The practice form may also serve as your backup copy, as some on-line forms do not permit saving or printing.) Follow instructions carefully; a direction not followed can eliminate your application. Read over the entire application and any accompanying instructions; you may find that the overview provides information about specific items. Answer all questions; if an item is not applicable, indicate that with "Not Applicable" or "NA." Proofread the application yourself and then ask another person to proofread it for you.

Mail and on-line submissions should be made according to instructions. Do not send extra copies and do not e-mail copies unless specifically requested. In-person delivery of applications may be invited. If you take advantage of this option, dress as if for an interview. A visit to the site always has the potential of turning into an in-person interview, and your first impression will be made that day.

Just as in an application for employment, answer all intern application questions honestly. Accurately describe previous experience with dates and times. Do not invent job titles for your previous employment; your interview will serve as opportunity to explain what you did in previous work. Similarly, do not overstate your GPA. While you might round a GPA of 2.99 to 3.0, this is not appropriate for the GPA of 2.8. If in doubt, state your exact GPA. Grades are not the only consideration in your application; other factors can often offset a low GPA. So, do not be discouraged if you must report a low GPA.

Experience in student organizations can be a good indicator of your work ethic and ability to work with others. Include membership years as well as leadership roles. Do not inflate titles of positions held; similarly, if your officer status lasted only one semester, identify that. Accurate reporting is expected for all items on the application, even those not associated with employment. Volunteer work can be listed as experience unless the application stipulates "paid employment."

List references on the application or on a resume, if requested. The list should include complete and current contact information; an e-mail address should be listed along with physical address and phone number. If the application instructions do not mention references, you can add a line such as "References upon request" to your resume. References may include instructors, employers (past and present), and even longtime family friends. Most reference checks (by the internship program) will ask what the relationship is between your reference person and you; thus, it is good to include people who know you in different capacities.

Before listing a person as a reference, ask permission of the person. This can be done in person or through e-mail, with opportunity for the person to

Volunteer work can be listed as experience on an internship application, unless the application stipulates "paid employment."

decline (see Figure 2-1). If you have not spoken with the person for a long time, or it is a professor who may have hundreds of students, reintroduce yourself and remind the person of your work. Attach a resume. If your request includes a letter of recommendation, provide enough details that the letter can be tailored to your need. Include the date needed and the format (print, e-mail, or fax). For your own peace of mind, create a list of references you can call on. That way, if you do not hear from some of them, you can move on down your list without delay.

Some applications require transcripts, official or unofficial. Official transcripts may need to be mailed or electronically transmitted directly from the university registrar's office to the site. Allow sufficient time for this process; check early with the registrar for the ordering requirements and cost. If at all

Dear Dr. Doe,

    I am making an application to the XYZ Intern Program and would like to list you as a reference. I was in your Introduction to Child Development class last year, and I made a final presentation on parent-child communication. My resume, with more details of my college experience, is attached. May I list you as a reference?

Sincerely,

Mary Jones

Figure 2-1 A sample reference request.

possible, choose a non-rush time for the processing; avoid the beginning and end of semesters. If you expect a delay in gathering official transcripts or need a transcript with the most recent grades, you can notify the internship of that and send an unofficial copy (or an electronic version). While your application will still require receipt of the official transcript, the intern site may be willing to continue processing your application with the unofficial transcript. An acceptance, then, may be conditional upon confirmation of grades as required through the official transcript.

Additional materials may be requested with an application. A writing sample or application essay is common. In some fields, a portfolio of products is appropriate. Typical contents of the portfolio are samples from your course work such as a parenting curriculum you created and examples of your writing. Just as electronic resumes are often welcome, so are electronic portfolios; essays can typically be e-mailed or attached to applications. (Chapter 8, "After the Internship," also addresses the creation and submission of portfolios.) The level of proofreading needed for essays and portfolios is high, just the same as for the application. These materials typically serve one of two (or both) purposes: to substitute for an interview, to provide a means to rank applicants. As you can imagine, the data collected on application forms document the background of applicants but do little to distinguish between applicants. Many work histories of students will be similar, as may their academic histories. The essay or portfolio, however, portrays each applicant as a unique individual. And, so, it is the review and ranking of essays and portfolios that may determine who is accepted and who is not.

Required Checks

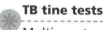

TB tine tests
Multipuncture skin
test for tuberculosis.

Some applications require health checks or proof of immunizations. Requirements such as **TB tine tests** are common for placement in schools and child care centers. More extensive health concerns and proof of immunizations may need to be addressed if your internship involves international travel. Beyond health matters, international travelers are advised to check advisories issued by the U.S. State Department and the destination country's government. Advisories include severe weather conditions (such as hurricanes and tsunamis), health alerts (disease outbreaks or warnings), and domestic unrest (police or military actions, civil war, terrorist activity). Passport and visa documentation may be required; these forms of identification can take many weeks to secure. Passports can be ordered through some U.S. Post Offices.

Criminal background checks can also be time-consuming, and at least several weeks should be allowed for such background verifications. Digital fingerprinting may be available as an option to satisfy requirements of a national criminal background check. Digital files dominate security recordkeeping today and supply immediate information about a person's record. Some internship sites run these checks themselves, and others rely on the college or university, which may have staff members who arrange for background checks. Security clearances may be accomplished in similar manner, but these will almost always be conducted by the site. In all settings, the intern's responsibility is to begin the paperwork as quickly as possible so that an application or start date does not have to be delayed.

Security forms, as well as application forms, for internships may include questions about conviction for a crime; it is essential to answer such questions honestly. If your background includes a criminal conviction or probation record, share that knowledge with your instructor. Full disclosure will permit your instructor to work with you on selecting an appropriate internship.

Sample Timelines

Securing your ideal internship sometimes comes down to having started the application process in a timely manner. Deadlines may be as much as a year ahead of the start date for a popular or competitive internship. Some sites may accept applications only once a year—perhaps because they use a committee to review submissions from all potential interns. Some sites publish their notification date, which is the applicant's assurance of knowing the answer by a certain date. Regional interview days are a feature of some internships; knowing the schedule well ahead of time is crucial.

Requirements by the site may demand advanced planning so that the hours of internship can be completed in the semester specified. Early action may be needed to meet the following requirements.

1. Placement interview at the site
2. Screening or background check by the site
3. Approval by the college or university
4. Screening or background check by the college or university
5. Immunizations specified by the site
6. Orientation or training prior to placement
7. Reading of compliance manual(s) prior to placement
8. Sequence of approvals (by site or by campus or by both)

Prior to placement, the intern may have to read compliance manuals relative to the site.

For some internships, an application must be made far in advance. Highly competitive internships include child life specialist at major medical centers, student research programs at colleges or government laboratories, legislative aide programs at state and national levels, and international placements. Planning such an application will involve additional steps such as

1. Researching the program online, by phone, and through mail
2. Securing application forms
3. Requesting and securing letters of recommendation
4. Requesting and securing campus documentation and transcripts
5. Creating a resume or portfolio or essay to submit with the application
6. Writing a cover letter to submit with the application
7. Arranging for housing or travel, depending on location of site
8. Planning appropriate wardrobe (for some settings)

The scope of planning is best understood through creation of a timeline (see Table 2-13). Although we usually think of time in terms of today versus tomorrow, the planning for an internship should begin with tomorrow! In short, the timeline should be created from the end point and work back to the beginning. This is the best way to determine *when* the planning should begin. A certain amount of research is needed just to construct the timeline, including identifying soft and hard deadlines. Deadlines called *soft* and *hard* refer to due date requirements that may be flexible (soft) or rigid (hard).

The number of approvals and deadlines varies greatly among campuses and sites, of course. Most internships must be approved by an instructor *before* application is made to the site, even if the approval is tentative. So,

---

Table 2-13 **Six-Month Timeline**
End Point: The Family Center Internship Will Begin on September 10.

Approval before logging hours: Goals must be approved by instructor on August 25.

Approval by campus: Instructor or coordinator signs off on internships on August 10.

Acceptance by site: The Family Center notifies interns of acceptance by August 1.

Interview at site: The Family Center schedules all interviews in the month of July.

Application deadline: The Family Center has a soft deadline of June 15.

Permission by campus: Instructor signs "Permission to Proceed" forms in June.

Application for Internship class: Instructor has a hard deadline of May 10.

Interview with campus instructor: Instructor meets with all applicants before May.

Research into potential sites: Conclude by April 30, at the latest.

Recommended start of process: March (about six months before start of internship).

> ## Table 2-14 **Nine-Month Timeline**
> ## End Point: The Elementary School Internship Will Begin on September 10.
>
> Approval before logging hours: Goals must be approved by instructor on August 25.
>
> Proof of TB tine test and health physical exam required before August 20.
>
> Orientation and CPR training required by the school district in early August.
>
> Acceptance by site: The elementary school notifies interns of acceptance by July 15.
>
> Submission of official transcripts and list of references by June 30.
>
> Interview at site: Principal or other official interviews during June.
>
> Application deadline: Elementary school has a soft deadline of May 15.
>
> Approval by instructor or college/university placement director by May 1.
>
> Application to instructor or placement director: Hard deadline of April 1.
>
> Interview with instructor: Instructor meets with all applicants before April.
>
> Research into potential elementary schools: Conclude by March 31, at the latest.
>
> Recommended start of process: January (about nine months before start of internship).

a September start date may require six to nine months of preparation. The least specific stages are the early ones. Researching sites could take 2 weeks or 12 weeks! Meeting with an instructor may not appear to have a set deadline, but there is a pragmatic deadline: making the contact before the instructor is too busy to accommodate all student requests. That aphorism about the early bird getting the worm is true. The student who takes measures early in the semester will be at the top of everyone's list all the way through the process. That student will be the first to meet with the instructor, first to interview at the site, first to submit an application, and first to receive notice of acceptance. The student is also self-protective: just in case the early notice is one of rejection instead of acceptance, the student will have time to either make corrections or apply to another site. Thus, with a January start date, the prospective intern can work one to two months ahead of every deadline.

The internship setting will dictate some of the timing. For placement at a public school, there is increased complexity as the intern must not only submit applications and health records, but also undergo a background or security check (see Table 2-14). There may be other populations that demand similar checking, such as child care facilities and youth probation centers.

The complexity increases even more if the intern adds the element of international travel and preparation. For some students, preparation must include learning a new language, in addition to the logistics of travel (see Table 2-15). Some university-sponsored programs abroad require a previous semester's course in cultural awareness or study specific to the country to be visited. Obviously, these activities would require even more advanced planning.

Table 2-15 **15-Month Timeline**

End Point: Guatamala Adoption Agency Internship Will Begin on September 10.

Approval before logging hours: Goals must be approved by instructor on September 5.
Orientation required by the agency by September 5.
Complete travel and move into local housing by September 1.
Check with U.S. State Department for travel advisories by August 1.
Submit application for passport (or renewal forms) by May 1.
Check for visa requirements and other special travel documentation by May 1.
Acceptance by site: Guatamala agency notifies interns of acceptance by April 15.
Submission of official transcripts and list of references by March 1.
Interview with local representative of agency during February.
Application deadline: Agency has a hard deadline of January 15.
Submit proof of immunizations with application by January 15.
Approval by university instructor or placement director by December 1.
Application to instructor or placement director: Hard deadline of October 15.
Interview with instructor: Early fall.
Research into potential international sites: Summer and fall.
Recommended start of process: July (14 to 15 months before start of internship).

⊙ SUMMARY OF CHAPTER CONTENTS

Typical Purposes of Field Experience: Although highly individual in meeting interns' needs, field experiences serve some common functions.

Self-Assessing: Self-analysis of strengths and weaknesses aids in the selection of an internship site.

Searching for Sites: The process of searching goes beyond preexisting lists of internships.

> *Resources for Site Selection:* Electronic, print, and people resources all deserve exploration.

> *How to Interpret Site Characteristics:* Vocabulary and unique jargon of site characteristics are clarified.

> *How to Interpret Job Listings:* Written job descriptions and their common phrases can be matched with your interests and qualifications.

> *How to Interpret Professional Credentials and Qualifications:* Acronyms are frequently used to describe and define training of professionals.

> *Local Sites for the Field Experience:* Common choices for internships are a starting point for determining an appropriate site.

Previewing and Interviewing: University policies may require obtaining permission before previewing an internship site.

> ***Planning the Interview:*** Advance research of a site can include anticipating the questions that may emerge in an interview.

> ***Ethical Considerations for the Interview:*** Applicants may face ethical decisions about scheduling interviews and presenting qualifications.

Evaluating Sites: The size of applicant pool and a site's selectivity are factors in evaluating sites.

> ***Matching Personal Characteristics with a Site:*** The personal match includes consideration of long-term career goals as well as site conditions.

> ***Expectations and Responsibilities of Stakeholders:*** Campus, community, the student, and the internship site comprise the stakeholders of a field experience.

Finalizing the Site Selection: Multiple steps are involved in the final selection and approval of the internship.

> ***Approvals:*** Preapprovals, screening, and final approvals may be required by both campus and internship site.

> ***Applications and References:*** Tracking applications and requesting references require recordkeeping and follow-up.

> ***Required Checks:*** Time must be allowed for site-relevant checks such as security clearance, health tests, and passports.

> ***Sample Timelines:*** Advance planning may begin as much as a year before the start date of a field experience.

⦿ DISCUSSION QUESTIONS

1. Using the opening case study of this chapter, describe the assessments that Stephen made in order to select an internship.

2. How might your expectations of on-the-job activities match those of your internship site supervisor? How might they be different?

3. If you had applied for internships a year ago, what would you have looked for? Is that different from what you look for now? What if you were to apply next year?

4. Make a review of two or three Web sites listed in this chapter. Compare them for ease of use, scope, and specificity.

5. What are advantages and disadvantages of having an internship at a site you are already familiar with (e.g., at your temple, where a friend works)?

6. What can you learn from an in-person interview or site visit that you cannot learn from an Internet search?

7. What are advantages and disadvantages of selecting an internship that requires skills you do not already have?

8. Should an internship be required for your degree? Why?

9. Construct sample timelines for your application to a local site, a regional site, and a national/international site.

10. Why are background and security checks required? What aspects could be revealed that would be relevant to sites you are most interested in?

GUIDED PRACTICES

Guided Practices offer structured exercises in critical thinking, observation (including self-observation), synthesis, and self-expression. The title of Guided Practice sums up the purpose of providing a guide: an opportunity that permits practice and does not require a final, ultimate effort.

All of the guided practices can be used by one person or by a group of people. The practices are designed as self-report instruments, meaning that answers are reported by the respondent and not collected by an interviewer or by another person who may speak with or observe the respondent.

There is not a standard amount of time to spend on the exercises. One person may use a guided practice for making a quick check while the next person may choose to spend hours on the same practice. Individual interest in a topic makes a difference in use, as does current need for the topic.

The greatest value is derived when the guided practice is completed with honest answers and observations. Any instrument may generate socially desirable answers, the kind of responses that a person thinks will be acceptable or expected. Especially when related to academic study, an instrument that calls for self-disclosure or self-evaluation risks being answered this way.

Guided Practice:
Self-Assessment of Strengths and Expectations

What are my strengths?

Place a check mark or number for ranking.

☐ Writing	☐ Listening	☐ Organizing
☐ Reading	☐ Researching	☐ Negotiating
☐ Speaking	☐ Planning	☐ Hosting
☐ Mentoring	☐ Tutoring	☐ Coaching
☐ _____ing	☐ _____ing	☐ _____ing
☐ _____ing	☐ _____ing	☐ _____ing
☐ _____ing	☐ _____ing	☐ _____ing
☐ _____ing	☐ _____ing	☐ _____ing

What do I hope to gain from the experience?

☐ to find a good "fit" for me for future employment

☐ to rule out an area of employment

☐ to work in a field I have always expected to work in

☐ to work with a population I have always expected to work with

☐ to work in a field very different from my previous experience

☐ to work with a population very different from my previous experience

☐ _____

☐ _____

☐ _____

**Guided Practice:
Self-Assessment of Work Style**

What kind of work do I want to do?

Place a check mark or number for ranking.

☐ Investigating ☐ Interviewing ☐ Fact-finding

☐ Curriculum writing ☐ Program planning ☐ Mentoring

☐ Meeting planning ☐ Report writing ☐ Facilitating

☐ Analyzing ☐ Coaching ☐ Teaching

☐ _____ ☐ _____ ☐ _____

☐ _____ ☐ _____ ☐ _____

☐ _____ ☐ _____ ☐ _____

☐ _____ ☐ _____ ☐ _____

What style of work suits me?

Place a check mark or number for ranking.

☐ Working alone as an individual contributor

    ☐ All of the time

    ☐ Most of the time

    ☐ Some of the time

☐ Working in a team with other people

    ☐ All of the time

    ☐ Most of the time

    ☐ Some of the time

Guided Practice:
Self-Analysis of Readiness for Internship

These abilities and levels of knowledge are often developed during an internship. No one expects the intern to be expert in all, or even many, of them.

	Expert	Developing	Novice
My ability to work independently			
My ability to introduce myself in a group			
My ability to introduce myself to people one-on-one			
My ability to set people at ease			
My ability to lead a group			
My understanding of professional ethics			
My understanding of professional conduct			
My understanding of _____			

> ### Guided Practice:
> ### Self-Assessment of Ecological Fit
>
> What population or sector do I want to serve?
>
> Place a check mark or number for ranking.
>
> ☐ Infants   ☐ Infants/Toddlers   ☐ Preschoolers
>
> ☐ Kindergarten age   ☐ Grades 1–3   ☐ Grades 4–6
>
> ☐ Early adolescence   ☐ Midadolescence   ☐ Young adults
>
> ☐ Middle adults   ☐ Older adults   ☐ College age
>
> ☐ Younger parents   ☐ Older parents   ☐ Single dads
>
> ☐ _____   ☐ _____   ☐ _____
>
> ☐ _____   ☐ _____   ☐ _____
>
> ☐ _____   ☐ _____   ☐ _____
>
> What level of relationship with customers or clients do I want?
>
> ☐ one-on-one   ☐ small group   ☐ large group
>
> What type of relationship with customers or clients do I want?
>
> ☐ program partner   ☐ teacher/mentor   ☐ group facilitator

Guided Practice forms are also included on the accompanying CD-ROM.

⬤ ADDITIONAL RESOURCES

Helpful Web Sites:

U.S. Congress, http://www.senate.gov, http://www.house.gov

U.S. Federal Reserve Banks, http://www.federalreserve.gov

U.S. Centers for Disease Control and Prevention, http://www.cdc.gov

National Head Start Association, http://www.nhsa.org

Families and Work Institute, http://www.familiesandwork.org

Smithsonian Institution and Museums, http://www.si.edu

Habitat for Humanity (worldwide), http://www.habitat.org

British National Health Service, http://www.nhs.uk

U.K. House of Commons, http:/www.parliament.uk

National Park Service, http://www.nps.gov

Education Regional Service Centers, http://dmoz.org/Regional/North_America/United_States/Education

World Health Organization, http://www.who.int

American Cancer Society, http://www.cancer.org

Ronald McDonald House, http://www.rmhc.com

Gilda's Club (cancer support organization), http://www.gildasclub.org

Make a Wish Foundation, http://www.wish.org

For additional material and resources to complement this chapter, the Online Companion Web site can be accessed at http://www.earlychilded.delmar.com.

CHAPTER 3

On the Job as an Intern

CASE STUDY: Tricia had trouble sleeping all weekend just thinking about her internship at CASA beginning on Monday. Unfortunately, she ignored her alarm and woke up late. She wasn't sure what she should wear at this new place, so she frantically tried several outfits before settling on her new sweater and skirt. As Tricia rushed out the door, she remembered her intention to print out a map of the best route, but there was no time for that now. The morning rush hour traffic was much worse than she had encountered when making afternoon observations the previous month. As she pulled into the parking lot, she had only a few minutes to wonder about where to park. Was there a special place for employees or interns?

Tricia was greeted warmly by her supervisor, who quickly asked her to accompany a caseworker to court to substitute for a sick colleague. Noting the supervisor's glance at her attire, Tricia realized her new short skirt wouldn't meet the dress code for court, so she had to decline the experience. She watched enviously as a fellow intern was asked to go instead. Tricia knew she would miss out on that case and have to wait for another assignment; her day would be spent reading old cases instead of observing a live-action new case.

When time for lunch came, Tricia was surprised to see her coworkers gathering in the conference room to eat the lunches they had brought. She had not known that the lunch break was only 30 minutes, not enough time to go out. Her supervisor shared her salad, so Tricia was spared from eating only snacks from the vending machine. She would be better prepared tomorrow.

✳ FIRST DAY AND FIRST IMPRESSIONS

The first day of the internship may start with an orientation like a new employee's first day of work. Tours, paperwork, and introductions may dominate the day. This chapter will detail many of the likely activities "on the job," and we'll begin with a clock-based view of the internship.

7:55 a.m.

Arrive early. First impressions do matter and promptness is a top concern at most work locations. To support the goal of a timely arrival, plan your route and anticipate delays and allow for extra time. You may need to drive the route to time it, taking note of parking availability or special requirements such as entry code or permit. If you are in a new city for the practicum, check traffic reports for several days to learn of local traffic patterns, especially during drive time.

If you plan to use mass transit or you are a cyclist or walker, timing is crucial. In the case of using mass transit, you will need to allow time for transfers. For biking or walking, you may need to include time to change clothes or at least change shoes. Your company may have a rideshare program you can utilize, especially for bad weather days. If no bike racks are obvious, make a call to the security department to enlist their help in finding storage space.

Some companies provide an allowance for parking or mass transit. However, most interns do not receive such support. If you do not know the cost of parking, have enough cash on hand to pay for a full day's charge.

Breakfast should be a before-arrival event. Even if you plan to eat on the way, or stop at a fast food restaurant, build in enough time so that you are not carrying food into the work facility. Drinks should also be disposed of before entering.

8:10 a.m.

If some other day you arrive late, apologize. Supervisors expect no less! Offer to stay late or work during the lunch break to make up the time. If work or a meeting is already underway, enter quietly and do not interrupt. In most cases, your apology can wait until after a meeting.

In most settings, professionalism dictates that you apologize but not necessarily provide a detailed reason. If lateness is very occasional, no reason may ever be discussed. If lateness becomes habitual, supervisors may very well ask about your reason.

When you are the one who is late, the reason is very important to you. You may even still have to take care of some logistics because of the reason (such as car repair, babysitter schedules). The less said, the better. If coworkers are interested, they will ask. If they do not ask, refrain from telling your story.

9:00 a.m.

Use your first day to observe as much as you can. Look for local customs of the site and listen. You may notice watercooler or hallway conversations that are more social than business. A good rule of thumb is to not initiate such conversations but participate when invited. On the first day, there may be many introductions as you tour offices. Most will be very short; see Chapter 5, "Communication and Networking," for tips on making the most of these opportunities.

Self-disclosure in such conversations deserves some planning on your part. A question about your family can be answered with minimal information, such as "We have a young child and a dog." Detailing the child's age and the dog's diet can wait until you are on a friendship level, which may not be appropriate for the workplace. A passing question of "How's life?" generally means how are you doing this hour, not expecting to hear your life history or your plans for the weekend. Answer simply and positively to conversational questions.

12:00 p.m.

Over lunch or scheduled breaks, chat in a friendly fashion. Don't try to learn everything in one day, but express interest in your new surroundings. Pay attention to the language around you. Every site has a culture that you can learn from.

A lunch break is a nice time for an intern to chat with others and express an interest in her new surroundings.

On the first day, you may be invited to lunch and even treated to lunch. But to be on the safe side, have cash to pay for your own meal. Whether you are paying or not, hold back to see what others order from the menu. There may be unspoken rules about ordering only fast sandwiches or everyone going for the buffet. Try to fit in as much as possible. Certainly, if you have dietary preferences, you can order something appropriate that still fits the group's schedule.

If you didn't know prior to the first day about lunch provisions or schedule, you could prepare for the possibility of providing for yourself onsite. Packing a bottle of water and several sealed food items that don't require refrigeration will get you through the day. You will probably find certain areas dedicated to mealtimes. You may or may not have access to a refrigerator; until you can determine that, pack food that won't spoil.

2:00 p.m.

A first day can seem very long: pace yourself. Create a revival kit for your backpack or car: *bottle of water, change of shoes, granola bar.* If you become drowsy, take a walk to wake up. Sleeping on the job is disallowed in almost all workplaces.

Stretch breaks are a good idea, especially if you are at a desk or computer for more than an hour. Change of focus is not only healthy but spurs productivity. The scheduling of such minibreaks is a personal matter; don't assume that others want to be interrupted on your stretch break.

4:30 p.m.

Do not think you have to work late at the site. Prompt leave-taking is your reward for prompt arrival. When special needs arise at the site, you will want to pitch in and work late or come an extra day: those are events that you and the site supervisor will discuss. Typically, you will know in advance if extra hours are requested of you.

An intern's hours may be shorter than everyone else's, and it can feel awkward leaving the site when everyone else is staying. You may want to find a routine task to do at the end of your shift that will help you stick to the schedule and exit on time. You may even need an exit line, such as, "I'm leaving for today; I'll be back tomorrow at 11."

The first day at the internship site can be exciting—and overwhelming. What is overwhelming at first becomes routine within a matter of weeks.

✳ WHAT INTERNS DO ON THE JOB

The range of internships is great and so will be the range of daily activities. This section addresses some of the most common activities dealt with daily: what you can learn from every task, defining roles and boundaries, attending meetings, and adjusting to work conditions.

Learning from Any Task

Tasks assigned to the intern may begin with grunt work and gophering that no one at the site wishes to do. The intern may be assigned the job of answering phones, covering for the receptionist, or other so-called filler tasks. Your attitude of readiness to learn in every setting should be conveyed both verbally

An intern may be assigned the job of answering phones or covering for the receptionist.

and nonverbally. Contrast the intern who can learn from any task—nothing is too menial—with the intern who is above filing or running errands.

Even phone duty can be a skill-building exercise worth the intern's attention. At a Salvation Army practicum site, an intern used time answering the receptionist phone to develop a protocol for handling incoming calls. The document was appreciated by the intern's mentor and was added to the training for volunteers at that site. At a family support agency, a **paraprofessional** explained her commitment to phone duty as the role of first contact for callers. She said that she knew each call provided just a few minutes of opportunity to make the caller comfortable about asking for help. Developing your own philosophy about telephone duty will help set the tone for cooperation and make the task more meaningful for you.

paraprofessional

Person in an assisting or support role.

Filing and paperwork organization at a site can be equally productive. Learning the basics about the site can be accomplished through organizing the agency's publication rack. Compiling a notebook of agency or community resources is a common practicum task, and one that yields not just local knowledge but appreciation for how organizations are related to each other. Gophering, or running errands, provides opportunity to learn the community and the chance to network with professionals at other agencies. For example, a CASA intern who moves paperwork from the courthouse to the attorney's office to CPS will see three very different venues for professionals who serve the same purpose. Similarly, making the run for donation pickup provides a view of shared activity across a community. Whether picking up donated diapers or delivering canned goods to a food bank, the intern is able to speak with professionals and make contacts for future opportunities. Gophering inside the agency is also valuable; you will meet many coworkers who were not included in your first-day introductions.

All of these examples reflect a reframing from *menial* to *productive*. Noted psychologist Martin Seligman wrote about this type of reframing in his research into optimism. He concluded that an optimistic attitude can be learned. Such an attitude can help the individual not just make the best of things but genuinely benefit from every task.

If your internship seems to feature a lot of menial work, you should take time to evaluate that. Finding a reasonable balance can be a challenge, especially at busy sites. Beginning the internship with such chores is common. They give the intern time to learn about the site and the local culture. However, when this level of work continues past a few weeks, the value of your internship is diminished. To protect against long-term assignment to routine chores, work with your advisor and supervisor to create realistic goals that limit the amount of time in introductory tasks.

Role Boundaries

By holding back on making too many unsolicited suggestions and by accepting all tasks, the intern acknowledges that the role has boundaries. Boundaries may sometimes feel constraining. A realistic question about a boundary is what is the chain of command at the site? Some organizations follow a rigid and obvious chain of command with job titles that communicate levels of authority. An example might be an "org chart," or organization or hierarchy structure, that details president on one line, several vice presidents on the next line, directors and assistant directors reporting to the vice presidents, and so forth. Familiar school titles are principal, assistant principals, deans of students or counselors, etc. In our egalitarian society, we increasingly see organizations where the levels are not so clearly delineated. Hierarchies are sometimes replaced by horizontal structures. The intern may need guidance from a mentor about whose directives receive priority.

Communication and interaction across levels may be driven by informal and unwritten customs. Access to authorities usually follows the hierarchical structure. When the levels of authority or chain of command are broken, it may be called "leapfrogging" (skipping up to the next person) or "golden-booting" (a boss skipping over a manager and speaking directly to workers). Communicating across levels is not always a problem, of course. An intern may benefit from interaction with authorities. Access and information are often gained through "gatekeepers," such as office managers, secretaries, and administrative assistants.

An intern's insight or new idea for a program should go up the ladder through the mentor and site supervisor, not directly to the top (such as the principal at a school). The intern may rightly worry that credit for his or her idea will not be properly attributed. The authorship may be assumed to be by someone higher up. This potential loss is real and reflects what also happens in employment sometimes. Your response will depend on your personality to some degree and, also, on your experience with such situations. Your future plans could dictate your response. Your response could range from demanding credit where credit is due, to accepting that your contribution to the site is not one for personal gain. In most employment situations, the ideas and words of an employee are seen as being owned by the company. This standard is not unusual and may be the case at a practicum site. The scenarios in Table 3-1 illustrate issues that you might encounter as you make the transition from student (where your words and ideas are clearly identified as your own) to intern (with unclear guidelines for attribution) to employee (with stated policies such as IP, intellectual property). Imagine yourself in these situations and how you might respond.

The intern benefits from boundaries because boundaries can serve as protection. The intern's role may be limited in scope of activity and authority, but it is also limited in liability. That is, an intern's errors are typically quickly forgiven and corrected. The intern's inexperience is acknowledged, and errors in judgment are seen as learning experiences.

Meetings in the Workplace

Work-related meetings range from weekly staff meetings to in-service trainings to all-employee communication meetings. The intern's participation depends on a supervisor's decision about the appropriateness of attendance and whether the internship hours can accommodate extra events.

Meeting protocol usually dictates that confidential information shared in a meeting not be shared outside, later. Similarly, documents distributed in a meeting

---

Table 3-1 **Claiming Ownership: Scenarios**

1. In a meeting, I hear a colleague presenting my idea as his or her own.

2. In a meeting, I hear my boss presenting my idea as his or her own.

3. I recognize my words (without acknowledgment) in printed materials being distributed publicly.

4. An idea that is *not* mine is credited to my name and receives accolades.

5. My software programming is incorporated in computer functions at the site, but my authorship is not acknowledged and I receive no compensation.

may not be for public distribution. Assume that you should not discuss the meeting with other coworkers unless your site supervisor initiates the discussion.

Clarify with your supervisor whether you are a listener or a participant in the meeting. If the supervisor asks you to just take notes, follow that instruction. Resist the impulse to add a comment and, even if asked, decline. Only if your supervisor asks you to contribute should you make a comment.

The meeting might be conducted more formally than you expect, and this would require equally formal conduct on your part. Participants may have assigned seating, and by holding back, you can likely discern where you should sit. If in question, you can always just take a seat at the back of the room or in a second row of chairs behind conference table seating. Don't take a seat at a conference table until invited. If your task is to take notes in the meeting, you may find that a back row seat is a good place to be. You can place supplies on the floor near you, use a computer or PDA unobtrusively, and even exit the room quietly if you need to.

Avoid eating, drinking, and texting in meetings. Meeting etiquette requires that you attend to the business at hand and focus on the speakers. Act interested even if the meeting has gone longer than it should. If people start leaving the meeting, maintain your poise and remain until the end.

Meeting etiquette requires that participants attend to the business at hand and focus on the speakers.

Ideally, you can turn off your cell phone or pager for the duration of the meeting. If you are expecting a call you must take, set the phone on vibrate or blinking light to signal you. If your call comes, step out of the room quickly before speaking into the phone. Return to the meeting quietly as soon as you can.

Regular meetings of all interns may also be a feature of the workplace. At some workplaces, you might be expected to make a presentation or share a progress report of your projects. Even though internships are of short duration, professional relationships may begin among interns and continue through their careers.

Adjusting to the Workplace

Sometimes your initial reaction to a workplace is feeling that you do not belong. A period of adjustment is almost always a feature of beginning an internship or job. You might feel lonely because you don't know your coworkers yet, or lonely because your work is isolated and you are expected to work independently of a group. It can take days or weeks to learn how to connect with others in the site. Some work assignments may remain "lonely" for the entire internship. You may need to compensate with social gatherings outside of work or resign yourself to a short-term condition. Sometimes the experience gained helps you realize that a solitary setting can be tolerated for three months but is something you will avoid in permanent employment.

Another problematic reaction is being bored. Initially, your supervisor may assign reading or observing, when you are more accustomed to having a more active role. There may be required orientation or preliminary qualification that prevents you from going straight into a hands-on assignment. In other instances, security clearances or checks on qualifications may prevent an immediate start. A not uncommon occurrence in internships is that the intern arrives when the site supervisor is on vacation or away on another assignment. Frequently, the *only* thing the intern can do is wait. After you have asked and determined that no other tasks can be assigned or you cannot observe in another site temporarily, you will simply have to bide your time. The mature response is to graciously acknowledge that such waiting periods are sometimes unavoidable.

Similarly, a mature response is required when you find the internship and its tasks not as advertised. Perhaps you expected a lively, stimulating assignment with close working relationships with professionals, but you arrive to find that you will work in a cubicle on menial projects of questionable value and seldom interact with the professionals on-site. You may rightly question whether the internship will be worth your time. You may conclude that no period of adjustment will change matters, and so you will want to consult your university instructor about the wisdom of staying in the internship or leaving it.

The benefit to your resume may be a reasonable trade-off for completing the internship. Your school calendar and schedule for graduation may not tolerate starting over in a new internship or new semester. For some interns, sticking it out is the best option.

Whether you decide to stay or change, your instructor should be your one confidante. You may feel a temptation to discuss your unhappiness with the site supervisor, other site professionals, or other interns. Complaining widely and loudly does not serve you well. Bad-mouthing the site is not appropriate. While this internship was not a good fit for you, it may be appropriate for someone else.

If your decision after consultation with your instructor is to leave the internship, consider how to make a good exit. That could include expressing appreciation for the opportunity and acknowledging the site's investment in offering you the internship. You will want to consider any commitments you have made in choosing your last day at the site. Leaving the site abruptly is rarely appropriate. Your instructor can guide you in deciding how much notice is needed before your exit.

✳ INTERNSHIP GOALS

The goals that you set for your field experience may develop from your preview of the site or may be tied specifically to career goals. What skills do you hope to develop? What type of clients do you hope to work with or observe? What kind of professionals do you hope to work alongside? For some interns, the preliminary goals of the internship perfectly match the final goals of the internship. For most, goals are best written after some time at the site. Your university program may require a schedule for goal writing that must be honored. You may even have to write initial goals before you can start your internship hours.

You may be joining a culture with well-defined goals for its interns. If this is the case, your strategies may already be planned for you. Rather than seeing this as a lack of freedom, you can assume that the professionals who designed the internship researched carefully to produce the best plan for you. You will still be able to apply creativity in how you relate your previous knowledge and training to the internship and how you benefit from the internship.

Prototype for Preliminary Goals

One of your first tasks in the internship will likely be to identify goals for your work at the site. Initially, you may not have enough information to formulate long-term goals and the objectives or strategies for reaching them. Until you have been at the site for some time, you may not be aware of your duties and responsibilities, ongoing projects, and all the opportunities that are open to you. The site supervisor isn't aware of all of your talents and skills, just as you are not aware of all that the new environment can offer you. Setting preliminary goals may allow you to explore all possibilities and be open to suggestions.

A preliminary internship goal may be "I will learn about the culture of the organization by attending meetings and interacting with co-workers."

Preliminary goals drawn from the prototype in Table 3-2 may be temporary, or they may form a foundation for your final goals for the internship. Some preliminary goals may appear universal, appropriate for any practicum site. At their best, they are exploratory and allow room for expansion and revision. As you select preliminary goals, you may already be thinking about how to transform them and formulate goals for your specific internship.

Use these preliminary goals as starting points; they can be your working model. When the time comes to formulate the goals specific to your internship, you will be able to draw on what you learned with the preliminary goals. This chapter includes an extensive guide to goal setting, using the 3-A model to articulate three aspects of each goal: what strength or skill does it help you acquire, can you adapt it to the unique environment of your internship, and can you assess or measure the **outcomes**?

outcomes

Measurable results of a process.

Table 3-2 **Prototype of Preliminary Goals**

1. I will aim to join the culture at a level appropriate for my status as intern and for my experience.

2. I will learn about the culture of the organization by attending meetings and interacting with coworkers.

3. I will understand the purpose of the agency by reading the mission statement and attending orientation or training.

4. I will become a member of a team by developing professional attributes appropriate to the workplace.

5. I will observe groups within the culture, noting stages of development and group dynamics.

6. I will observe the variety of ways that problems are addressed in the culture.

7. I will be sensitive to differences in communication style, work style, etc., exhibited by workers in this culture.

8. I will be sensitive to differences among the clients or populations served by this culture.

9. I will be aware of developmentally appropriate interactions taking place in the culture.

10. I will strive to synthesize the observations and information to create a coherent **knowledge base** of the culture.

knowledge base

Understanding of essential elements of a phenomenon or setting that lead to further learning and expansion.

Goal Writing

Express your goals in positive language. Statements that assume success is possible set the tone for consistent efforts toward accomplishment. State what you want to happen, not what you don't want to happen.

Be precise in stating goals so that your results are measurable. Include dates, times, numbers, and as many specific details as possible. Don't be afraid of being trapped by dates or numbers, as every element can be amended.

Prioritize your goals. Priorities may be set according to time and resources available; when either is depleted or unavailable, the order of priority may shift. Compare your goals with the practicum site's. Organization goals are typically found in strategic plans, and the goals are usually tied to the organization's mission statement. Your review of these documents will allow you to see how your aims coincide or conflict with the larger organization's. For example, if the number one focus of the organization is fund-raising, one of your goals may, of necessity, be assisting with a fund-raising event. Even a related task, such as updating a mailing list or soliciting door prizes, would be supportive of the larger goal.

Put the goals in writing, not just in your head. Recording goals helps to organize them and monitor progress. When revisions must be made, those, too, should be written. The process of writing implies commitment and serves as a visible reminder.

Goals should concern aspects of the organization within your control, not beyond your level of activity or influence. Setting a goal for the team or unit is not appropriate, but focusing on what you can contribute to a team goal is appropriate.

Set goals that reflect your genuine interests—something you have chosen and can relate to. The instructor and supervisor are approvers, not creators, of your goals. You will be more motivated to reach goals of your own design rather than meeting someone else's plan for you.

Look for categories that your goals may fit into. When you see them organized in a new way, you will be able to see additional possibilities or confirm that your goals are appropriate. One approach is to categorize by time frame (short-term, long-term) or by level within the agency (local, national). Different aspects (administrative, professional) of the organization may be addressed, too. Thematic organization might be identifying goals in terms of their products (making puppets for the child care center, making your own set of teaching materials for your library) or processes (joint project, individual activity).

Sharing a goal and announcing it makes the goal more likely to be attained. Discussion brings focus to the goal, and other people may make suggestions that speed your accomplishment of the goal. Just talking about it makes the goal more concrete in your mind and helps you to commit the time and effort needed to meet it.

Structure of Goals

Your academic program may prescribe a structure for goals and objectives. If you are not given a model to work from, you may still find that your program uses certain terminology that you should adopt. Two samples are constructed below using a model that is outcome based. An assessment outcome will be the measurable product or result at the end of the project or the completion of your internship. By naming the outcome at the start, you will begin with the end in mind. This is a specific knowledge or ability that you will be able to demonstrate at the conclusion of your internship. The next items focus on the steps to achieve that end, using the typical terms of goals and objectives. Variations in the terms are aims (goals), tasks (objectives), strategies (objectives).

#1 Sample

Outcome:
Identify and list professional organizations and credentials.

Goal:
Determine what credentials the professionals at the site hold.

Objectives:
two objectives to meet this goal:

1. Through informal interviews and observation, determine what credentials the professionals at the site hold.
2. Relate the credentials to my own career plans.

#2 Sample

Outcome:
Identify and describe diverse community populations and programs.

Goal:
Identify populations or clients served at the worksite and interact with them.

Table 3-3

Starter Words for Goals	Starter Phrases for Objectives
Acquire . . .	In observing the staff of _____, I will record in my journal . . .
Develop . . .	For a special project I can create and leave at the center, I will . . .
Demonstrate . . .	To learn about this special population, I will . . .
Understand . . .	To gain a view of agency hiring standards, I will . . .
Assess . . .	For an analysis of benefits to the clients, I will . . .
Evaluate . . .	To learn about community resources, I will . . .
Interpret . . .	To assess my skill level in _____, I will . . .
Apply . . .	

Objectives:
three objectives to meet this goal:

1. Observe and query about the client base.
2. Research typical clients through Web site, brochure, annual report, etc.
3. Participate in program activities that allow interaction with clients.

Sample Language for Goals and Objectives

Action verbs dominate the language of goal setting. Words such as *demonstrate* and *apply* lead to results that can be tested. If a goal is to demonstrate oral communication skills, the demonstration will be an actual event (or series of events) that can be evaluated. See Table 3-3 for examples of starter words and phrases that can be used in developing goals and objectives. Chapter 7, "Assessment and Evaluation," details means for measuring goals.

Finalizing Goals

In the process of finalizing your goals, it is useful to articulate three aspects of each goal, as shown in Table 3-4: what strength or skill does it help you acquire; can you adapt it to the unique environment of your internship; and can you assess or measure the outcomes? These concerns will have to be answered when you share goals with your instructor and site supervisor.

Table 3-4

	Critique of Goals
Acquire	Does the goal reflect a strength or skill that I hope to acquire during the internship?
Adapt	Can I adapt the goal to time and resource conditions of the environment?
Assess	Can I assess the goal? Have I identified measurable outcomes?

Acquire. Your career goals may dictate a skill set that can be acquired or begun in the internship. A review of your strengths and skills identified with the Guided Practice in Chapter 2 probably revealed your areas for development. You can ask yourself the question, "Does the goal reflect a strength or skill that I hope to acquire during the internship?" The stage of critiquing your goals is focused on you and what is important to you. The more specific you can be about that focus, the more likely you will be able to match your goals with the environment. Others will be able to add suggestions in response to your specific and concrete statements.

Adapt. The critique of goals also includes asking yourself, "Can I adapt the goal to time and resource conditions of the environment?" This question moves your focus from your dream to the real conditions. You will have to take the environment as is, which may or may not support your goals. For example, if your goal were to create a digital photo inventory of resources, you would have to consider what equipment would be used. If there is no computer available for your use on-site, you will have to adapt by bringing your own laptop or modifying the goal. In the case of resources, a modification would involve the site supervisor as well as the academic instructor. This three-way discussion of each of your goals is crucial to the critique.

Feasibility asks the question, is this possible? Can it be done? Can it be achieved in this place, in this time frame? Major initiatives in industry often conduct feasibility studies assessing resources, staffing, equipment, funding, deadlines, and schedules. Managing the intersection of these demands determines the outcome or dictates changes. Feasibility studies also include contingency plans, which identify potential problems and solutions. In considering the feasibility of your internship goals, you, too, can develop contingency plans. For example, does your goal for observing and assisting in four programs in a month allow for your supervisor's two-week vacation (something you would not know about in your goal-planning stage)? Contingencies could include scaling back the number of programs, or asking for permission to visit a site in another county. Flexibility is usually a key component to feasibility.

✳ **feasibility**
Ability to be accomplished.

The adaptations you make to environmental conditions are an example of bidirectional influence. You react to a condition and adapt your plan or behavior, and the environment is then influenced by your adaptation. Social environments are especially responsive to the influences. For example, in a training situation, you may intend to use a digital display of information to stimulate discussion by participants. You discover that you cannot access your computer files at the site. Your contingency plan is small group discussion, using the technique of buzz groups. That technique does stimulate discussion and has the side effect of generating new friendships among participants. Both you and the environment have adapted.

Assess. Finalizing a goal includes planning its measure. You will want to ask yourself, "Can I assess the goal? Have I identified measurable outcomes?" Outcomes represent how you, the site supervisor, and the instructor will know when you've accomplished the goal. Determine in advance what evidence will document success.

An outcome's measure may be as simple as noting if a product was created or not. At a higher level of evaluation, the quality of the product is assessed. If the outcome were to be your increased knowledge of something, the measure would be how much knowledge you gained, which could be demonstrated with a pre- and posttest, or an essay or report to your university class. Your university instructor may be concerned with your achievement compared to a benchmark established for your cohort or an assessment of your starting competency and ending competency. A tangible measure could be a certificate earned in CPR training or your score on a licensure test.

✳ UNDERSTANDING THE CULTURE

culture
Shared knowledge and practices in a defined setting.

assimilation
Process of adopting the characteristics and norms of the organization.

acculturation
Process of adapting to a different set of rules and behaviors.

collaborative work
Professional activity conducted in small groups or teams, in concert with colleagues or coworkers, toward common program goals.

Understanding and, ideally, joining the **culture** of the internship site is one of the universal goals that interns share. Just as your classroom is a subculture of the campus culture, the worksite is a unique subculture. Rarely can a person step into a new culture without learning the rules for behavior and expectations. Guidelines can be as simple as how to dress or as complex as how to communicate with multiple stakeholders in the business of the agency. Learning what messages are appropriate and the preferred means of delivery are keys to fitting in.

In a new field experience, you will surely meet new people, new behaviors, and new thinking. As you become aware of and familiar with these new elements, you will begin to **assimilate** them into your own thinking. From the perspective of your practicum site, you will be assimilated into the new setting. Through **acculturation,** a person adapts to the behaviors of people in the surrounding culture (see Table 3-5). The idea of your practicum site as a culture (or subculture of a larger community) can help you decide how you will fit in.

Another aspect of workplace culture is who you work with. Some workplaces thrive on **collaborative work,** while others are designed around individual contributions (see Table 3-6). How you adapt to either of these settings may not only depend on your own work style but also on the cultural expectations. A frequent change in thinking revolves around working in a group. In college, you may have dreaded group work and avoided it when possible. In the workplace, your success may depend on not just the ability to tolerate this work style but to learn how to be both a leader and a follower in collaborations. Your collaborative group might be other interns. Different skills may be developed based on whether you work primarily with interns or primarily with professionals. Each setting has strengths.

Just as the size of the intern cohort should be considered, so should the size of the professional staff. Will you have the opportunity to work with one or more mentors? A large staff may represent many professional specialties at

Table 3-5 **Applications of Assimilation and Acculturation**

Assimilation	Acculturation
Scenario: Lunch at a New Time	
Assimilation means adjusting to your assigned lunch period of 10:30 a.m.	Acculturation means delaying lunch until after you leave the site for the day.
Scenario: Teaching Divorce Education	
Assimilation means presenting the benefits of divorce and identifying benefits for children in shared custody households.	Acculturation means changing language to refer to the families represented as *single parent households* rather than *broken families.*

Table 3-6 **Collaboration vs. Individual Work Environments**	
Working with Other Interns	**Being the Only Intern**
Collaborative work	One-on-one work with mentors
Shared experience	Making an individual contribution
Social group	Focused experience
Exposure to different perspectives	Independence
Learning with peers and from peers	Self-initiative
Communication skills for shared tasks	Self-pacing
Sharing accolades *and* criticism	Collaborative work with professionals

a site. If the intern program permits movement through the site, you may be exposed to many career possibilities. Similarly, the overall size of the site and its **clientele** will affect the practicum experience.

In the helping professions, joining the culture also requires examination of personal boundaries. Some professions address this question in a code of ethics. For example, a counselor may be trained to maintain distance from clients when a **dual relationship** exists. This means that the counselor who has a helping or consulting relationship with a client may find herself in a dual relationship through shared membership in a second setting, such as church or temple. In such a situation, the counselor may choose to refer a client to another resource. Or, in some settings, such as rural communities, the counselor may decide to acknowledge and manage the overlap. Awareness of any power differential and chance of exploitation is key to the professional's responsible handling of dual roles.

Dual roles are not always a threat. Some may be helpful. For example, a caseworker may serve on the board of a local housing initiative and have contacts that could benefit a client who has a housing emergency. As long as no conflict of interest arises in conducting business, the roles may be blended successfully. Similarly, the role of mentor blends friendship with professional guidance. Thus, as an intern, you may benefit greatly from working with professionals in dual roles.

clientele

Target audience (such as a school population), clients, patients, program participants, customers, service recipients. (Terms are program-specific.)

dual relationship

Overlapping personal and professional relationships, or overlapping multiple professional roles.

Models of Relating to a New Culture

Three models illustrate how a professional may relate to the culture or community he or she serves: as a participant, as a partner, or as a consultant. No one model is more correct than another, but you may find yourself relating to one model more than another. Individual personality may influence the professional's approach to the community, and over the course of a career, the professional might serve in roles that cross over the models. Some workplaces specify the model that the professional is expected to follow. For example, caseworkers in one community may be instructed to avoid personal connections (as in the participant model), but in another community, caseworkers may be encouraged to live in the same neighborhood and participate in community building. In schools, professionals often have relatives or their own children among the student body. Maintaining professional relationships with the young people's teachers may cross the boundaries of parent, professional, and colleague.

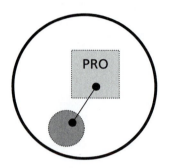

Figure 3-1 In the participant model, the professional is a member of the community being served.

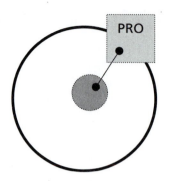

Figure 3-2 In the partner model, the professional may join in community activities but clearly has other responsibilities beyond the community borders.

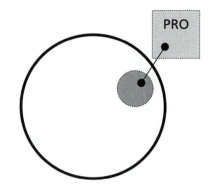

Figure 3-3 In the consultant model, the professional may be in the role of "outside expert" and clearly from another environment.

Participant Model. In the participant model illustrated in Figure 3-1, the professional is a member of the community being served. For example, the school's parenting educator is a parent of a child in the same school. This professional may not only face the challenge of dual relationships (and attendant ethical concerns) but also enjoy sure knowledge of the school culture and the community. The participant model is justified through the same reasons acknowledged in participant-observer research traditions in anthropology and sociology. Briefly, the researcher takes a place alongside the people being studied. Through daily activity and conversation, the researcher comes to understand the experience of the people.

Partner Model. In the partner model illustrated in Figure 3-2, the professional may join in community activities but clearly has other responsibilities beyond the community borders. Sometimes, the partnership is described in terms of the contribution the professional brings to the setting. For example, the sexuality educator at a parenting center partners with clients or professionals to deliver programs to various audiences, often with a goal of empowering clients to move forward on their own after the partnership ends. The professional partner may work with a community gatekeeper, or another professional in a complementary field, or clients who will also serve as facilitators with other clients. The partner model does not have to be built on fifty-fifty contributions, but regardless of the proportion of contribution, each partner's knowledge or skill is highly valued and seen as part of the whole of the program.

Consultant Model. In the consultant model illustrated in Figure 3-3, the professional may be in the role of the outside expert and clearly from another environment. As consultants, family professionals might be referred to with these labels: *guest speaker, program evaluator, curriculum author, in-service trainer, content expert, support specialist,* etc. While the consultant may be well known to an agency or program, she is typically not a member of the regular team. For example, the program evaluator may be on-site for only two weeks of the year, but when he is present, he interviews or conferences with most of the staff and then writes a report that affects the agency for the other fifty weeks of the year.

✳ OBSERVATION SKILL AND TECHNIQUE

Observation is the means by which you can study the culture before attempting to join. Observation is a form of active learning. While the word *observation* implies watching or looking (not taking action), much more is involved. It is a process, not a one-time event, that provides insight into the people and environment of a culture. An initial goal of observation is to take the emic point of view. This means seeing the environment as the person living there sees it.

You can train yourself—you may see a lot at first glance and think the job of observation is done. But look deeper: even the best observer will find a need for new skills when the task is cultural understanding. And even if you know the culture or community well, your observation now will produce new knowledge.

Even a familiar scene has the potential to yield new information. An intern at a child care center may report, "They do the same thing every day." That conclusion may be prompted by regular schedules and routines typical in early childhood settings. But it is unlikely (maybe even impossible) that a group of four-year-olds is repeating exact behaviors from previous days. The nuances of change will emerge after you set aside any preconceived expectations of their behaviors.

This section introduces ways to approach the observation process. Time considerations can guide you, as well as understanding the two types of observation, descriptive and reflective. Strategies for effective observing are described, as well as skill levels. You may also want to apply your observations to evaluate a site as a potential workplace.

Time Model for Observation

The observation process requires preparation and forethought. Preparation is not necessarily planning, but orienting yourself to what you may see and what you may need to do at each stage before, during, and after the observation.

Before the Observation

- Clarify purposes of observation.
- Read background information such as the site's Web site, mission statement, brochures.
- Secure permission to visit and observe, and comply with any security or health requirements.
- Talk with others who have completed internship at the same or similar site.
- List questions about the site.
- Schedule time when an appropriate supervisor is available.
- Practice a self-introduction.

During Observation

- Make an appropriate introduction of self and purpose.
- Dress appropriately.
- Take notes.
- Observe people, facilities, dialogue.
- Schedule time when an appropriate supervisor is available.

After Observation

- Record impressions while fresh in your mind.
- Write up notes soon after visit.

- Add reflective notes.
- Generate new questions from your reflection.
- Send appropriate thank-you notes.

Descriptive Observation

The simplest observations describe a setting. Identifying the physical attributes or characteristics is a good beginning place. Making a record of the physical setting can include video and photographs, both very affordable with digital equipment. Although immediately produced, such records must not invade privacy or violate any policies of the site. For example, people appearing in any picture must be asked for permission to photograph or film them, and some sites do not allow any recording of any kind. For some sites, even an address cannot be made public, and so a description should not include exterior features or landmarks. With these safety precautions in mind, recorded observations can serve as a rich resource.

Entering a site, describe what you see. In a school setting, you might start by looking for public and private spaces. Are there spaces where a child could be hiding? Can every child be seen at all times? Apply the same inquiry in a setting for adults. In an adult environment, private spaces may be highly valued. Look for quiet, out-of-the-way spots for consultation and meetings. Scan the environment for obvious social conversation areas. Traffic patterns and safety features are other obvious clues to activity.

Descriptive observation involves describing what one sees in a given environment, such as a dedicated reading area for students.

Listen for background sounds. Is the outside world noticeable? Do people speak in hushed tones? Do people shout? Are signals such as bells or public announcements prominent in the environment? Does equipment make noise? Are phones being answered? Are babies crying? Is there laughter?

Can weather be observed? Are offices light or dark? What colors are dominant among the furnishings? Are employees dressed in uniforms that are colorful?

If you enter the site with suspicious eyes, what do you find? If you were the inspector from the health department or the fire marshal, what would you focus on? Would you immediately see problems? Would you immediately see safeguards? Would you see only part of the environment?

After recording your description, based on what you see, consider what is missing. This is one of the greatest challenges of observation.

Reflective Observation

This type of observation draws from the participant-observer tradition in research. Some of the techniques are similar, but for the intern attempting reflection in observation, the focus is not on the participants as it would be for a researcher. The focus is on the environment as a context with the intern at its center. The purpose is a personal one rather than the study of others. The purpose of reflective observation is to determine your place in the culture.

Observing yourself as an actor allows you to imagine how you might fit into that space or a similar one on a long-term basis. Does it bring out the best in you? Are you energized? Do you feel creative? Do you feel like an insider? Or are you on the "outside looking in"? Some environments create a climate of immediate friendliness and others need a warming-up period.

Part of the reflective observation is to note your own reaction to a place or its people. Overall, how do you feel? You may not be able to tie your reaction to a concrete observation or articulate why you feel a certain way. You may feel a rapport that is expressed through statements such as, "I felt comfortable"; "I felt connected to the children there"; "I want to be there"; "I want to go back." Sometimes you need to trust those feelings as a valid part of your observation.

Reflective observation places evaluative meaning on the environment you have observed. While feelings are important, tangible signals will also be instructive. A waiting list for services could indicate high need in the community or high perceived value of facility. For example, child care centers, mothers' day programs, early childhood schools may be described by the length of their waiting list before any other criterion is mentioned. Your reflection on this circumstance would include evaluating the meaning of this criterion. You might decide that it is a valid measure, or you might discount it based on other indicators of quality. The appreciative observer notes the ratio of adults per child, or books per child, and so forth, and then sets about looking for more.

Observation Strategies

Observation depends on the skills and techniques we bring to the process. Training in observation can enhance your natural ability. You can learn to look beyond first glance and see the full environment. By using different lenses, you can examine details, as well as the big picture. Researchers in many fields use specific techniques to observe clients, customers, shoppers, ordinary people on the street. Marketers have studied shoppers in the mall; researchers have videotaped couples as they argue; social scientists have observed gang behaviors in neighborhoods. Even popular TV shows and movies have capitalized on our interest in watching 24-hour Webcam sites. Your internship will have opportunities for similarly informative and valuable observation. By learning diverse strategies, such as those listed in Table 3-7 and described below, you can adapt the approach to suit your site and your goals. Whether at a preschool with one-way observation booths or a site with video recordings of victim interviews, you will appreciate the information acquired through systematic observation.

Survey Whole Communities. In other classes, you may have observed in a different way, for example, looking through a one-way mirror, watching one child in one center. Your purpose in that setting was to focus on a single child or a single class in a designated center. Now, your scope widens. The

> ### Table 3-7 **Observation Strategies**
>
> Survey whole communities.
>
> Research the culture's history.
>
> Investigate through publications.
>
> Observe from a distance.
>
> Zoom for details.
>
> Bracket your expectations.
>
> Use all senses.
>
> Sketch the scene.
>
> Detail dimensions.
>
> Notice what's missing.

purpose is to look beyond one setting or one individual to the broader context of community.

Street maps and on-line software such as Google Earth provide different perspectives of the community—they are in contrast to your view from standing on a street corner. Satellite views from space display the general forms on the landscape such as natural elements of rivers, lakes, sinkholes, trees. Boundaries may have been created by farming crops or tree lines planted a century ago. Political boundaries appear on handmade drawings, from street maps to zoning maps.

Research the Culture's History. While history may not be evident in a community's everyday life, historical forces surely influence how a community develops. Where did the people come from? What was in that building? Finding the answers may require research through historical documents. A local historical society may provide the information that helps you understand the why behind a community.

Visual cues are age of buildings, new roads intersecting old roads, new schools, newly renovated spaces, or whole neighborhoods that have been renovated through the process of **gentrification.** Flowers and plants may be recent additions, or perennial bulbs emerging in spring may indicate where a homestead once was. Styles of architecture are obvious signs about the history, as are cemeteries and historical districts.

A community's culture will be represented in many artifacts housed by both local and nonlocal institutions. For example, you might view scrapbooks at a Boys & Girls Club showing the matches between children and mentors over the years. This would give you a sense of the history of the agency. Preservation of such records is difficult, and you may find few originals to view. (Acid-free paper is a relatively new standard for extending the life of documents and photographs.) Digitized images of historical documents may be the only way to view some things, as their original form has decayed. You could even look at original Web sites through the Wayback Machine, which is part of the Internet Archive.

Other artifacts include photographs, diaries, memoirs, letters, collections of symbols of an era, sound recordings, and film. You could review the local

✳ **gentrification**

Restoration of deteriorated neighborhoods, replacing old buildings through renovation or new construction. Typically, property values increase, necessitating a change in residence for some of the original owners.

high school yearbook or annual in its historical and current formats. Yearbooks display local customs year to year as well as national and local trends in fashion, hobbies, and language.

Investigate through Publications. Has a daily newspaper survived in the community? Both daily and weekly papers provide insights into current events and the flavor of the community. The classified ads, as well as the feature stories, profile the local culture. Subcommunities are represented through **internal organs,** publications such as employee newsletters, outreach newsletters, brochures, and public reports. These are easily found today through on-line sources.

Public documents such as tax records and property appraisals are also available on-line for clues to the culture. These are often housed by county governments. You can discover who the contributors to the local tax base are. Some will be obvious, such as a large employer or university. Who supports the community? In a small town, there may be one dominant employer; in a large city, there is a broader base. Cities often target a desired industry and create a city identity associated with it. For example, a high tech corridor is an area where technology companies cluster. The tax base influences the social service agencies that are needed and supported.

Your community might be represented on craigslist and other Internet sources of information. Although younger audiences increasingly rely on the Internet for information, some print publications persist, such as the high school newspaper. In some communities, this high school publication may be the best read, meaning that research documents that teenagers read their high school newspaper completely (and numerous times).

Observe from a Distance. Learning about a community without being onsite produces another view. A bird's-eye view may include third-party reports, the reputation of a town, and published rankings on things such as most desirable place to retire and most outstanding schools. You might find specific rankings for charitable organizations in terms of their efficiency or historical use of funds.

Some of the community services that can be researched at arm's length include:

Health services, hospitals, hospices, assisted living facilities, dependent care facilites, free clinics

Schools (exemplary ratings, size, attendance zones, busing, subsidized lunch and breakfast programs)

Libraries and their services, including bookmobiles

Cultural opportunities, such as community theatre, symphony, museums

Parks, green areas, public recreation facilities

Public transit, airports, other transportation centers

Zoom for Details. Through public events, as well as visits with gatekeepers, you can learn about the priorities of the community. Public events include open houses, receptions, virtual tours, local festivals, and holiday celebrations. Athletic events, including local high school games, are another source of detail about community life. A calendar of events published on-line or by a local newspaper can guide you. On-line city guides include visitors bureaus, city governments, chambers of commerce, and commercial Web sites, such as travel services and tourist attractions. Listings will include lodging and nearby attractions and landmarks.

✳ **internal organs**

Communication publications created by businesses and agencies for targeted internal and external audiences.

The up close look will allow you to think about what life is like for residents. What are the implications of what you have observed? A list of questions about a detailed view may look something like the following:

What is free? Is it expensive for families to eat out in this town?

What public buildings and facilities are available? What is their accessibility? How well are they maintained?

Is a homeless population obvious? Is such a population hidden? Are there shelters and food kitchens?

Does the community offer subsidized housing? Habitat for Humanity projects?

How literate is the population? What are reading and viewing trends (available through lists of most frequently rented videos and most frequently loaned library books)?

Is there a shopping center or mall? How would you describe its stores, prices, and policies (for example, bans on unaccompanied adolescents after certain hours)? Is the mall used by different populations at different times (early morning by walkers, midmorning by shoppers with young children, after-school hours by teenagers)?

Zooming for details for a specific agency may include a scan of the magazines in the waiting room. (In some places, the client will spend more time in this space than in any other.) How do people spend their time in the waiting room? Do they have freedom to leave and return? Do they need to be close by at all times? Do clients know what to do? Do they sign in? Do they speak up? Can they ask for a restroom? If they have children with them, are they welcomed and included?

Bracket Your Expectations. One of the techniques of observation is to enter the culture free from preconceived ideas. This is more difficult than it sounds because through selection of an internship, you may have learned a lot about the site already. You may have imagined the site, both in terms of physical appearance and activity. The imagery that comes with planning and anticipating produces the preconceived ideas that you should be aware of. The technique called for is *bracketing*. This means setting aside your expectations and acknowledging your biases. You cannot eliminate those ideas, but you can be aware of their influence.

Use All Senses. Using all of your senses—seeing, hearing, feeling, tasting, smelling—enhances observation. You want to observe activities, actors, times, space, objects, and feelings in as many ways as possible. Later, in your journaling, you will be able to not only describe what someone was doing in a specific moment, but re-create the entire context, either in your words or in your own mind.

Notice the noises. Think about details such as decibel level, background street noise, voices in hushed tones, elevator music, intercom announcements, phone rings. Do you hear multiple languages and dialects? How many can be heard in a single day?

Be aware of the aesthetics of the environment. Can you discern if there is a standard decorating scheme for all offices or are employees allowed to personalize their space? Do lighting, color, and window coverings create a warm setting?

Do you see break rooms and open spaces that support social interaction? What are the traffic patterns in buildings? The physical structure and its spaces may dictate activity or have been planned to support certain activity. For example, a children's hospital may be designed with an inner hallway and an outer hallway so that child patients and their families have privacy apart from hurrying professionals. Doctors and nurses populate the inner hallway with a different noise level, pace, and language.

During a site observation, be aware of the aesthetics of the environment. For example, do lighting, color, and window coverings create a warm setting?

Another thing to observe is overall cleanliness, sometimes represented most obviously in the public restrooms. Litter or trash, including overflowing ashtrays, might be indicative of the priorities of the site. A government agency may actually have no control of the frequency of painting or refurbishing. Even carpet cleaning may be a schedule set by someone who is not onsite.

A building's comfort can be observed in its furnishings. Padded chairs may be inviting, but they may also require frequent cleaning. Similar trade-offs are made in floor surfaces: hard flooring versus carpeting. A detail such as floor mats may indicate interest in whether workers' fatigue from standing is acknowledged. A floor space or dedicated area for children's play also indicates priorities. Providing furniture appropriate for both children and adults prevents either from having to use uncomfortable seating.

Using all of your senses, observe the welcoming tone of the site. What do you notice first? A smell or a noise may create your first impression. Is it easy to navigate doors and hallways? Do you feel lost? Are signs posted in more than one language? All of these markers create the overall atmosphere and contribute to your job satisfaction.

Sketch the Scene. Sometimes it is helpful to sketch or map what you are observing. Sketch a scene one day (regardless of your artistic skill) and then revisit it the next day—what did you leave out?

A classroom exercise is to review the contents of a room. What can you recreate from memory? By making a list of the contents or by mapping them to a diagram of the room, you are not only testing your first observation but you are also making a record of it.

Table 3-8	
Classroom Dimensions to Detail	
Wide array of objects	Narrow array of objects
Male focused	Female focused
Familiar	Novel
Child focused	Adult focused
Warm colors	Cool colors
Inviting	Closed
Informal	Formal
Noisy	Quiet
Lively	Subdued
Clean	Dirty
Cluttered	Orderly
Lived-in	Organized
Old	New
Outdated	Up to date
Antique	Modern

Consider that your sketch is also an interpretation. Would different people draw the sketch the same way? Think of a map of a classroom from others' views: the teacher's, the aide's, the parent's, the student's, the principal's, the visiting nurse's. Their views will have a different focus. They see the classroom in terms of specific functions. You can sketch in words (highly descriptive text as a novelist might), in drawings, on a palm (PDA), on a computer tablet, or as a narrative into your iPod. Sketch in poetry, in prose, in rap—whatever is most descriptive for you.

Detail Dimensions. Another way to stretch your power of observation is to think in different dimensions. Detailing a dimension is thinking of the extremes of a continuum and then identifying where on that continuum your observation would fall. For example, a classroom could be described as student-centered or teacher-centered (the extremes of the continuum) (see Table 3-8). As you enter the room, what do you see first: the teacher's desk or the child's reading center? Are objects and wall hangings at a child's eye level or are they at an adult's level? Your observation will place the classroom at a point somewhere between completely child-centered and completely teacher-centered. The intent of this exercise is not to determine a ranking, but to observe more details.

Notice What's Missing. One of the most difficult observations is to consider what you do not see or hear or feel. Especially if you are new to a type of environment, you may not have a frame of reference for all that is possible to be in a setting. (For example, an experienced teacher may be an expert observer of facilities for children. You might not notice the lack of learning centers or children's books if you have not worked with children using those materials.) In terms of clients, you might notice a lack of diversity of ages, ethnicities, abilities, and so forth. Interaction is difficult to gauge, and you may struggle to decide if that is missing. An added reflection to the question of what is missing is to consider if that element is always missing or is present only at certain times. A risk of noting missing elements is to jump to a conclusion without gathering more data. For example, you may have been trained to look for adherence to standards such as NAEYC teacher to child ratios. While you are looking for the ideal, all centers will not meet that standard.

Levels of Observation Skill

Observation is a skill that can be developed. You may start out as a novice but with practice move to higher skill levels. This breakdown describes just three levels: novice, intermediate, and expert. The novice observer most frequently makes subjective, emotional responses to the environment. The focus for the observation may be unclear and the purpose not identified. Observation is not systematic and, therefore, the set of descriptions may appear to be random and unconnected.

The intermediate level of skill is represented by a greater focus, with a plan for what type of information is desired. The observer makes appropriate scans of the environment but may be limited in technique or strategy. The intermediate observer may rely on just one or two strategies and think that's complete.

In contrast, the expert observer draws from multiple strategies and understands the need for both detail and the big picture. The work is begun with an organized plan or systematic method. The focus is identified and strategies are selected that will support accurate observation. The expert uses both descriptive and reflective observations, making a record throughout the process.

Based on prior experience and study, the expert routinely incorporates **triangulation** of data sources. The use of multiple indicators allows the observer to confirm personal observation. For example, an expert observer at a child care center would do more than watch the children to assess quality. Measures would include teacher-child ratio, number of children on the waiting list, anecdotal stories about the center and its reputation, welcoming atmosphere for families, parent newsletters and other communication, and the physical environment. All of these indicators would be considered with the curriculum, use of time, and similar measures to produce a full description of the center.

Observation skill includes the ability to articulate and share those observations. In many professional settings, multiple observations inform a decision that may be crucial. For example, cooperating teachers benefit from interns' observations in the classroom. The extra source of information coming from an extra set of trained eyes typically provides new perspective that teachers appreciate. In a child advocacy setting, an intern's observation could include debriefing with the case management team after a home visit when parental rights are being questioned. The intern may be invited to participate in that discussion, contributing the detail or the insight that assists in critical decision making. A key skill is to articulate not all that was observed, but selected evidences that are relevant.

Observing Internal Dynamics

The internal dynamics of a workplace refer to the people and their collegiality, or how they get along. The size and functioning of work groups, as well as the methods by which teams are built, influence dynamics. The demographics

triangulation

Use of multiple methods and data sources to form conclusions.

The internal dynamics of a workplace refer to the people and their collegiality.

of the workforce also influence dynamics, especially in terms of generational work styles. As an intern, you can observe these dynamics and imagine yourself in that group. You can estimate how you would contribute in such a work group and whether your voice would be heard. A group's openness to newcomers can also be observed.

Look for groups that can be identified as to their stage of development. A common staging model of group formation is "form, storm, norm, perform, and adjourn." This model predicts the typical processes of group work. First, the group must *form,* either voluntarily or by assignment. Roles are created or assigned at this stage. At the stage of *storm,* group members may bid for attention, compete for power, and emotions could be high. The third stage is *norm,* meaning that group members start listening to each other. Roles are clarified and jobs are defined. The next stage of *perform* refers to the actual work of the group. Usually, strong loyalty and group spirit develop. A final stage is *adjourn,* where the group may be dissolved because its work is done. In some workplaces, the adjournment is a period of reassignment as new groups are formed for new projects. The intern's observation can include a personal image: how might you work in a group at these stages?

You may see examples of intentional team building. The workplace may sponsor recreational activities or retreats. Such events may be designed to increase team interaction in order to promote work productivity. These activities exclude family members and friends. You can decide how you feel about such activity. Some may be scheduled only during working hours, but some sites schedule team-building events in evenings and weekends, with attendance expected.

Observing the workplace from a generational view, you can expect that most site supervisors are of the baby boomer generation, meaning that they were born between 1946 and 1964. The next generation is called Generation X, meaning that members were born between 1961 and 1981. Generation Y was named by marketers to reflect birth years of 1977 to 2003, but newer names are emerging for the next cohort: Millennial Kids, NetGens, and the iGeneration. The birth years to describe these groups will probably shift in the next decade. For example, right now, iGeneration reflects birth years beginning in 1982. So, there is overlap between this group and the Generation Y group. Describing a workforce in sociohistorical terms means that we

Table 3-9 **Potential Workplace Aspects**

Working Conditions	Opportunities for Professional Development	Management Style
Pay scale (published/nonpublished)	Opportunity for promotion	Management model
Raises (merit/cost-of-living)	Support for continuing education, tuition reimbursement	Hierarchy or career ladder
Overtime pay or compensation time	Training (in-house/outside agency)	Guidance from management
Provision for occasional time off: for vacation, for illness	Support for conference attendance	Receptivity to suggestions
Benefits, including retirement account		Open door policies
Provisions for flextime and job-sharing		
Evaluation methods		
Hours of work		

expect the age cohort to influence how workplaces operate. It may be more accurate to say that your cohort *and* your training in technology influence your work style.

Observation of Potential Workplace

The internship provides opportunity to see a workplace in action. Your site supervisor may also talk about the site as a possible source of employment. Most internships do not turn into paid employment after graduation, but all have the potential to display up close views of working conditions and professional standards. Three aspects of the workplace to consider are its working conditions, the opportunities for professional development, and the management style utilized (see Table 3-9).

Working conditions may be hard to discern. For some public employment, pay scales are published; in others, discussion of compensation is discouraged. You may be unable to have a conversation about raises and overtime pay. Questions about benefits can be answered by a human resources department or in published manuals, but policy may not tell the whole story. In some environments, taking vacation days or leave time is discouraged; in others, taking time off is facilitated by agreeable coworkers or flexible schedules.

Opportunities for professional development may not be a part of written policy, but you can ask questions of the professionals about whether they travel to conferences regularly. Most agencies and businesses that offer tuition reimbursement for furthering education share that information openly. On-the-job training and in-service days also serve as professional development and are an added benefit for the workplace. Usually, management style will be obvious to the intern-observer. Notice the forms of address used among colleagues and use of titles. A hierarchy may be evident through seating, deference in the hallway, or office furnishings.

Management style may be observed in meetings or in how information is communicated. You may see a top-down approach or a lateral organization that allows all employees to approach the boss. A supervisor with an open-door policy invites workers to share their ideas and suggestions. Your reaction to the different styles might influence your career plans.

✳ PROCESSING FEELINGS AND PERSONAL REACTIONS

Especially in the helping professions, it is not unusual for interns to feel some sense of overwhelm or even personal inadequacy at the needs of clients they work with. Many social service agencies are understaffed and may obviously be lacking in resources. There may be no easy solutions to clients' problems, or there may be no solutions at all. In some situations, the intern may be frustrated by slow processes or concerned that things aren't happening fast enough.

The historical perspective is more positive. We know that populations that were underserved in generations past are now addressed, even if sometimes inadequately. Over time, progress is made and the professional whose career spans decades is more likely to be able to see this. For the new professional and the intern, the big picture may be obscured by pervasive problems.

What the intern sees up close becomes the focus of the internship, and this may include feelings that must be processed. The working professional has to separate personal reaction from professional reaction, knowing that the two are intertwined. If the professional reaction is primary, personal distress is alleviated. For example, processing a death while working at the hospice evokes both professional and personal feelings. The professional reaction includes calling in resources, arranging grief counseling for the family, and maintaining perspective on the person's overall life. If the hospice worker's focus were only on a personal reaction of sadness and grief, the emotional toll would preclude helping the client or the client's family. The worker may still experience sadness at the client's death, but that sadness does not carry a long-term cost such as professional burnout.

Some of the emotions specific to different situations include anger about family violence and frustration at victims' seeming helplessness. Victim advocates at a police department see the worst examples of inhumanity, including extreme cases of child abuse and rape. Professionals in many settings deal with the frustration of clients', students', or families' inability to address or overcome problems. Even the emotional task of accepting limitations of yourself and others must be processed. Some clients resist help from professionals and choose their own path.

One of the challenges for the intern or new professional is the personal connection that may develop with a client. The intern may begin to serve in the role of therapist or confidante. This relationship can form quickly before the intern is fully aware of the risks. Teachers are frequently in this position when a student forms a bond with them. In an effort to help a child, the intern may feel the impulse to house or feed the child or provide recreation such as swimming or games. In most cases, the resulting bond creates new problems and risks, losing the ethical distance between the provider and recipient.

A personal connection may also be heightened when a client shares personal details in confidence. The trap is that the intern then reciprocates with a personal story. The professional finds a way to empathize without self-disclosure. Resist sharing details of your own history, which might include similar issues of abuse or divorce or poverty. Helping professionals work in settings that promote sharing and that honor clients' stories. The professional does not use that setting to address personal issues or problems.

Managing Emotions

A valuable outcome of the internship is developing strategies for managing your emotions in a professional manner. Mentors are appropriate resources for learning strategies and also for guidance about boundaries, emotion processing, and circumstances that demand referral. Before the field experience, the intern may have had only a personal reaction to a client's situation. With experience, the intern begins to adopt the professional's perspective, eventually prompting a shift in identity. This shift signals the integration of classroom knowledge and professional **praxis.**

Many interns find that documenting their field experience through a **journal** also helps to process feelings and reactions to the experiences and people encountered. Interns use the journal to support their transition to praxis. The journal also serves to document the experience for academic purposes. Journal assignments are a requirement in some internships, typically written weekly and increasingly submitted through electronic means. Their usefulness extends beyond the logging of internship hours and, for some, introduces their writers to the value of journaling. Chapter 5, "Communication and Networking," will discuss the process of journaling in depth.

praxis

The integration of ideas and practice; typically, the application of theory or knowledge such as in a field experience. Also a commercial test series.

journal

Record of events, typically written daily or weekly.

● SUMMARY OF CHAPTER CONTENTS

First Day and First Impressions: Preparation for the first day at the site supports making a good first impression.

What Interns Do on the Job: A range of activities will face most interns, but some common concerns can be identified across sites.

> *Learning from Any Task:* Even the least favored task has potential for providing a learning experience.

> *Role Boundaries:* The observant intern learns informal and formal rules for communication and interaction with colleagues, families, students, and clients.

> *Meetings in the Workplace:* Protocol for attending and participating in meetings should be clarified.

> *Adjusting to the Workplace:* A period of adjustment is common for interns and new employees.

Internship Goals: While interns may set goals specific to a site, a common universal goal is to apply knowledge and theory while learning new skills in a workplace.

> *Prototype for Preliminary Goals:* A preliminary set of goals is a working model that allows for revision and expansion.

Goal Writing: The writing of goals incorporates stating what you want to happen, prioritizing, and sharing with mentors.

Structure of Goals: An outcome-based model integrates outcomes, goals, and objectives.

Sample Language for Goals and Objectives: Starter words and phrases, emphasizing action verbs, lay a foundation for goals and objectives.

Finalizing Goals: Critique three aspects of goals: acquisition of strengths or skills, adaptation of time and resources, assessment of outcomes.

Understanding the Culture: Assimilation and acculturation are major processes of entering the culture at an internship site.

Models of Relating to a New Culture: Three models illustrate how an intern or new professional may approach a new environment: participant, partner, and consultant.

Observation Skill and Technique: Observation is an active process crucial to entering new environments.

Time Model for Observation: Observation can be based on sequential steps.

Descriptive Observation: A full description articulates both what is present and what is not present.

Reflective Observation: The participant-observer tradition undergirds the evaluative processes of reflective observation.

Observation Strategies: Training can develop natural observation skills.

Levels of Observation Skill: Observers advance through skill levels of novice, intermediate, and expert.

Observing Internal Dynamics: Processes of group formation and teaming can be observed in workplaces and classrooms.

Observation of Potential Workplace: Internships provide a view of a workplace's working conditions, opportunities for professional development, and management style.

Processing Feelings and Personal Reaction: Learning to manage emotions in a professional manner is one outcome of a successful internship.

◉ DISCUSSION QUESTIONS

1. Using the opening case study of this chapter, itemize Tricia's errors and suggest strategies you would recommend to a new intern.
2. Five scenarios are presented in Table 3-1, "Claiming Ownership." Select at least one and develop it with hypothetical context, including specific responses that are appropriate.
3. Write a case study in which an intern is requested to perform a task beyond his or her job description.
4. Sketch or re-create a room's contents. What can you re-create from memory? Revisit the room to check on your observation skills.
5. Using the samples in this chapter, write three goals for your next professional experience after completing this internship.

6. Recalling a group you joined in the past, identify the stages of group formation and compare it with the group dynamics at your internship site.

7. Give examples of professional behavior in workplace meetings.

8. Identify processes of assimilation and acculturation that you have experienced in the internship or elsewhere.

9. Explain what is meant by managing personal emotions on the job.

10. Explain what is meant by processing personal emotions resulting from the job.

⊙ GUIDED PRACTICES

Guided Practices offer structured exercises in critical thinking, observation (including self-observation), synthesis, and self-expression. The title of Guided Practice sums up the purpose of providing a guide: an opportunity that permits practice and does not require a final, ultimate effort.

All of the guided practices can be used by one person or by a group of people. The practices are designed as self-report instruments, meaning that answers are reported by the respondent and not collected by an interviewer or by another person who may speak with or observe the respondent.

There is not a standard amount of time to spend on the exercises. One person may use a guided practice for making a quick check while the next person may choose to spend hours on the same practice. Individual interest in a topic makes a difference in use, as does current need for the topic.

The greatest value is derived when the guided practice is completed with honest answers and observations. Any instrument may generate socially desirable answers, the kind of responses that a person thinks will be acceptable or expected. Especially when related to academic study, an instrument that calls for self-disclosure or self-evaluation risks being answered this way.

Guided Practice:
Observation at a Worksite

To sharpen your observation skills, use this framework at a site other than your internship or field experience location. For this exercise, focus on the environment rather than the people. Answer the questions first as a potential employee, and then as a client or student being served at that facility. Another comparison might be to observe early in the morning compared with late at night. How do your observations differ by time or perspective? What other important characteristics do you notice?

Physical environment?
Feel of the neighborhood?
Overall first impression of building exterior?
First impression of entrance or reception area?
Ease of access?
Signage?
Entrances clearly labeled?
Parking for visitors?
Sounds?
Background noises?
Talking?
Equipment sounds?
Smells?
Feelings of security?
Comfort?
Cleanliness?
Welcome?

Guided Practice:
Learning from Any Task

While many tasks assigned to interns can seem routine or menial, each task can lead to productive outcomes. List potentially productive benefits from each task suggested below.

Routine Task:	Potential Productive Outcome:
Answering the phone	
Serving as receptionist	
Filing	
Updating Web site	
Cleaning storage closet	
Organizing publicity brochures	
Collating handouts for program	

What is the overall balance of routine tasks with more challenging assignments?

Daily?	
Weekly?	
Monthly?	

Guided Practice:
Organization Chart

Some organizations have clear chains of command with positions and job titles that leave little doubt about boundaries. Using the sample sketch begun below, or a framework appropriate for your organization, fill in the positions of authority with names and titles. After sketching the chart for your site, ask your mentor or site supervisor to help answer your questions.

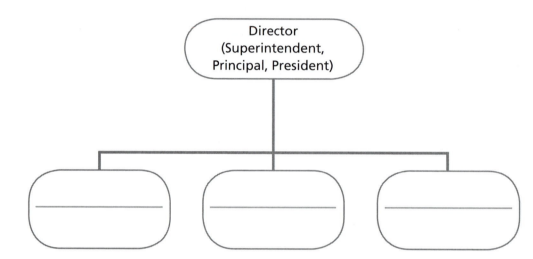

What is the appropriate method of communicating with your immediate supervisor?

_____

_____

How should you communicate with your supervisor's boss?

_____

_____

How does the staff communicate with the agency director (superintendent, principal, or other top official)?

_____

_____

What credentials or training are required at each level in the organization?

_____

_____

How is one promoted from one level to another? Is there a set time period "in rank" before being eligible for promotion?

_____

_____

Guided Practice:
Focus on Meetings

Attend one meeting at your worksite as an observer rather than a participant. Take notes during the meeting by answering the following questions.

3 new ideas of ways I can help the organization:

_____

_____

_____

3 ways I could participate (rather than observe) in a similar meeting:

_____

_____

_____

3 questions I want to follow up on after the meeting:

_____

_____

_____

3 new persons I met or talked with:

_____

_____

_____

3 ideas for projects or research:

_____

_____

_____

3 benefits from observing this meeting:

_____

_____

_____

Guided Practice forms are also included on the accompanying CD-ROM.

⦿ ADDITIONAL RESOURCES

Recommended Reading: Observation skills are an important part of research methodology that can serve professionals well in their fieldwork. A classic book, *Ethnographic Eyes: A Teacher's Guide to Classroom Observation,* by Carolyn Frank, introduces the process of observing classroom surroundings.

⦿ REFERENCE

Seligman, M. E. P. (1990). *Learned optimism.* New York: Knopf.

For additional material and resources to complement this chapter, the Online Companion Web site can be accessed at http://www.earlychilded.delmar.com.

CHAPTER 4

Knowledge to Practice

Major Points in This Chapter:

Transition from Preparation to Application
Intervention and Prevention
Theory and Perspective
Understanding Audiences through Theory

CASE STUDY: Matthew had a lightbulb moment in his junior year: Theories of the Family came into focus suddenly, with his own extended family as example. He had never thought about why families were so different but was certainly aware of his and his best friend Jim's differences in how they spent family holidays. In that theories class, the lightbulb was switched on by a life course trajectory—a big graphic illustrating a theorist's view of a person's transitions over a lifespan—that made Matthew aware of the differences between the turning points for himself, as a child in a small family with few extended relatives, and Jim, who was the youngest of four children and had weekly dinners with cousins and grandparents.

From that moment of realization, Matthew used theory to describe other aspects of his life. His choice of college could be understood when he considered exchange theory; his anger about labels of "broken families" could be understood in light of resilience and the study of how families respond to crises. As he continued to study theory and human development, Matthew appreciated how his textbooks related to real life. With new understanding that theories evolve from observation of reality, he entered his internship at Big Brothers Big Sisters eager to see theories in practice. He even saw the possibility of generating new theory through his own observations of the successful matches between mentors and children.

✳ TRANSITION FROM PREPARATION TO APPLICATION

For many students, the internship is the first opportunity to apply what they've learned in classes, from human development to communications. Some book learning has prepared you for working with people, solving problems, and applying research-based strategies to real life situations. You may be eager to move from the time of preparation and knowledge acquisition to practice and performance in the workplace.

Some people in the community may view college life as an ivory tower, a place isolated from real life pressures. Most campuses employ professors who do have experience to share with students, but campuses frequently have boundaries, real or imagined, that separate them from the community. The phrase "town and gown" is sometimes used to distinguish between community life (town) and campus life (gown). The perception is that walls or hedges or fences around a college or university are more than physical barriers. The internship is your opportunity as a representative of your school to contribute to the community and integrate your knowledge and your work life.

Attitudes are important in making the move from knowledge to practice, from classroom to community. The intern is expected to continue in a learner role but may also want to contribute knowledge from the classroom. Enthusiasm for your book learning may be met by resistance. A student knowing a newer theory may come across as being a know-it-all. The observant intern will adopt a technique of tact and timing: resist sharing your point of view until you are sure of how to introduce it, or wait for the right time to discuss with a mentor whether your contribution will be welcomed.

The matter about which you want to contribute might be central to the site's mission, or it could be a clerical task that you think should be improved. For example, you might see a technological alternative to a site's practice of scheduling breaks or days off. You might suggest that an on-line shared calendar replace the site's physical whiteboard for that purpose. Reactions could include, "Great idea," or "That's not how we do things here." An intern who does not possess tact might exclaim, "At my school (or former worksite), we did it this way. . ." Your new coworkers might tolerate such a statement—once or twice. Beyond that, you could be ridiculed and even considered a nuisance.

From the intern's perspective, you might find equally irritating a phrase such as, "No, this is how we've always done it." It is natural for you to want to offer suggestions, but recognize that resistance to change is also natural. A suggestion may carry the implication that things are being done poorly and thus may offend your coworkers. Don't assume that other people haven't thought of your suggestion before; they may have even tried and rejected several alternatives. There may be unseen barriers to the change that you could not be aware of: budget constraints, a previous mandate from a manager, anticipation of greater changes that make the suggested change unnecessary or impractical.

Resistance to change is a well-documented human response. You might consider what your own **change model** is. For some people, change is exciting and viewed as opportunity to try new things. For others, change is threatening or at least disturbing. While habit and usual practices are altered when making change, the process involves more than just new procedures. Change requires learning and taking a new perspective. The book by Spencer Johnson, (1998) MD on change, *Who Moved My Cheese?,* explained response to change with characters named Sniff, Scurry, Hem, and Haw. Through a maze in search of new cheese, the two mice and two humans display their tendencies to

✳ **change model**

Unique set of processes that describe how an individual or institution adapts to a changing environment.

welcome or fight change. The author advises that humans should expect that change will be necessary (someone will eventually move your cheese, or it will run out) and respond positively to the need for change, without fear. The maze parable illustrates the value of an open attitude. A loss cannot be ignored: change requires letting go of the familiar and sometimes cherished past. The person who does not let go of the past may become stagnant and unable to move forward. Johnson's characters in the maze eventually become unstuck and focus on their goals. To conquer fear, they answer signposts in the maze, such as "What would you do if you were not afraid?"

For some people, starting a new teaching position can be an exciting opportunity to try new things.

In your own life, you may have experienced change that was frightening as well as change that was enjoyable. The big changes are easy to recall: moving to a new house, changing schools, welcoming new family members. But daily life is full of change, also, and it can provide insight into how you adapt to change. In college, some students delight at having a new schedule every semester. Other students struggle with finding new routines every four or five months. You also have clues about your change model from the people around you: When a friend announces a move to a new city, do you adjust quickly to the idea of your relationship needing to change? Or do you feel irritation at having to find new ways to maintain the friendship? Being resistant to change does not necessarily mean a person is pessimistic or irritable about it. Optimistic people can resist change, too. And even a welcomed change can be resisted. Resistance is usually marked by slower change, slower transition to the new situation. Age plays a part in personal change models but does not fully explain how a person will react. A young person, flexible about many things, can still resist change. An older person, even if apparently set in his ways, may be open to change. Response to change may be more a matter of temperament than age or experience. But there is one important value of experience: the person who undergoes a lot of change may become more adept at adjusting to new environments. Skills can be developed that promote adjustment and ease the agony of change for even the most resistant person. For example, an intern or new professional may regret having to leave a comfortable assignment to start a new one. By focusing on the start-up skills noted in Table 4-1, rather than feelings, the intern can quickly adjust.

Personal change models, as well as societal change, are described by **diffusion theory**. Everett Rogers (2003) charted diffusion of ideas about

✳ diffusion theory

Description of how a new technology, idea, or approach is adopted, typically over time and across an entire population.

Table 4-1 **Start-Up Skills for Adapting to New Environments**

1. Introduce yourself to new coworkers, handing a business card to each one.

2. On your new computer, import familiar browser settings and even saved Favorites.

3. Schedule a lunch date with coworkers at your prior assignment; if that is not physically possible, schedule a telephone or an instant message session.

4. Adopt your own set of tools to carry with you, rather than starting with new supplies at each assignment. A small supply set, such as your favorite graph paper or your favorite style of legal pad, or your own pens and pencils, serves as both tools and symbols of your work ability, regardless of where you are.

5. Immediately add new phone numbers and e-mail addresses to your cell phone or computer contact list.

6. Give your new phone number or e-mail address to people who will need it to contact you.

7. Make a test run to determine the length of time needed for a new commute; while in the neighborhood, look for likely lunch spots, and even try one out.

8. If you know that you dislike starting over in new settings, adopt a special wardrobe for the occasion. By wearing a familiar outfit for Day 1, for Day 2, and so forth, you can create a routine that will make you feel in control of the change.

---

innovators

Inventors or creators of new technology or ideas.

early adopters

First people in a group to adopt a new technology or idea.

middle majority

The largest number of group members who accept change and adopt new standards or products.

late adopters

Those members of a group who are slow to adopt changes.

laggards

People who resist change and delay adoption.

farming methods, and his work is used more generally to explain how adoption of new ideas and products spread across society. Rogers' phrase, "diffusion of technology," is especially apt to describe how computers and the Internet have been adopted, both by individuals and by society. A new technology is introduced to a society by **innovators**, the people who invent or modify the prototypes of new hardware and software. Innovators of computers (the hardware) worked in laboratories and home garages. Innovators of the Internet worked primarily in government and university labs; the next group of innovators built the dot-com industry. While innovators number very few (and most of us never meet them), the more visible spreaders of technology are **early adopters**. These are the individuals who bought the first computers available for desktop use. Early adopters share information about their experience and spur adoption by the next group: the **middle majority**. While the technology spreads across society, not everyone is ready to jump on board. **Late adopters** wait until "the price comes down" or "the kinks are worked out." Last to adopt are **laggards**. They trail behind all the rest and a very few resist ever using a computer. (A laggard will likely never buy an iPod.) As Figure 4-1 shows, the smaller number of laggards is similar to the size of the early adopters, forming a normal distribution of the population.

Most people do not ever relate their technology adoption to the society's rate of adoption. An early adopter, for example, does not say, "I don't mind paying a premium price for my laptop in order to spread the word across society." The early adopter simply anticipates a new technology and orders before it hits the shelves. Similarly, the late adopter borrows a relative's laptop to try it out, not much aware of the role that it plays in the societal adoption of laptops. If you can pinpoint your position on the technology diffusion curve, you may be able to describe your response to change.

Diffusion theory is not limited to discussion of computer technology, of course. The theory helps us understand how any group adopts any change. In the workplace, the institution may also be described by a change model. Certainly, in education, some schools are described as innovators. Workplace

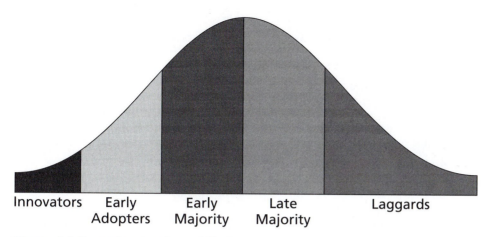

Innovators | Early Adopters | Early Majority | Late Majority | Laggards

Figure 4-1 Rogers' technology diffusion curve.

practices could be charted: some institutions are early adopters of family friendly policies, such as flexible hours and locations, on-site child care, leave time for dependent care.

Readiness for the Real World

Soon-to-be college graduates who are anticipating the accomplishment of a degree may find a sudden change in status upon entering the internship. In school, the intern has achieved the rank of junior or senior and suddenly drops back down to the status of novice in the workplace or internship site. Workplace vocabulary that you may have heard referring to the novice status include: *start at the bottom, newbie, green, greenhorn, getting your feet wet*. Being the novice sometimes means being introduced as such for a very long time. Interns are not surprised when they are introduced as "our intern" for the duration of the internship. New professionals, however, may be startled at still being called "our new caseworker" or "our new teacher" for two or three years! Each setting is different, of course, and "new" may last for six months or for six years, depending on how often new employees are hired in that setting.

A shift in status may necessitate a change in self-identity for the intern. While in college, you may be able to express yourself as a free-spirited, nonconformist through your dress or speech or behavior. At the internship site, you are likely going to need to blend in, at least initially. Joining the culture is the first goal, rather than changing the culture. Some adjustments may be more difficult than others; and for some interns, the adjustments may mean coming to terms with the need to conform.

The vegetarian whose food choices are honored in the campus cafeteria may have to adjust to an environment where vegetarianism is never even acknowledged. When meals are catered on the job, perhaps only meat-based entrees are provided. Besides the inconvenience of meeting your own dietary needs, you will have to accept others' attitudes and choices. If you make suggestions about increasing menu choices, for example, your remarks may be misinterpreted as criticism or a demand.

Similarly, clothing may differ dramatically from campus to workplace. A T-shirt with a commercial slogan or a political statement may be admired on campus but create conflict on the job. Changing your attire represents a change in role; for some college students, it is also the merging of adolescence into adulthood.

> **Technology Diffusion Curve**
>
> Where does your current agency or worksite fall on the curve?
>
> Where do you personally fall on the curve?
>
> Where does your ideal job fall on the curve?

Table 4-2 **Trade-offs: Discussion Points**
1. What constitutes selling out?
2. What changes am I willing to make for an internship, for a regular paycheck, for a job with benefits?
3. What subjects are off-limits at the site? Religion, politics, personal life?
4. What priority do I place on my personal freedom?

prevention program

Research-based and goal-focused program incorporating family support measures through which professionals assist groups, families, or individuals.

intervention program

Crisis- or problem-focused program incorporating clinical techniques through which professionals treat individuals, families, or groups.

interventionist

Professional whose work is primarily in making interventions when individuals' crises interfere with daily functioning and require external help. Example careers include Child Protective Services caseworker, CASA family advocate in the courts, victims services coordinator for the police department, disaster response team member for Red Cross or FEMA, substance abuse counselor, and adolescent suicide prevention counselor.

These examples depict what some interns may consider selling out, or selling your soul, or making trade-offs. You may feel a loss in freedom and self-expression. This dilemma is part of the real world and part of readying yourself to make life decisions. If you struggle with this issue, the place for discussion is likely to be in a campus class or with your instructor. Table 4-2 offers possible topics of discussion.

✳ INTERVENTION AND PREVENTION

Helping professionals are often characterized in one of two spheres: **prevention** or **intervention** (see Table 4-3). While emphases of educational preparation differ for these spheres (as do the professional credentials), there is also overlap and collaboration. Speaking generally, intervention refers to treatment taken after problems or at-risk populations are identified. Prevention typically refers to educational efforts to strengthen communities and families. Interventions tend to be made on the individual level; preventions often address groups or families.

In some settings, prevention and intervention are the focus of a single professional. For example, school counselors work with such large numbers of children that they must be prepared to offer services of both types. In contrast, a caseworker for Child Protective Services works almost entirely as an **interventionist**. These professionals have to consider how their interests and personalities would be put to best use in the sphere of prevention or intervention. As an intern, you may be able to observe the pressures of each sphere before making the choice of career. In fact, your observations in the field will be superior to simply reading about the careers. By observing a caseworker make the hard choice to remove a child from a home, you will be

Table 4-3 **Prevention/Intervention**
groups/individuals
before crisis/after or during crisis
parent educators/counselors or therapists
strengths focus/problem focus
ecological/pathological

able to picture yourself in that situation. By observing a teacher in a classroom, you will be able to imagine how you might react to 22 kindergarteners and the noise they sometimes generate. Just watching professionals work one-on-one versus facilitating a large group can bring into focus for the intern the demands of each approach. And while professionals' burnout may not be exhibited during your internship, the pressures that produce burnout in a workplace may be visible to you.

One approach to distinguishing between interventionists and preventionists is the best use of their strengths across what William Doherty calls levels of family involvement. Doherty's (1999) model describes five levels of participation or involvement with families or individuals by service providers (see Table 4-4). At level one, the agency has little emphasis on family involvement. Parents or family are involved for legal reasons or for purely practical considerations to promote coordination with absent family members. Such coordination could consist of permission forms for a field trip, signing photo release forms, and similar minimal efforts.

At level two, the focus is on information and advice. The family professional communicates knowledge about child development, early childhood education, parenting, or family life in an efficient setting that allows wide dissemination of information. Such a setting might be a school auditorium for a hundred parents attending an information session about school uniforms or an orientation to the school year. Typically, the communication is one way, with little dialogue between the professional and the family members. Some professionals even refer to such communications as *one-shot* or the *inoculation approach*, meaning that the audience needs only one contact. While such communication could also be conducted one-on-one, the fact that it is expected to be one-way communication promotes the use of group settings at this level.

Table 4-4 **Levels of Family Involvement**

Program Emphasis	Clients Served	Service Provider's Role
Level one Minimally involves family	Individuals, for example, children attending camp	Preventionist
Level two Provides information and advice to families	Parents attending orientation at elementary school	Preventionist
Level three Supports clients' feelings	New parents participating in a parenting skills class; Parents seeking help with a child's typical behavior issue (such as biting, thumb-sucking)	Preventionist
Level four Brief focused intervention	Parents seeking help with a child's atypical behavior or a typical behavior that is interfering with daily life	Trained preventionist, Interventionist
Level five Family therapy or counseling	Parents seeking help with crisis or chronic problem	Interventionist

normative events

Typical events or transitions experienced in human development or in family life.

family life educators

Professionals whose knowledge base includes human development and family processes.

needs assessment

Analysis of the state of current conditions or services (or lack of) in the community and/or survey of needs for a specific population. Common outcomes of such assessments are identification of program topics or goals, grant applications, and strategies for recruiting program participants and volunteers.

Level three marks a distinct change in approach or involvement. At this level, programs are more likely to be ongoing or be conducted over several planned sessions. Programs focus on **normative events** and pressures that are common to most families, or most parents, or most individuals. An example is parenting education for welcoming a new sibling into the home. In a preschool setting, the level three program might be an educational forum on parent-child communication; at a middle school, the focus might be on a parent workshop for "Talking with Your Teen." Most frequently in a group, participants are invited to share their feelings about the topic under discussion. The group serves a supportive role for its members and sometimes even takes on the function and descriptor of support group. It is common in such settings that participants disclose sensitive information. The facilitator of such groups must be adept at methods of handling sensitive and personal information. Leadership skills include helping the group when a participant cries openly, or promoting and maintaining standards of confidentiality of information. Because personal stories are so common in groups operating at level three, programs may specify that facilitators are trained **family life educators** or counselors.

Level four is brief focused intervention with intense emphasis on family or parenting problems. While of short duration, the program or treatment is facilitated by an interventionist or trained preventionist. For a typically developing child, such an intervention might be parents needing help in getting the child up and ready for school on time. Atypical behaviors may also be addressed at this level. For example, if a child refuses to cooperate in following school rules, the issue may lie outside typical development. Program participants may be in high risk populations, a status that supports use of both prevention and intervention methods.

Level five programs move beyond the scope of most preventionists. Both in range of topics and intensity, this level calls for professionals who are licensed in therapy or counseling. The preventionist may still play a role in making referrals for treatment or in collaborating with counselors.

It is difficult for both preventionists and interventionists to objectively rate the level at which they are providing service. For example, a preventionist might identify an exchange in a parenting class as level four, but a trained observer might call it level three. Knowing the differences in the levels influences how professionals identify their own role boundaries. The professional who can acknowledge his or her strengths is the professional who can deliver the highest service to clients.

While the new professional may aspire to function expertly at all levels, this is not a practical or even desired goal. The levels do not have to be viewed as a hierarchy. A preventionist who facilitates a parenting support group for typically developing children might not be effective in a counseling setting, just as an interventionist might not be effective in the parenting group. Find where your strength lies and seek out workplaces where the mission is congruent with your skills.

The family involvement levels reflect differing levels of need, also. For example, at the information level, families need specific facts or details, but do not seek support or guidance. At the counseling level, families may need ongoing support more than factual information. Populations (or target audiences) are rarely neatly identified or categorized by needs. Professionals must make those identifications through a needs analysis or **needs assessment**. This may be as straightforward as asking clients, "How may I help?" Other times, the process is more complex and could involve surveying the community, interviewing selected stakeholders or community leaders, or otherwise documenting the priority of needs. When needs assessment is not a formal process, the appearance may be that the professional is deciding what other people need. More likely, the professional is basing program decisions on previous experience and knowledge of the community. As programs are increasingly required to demonstrate effectiveness, formal documentation is required. From the intern's perspective, it is valuable to ask questions about the population rather than form opinions about their needs.

✳ THEORY AND PERSPECTIVE

Ways to view families have emerged in the literature as well as in practice. Some are formal theories that have been tested in empirical research and provide a lens for observing and predicting behavior in individuals and families. Other frameworks for understanding behavior are described as *perspectives*; often, this terminology is used to describe those explanations not yet thoroughly tested or those that blend several approaches in practice. Some perspectives have a basis in theory and are still developing. A key element to all of these is that their foundation is in professionals observing human behavior.

Some lenses work in one setting and not others. Context is key: a theory may specify that it describes and predicts behavior in *typically developing children*. Another theory may apply *only to children who are delayed developmentally*. A theory is not weakened by the exceptions that the context requires. Rather, a good theory is specific to the population that was observed when the theory was conceived and constructed. Sometimes students are frustrated that a theory has such limits and wish for a global explanation (or set of explanations) for all human behavior. In the social sciences, just a few attempts have been made at constructing grand, overarching theory, and those attempts have run into problems of universal application. In the physical sciences, the pursuit of unifying theory has been more accepted, and the current thinking on the theory of everything (TOE) suggests that conclusions about the physical world may be possible. But even in the so-called hard sciences, context is still considered: Newton's explanation of gravity in an apple's fall cannot alone describe the complicated motion of subatomic particles within the apple. For theories about human behavior, in the realm of the social sciences, researchers have even more contexts to contend with. We are likely to have more theories, rather than fewer.

From a practical standpoint, professionals adopt and adapt theories and frameworks that are useful in the context of their work. Usefulness, then,

A theory may specify that it describes and predicts behavior in *typically developing* children only.

sociohistorical

View that takes into account the larger social setting as well as the historical era.

zeitgeist

Spirit of the time. The German word is pronounced "Zite-guyst."

theoretical assumption

Statement of a premise that is accepted to be true, on which a theory's rationale is based. For example, social cognitive theory predicts that toddlers learn by observing other people's behaviors; a theoretical assumption is that toddlers have the capacity to observe behaviors.

eclectic method

Making decisions or selections in terms of what is best for that situation (drawing from multiple sources, theories, or styles) rather than following one doctrine (or theory, or style) when a decision or selection is needed.

family strengths

Characteristics of a family that enable them to meet challenges and function on a daily basis. Examples of strengths: resilient attitude, sense of humor, resources such as employment or emergency savings, shared sense of purpose or goals.

becomes the best measure of a theory (Burr, 1995). If a theory is useful, it will survive. Some scholars of theory say that a theory may be useful for a limited time, perhaps just a generation or two. This view is based not just on local context or setting of use, but also on **sociohistorical** context. A theory that assumes high connectedness among peers (for example, among children in school), such as group socialization theory, logically emerged in the 1990s, not the 1890s (when the school day and the school year were shorter). It may be possible that the principles of the theory would have been applicable a hundred years earlier—but the **Zeitgeist** was so different that the principles would not have been articulated as they are currently. The sociohistorical context thus determines the **theoretical assumptions** that are the bases for a theory's explanations and predictions. The assumptions are the conditions that are accepted as fact, and they may both underlie and limit the theory's predictions of human behavior.

For many family professionals, both preventionists and interventionists, the most pragmatic approach to theory is eclecticism, or the **eclectic method**. An eclectic approach allows freedom to select theory and research pertinent to a specific context. It also requires that the professional be aware of more than just one theory. Through education, professional development, and personal reading, professionals extend their knowledge of theory and build a storehouse of resources to draw from. To do this, the professional must remain open to new theory, which is easier said than done. Just as our discussion of change models indicated, some people are more willing and able to adapt and adjust than are other people. Too, the spread of a theory can be traced, just as we discussed the spread of technology. Innovators first craft a theory and launch it. Early adopters begin to use it, even if research has not yet confirmed its usefulness and even if context is not yet established. The middle majority wait to adopt a new theory, wanting its usefulness to be obvious before committing time and thought to learning how to use it. Late adopters and laggards resist a new theory, preferring to use more familiar frameworks.

This section reviews ten theories and perspectives that are dominant in the helping professions. Interns may be familiar with some of these and not others, just as professionals at internship sites may have been introduced to some but not all. Familiarity and use depend on the individual's exposure to the theories, training in theory, and the internship site's or agency's formal and informal adoption of theory. Your internship is an opportunity for you to practice multiple lenses *in the field,* the best place to test usefulness of theories.

Family Strengths Model

The **family strengths** approach is popular in helping programs, both in prevention and intervention. Program professionals focus on the strengths that clients bring and, on that basis, create programs that promote empowerment of the clients. Program design and direction are often shared between professional and client. This approach is in direct reaction to an older approach often called **deficit model**. In operating from a deficit model, the professional was thought to have known what was best for clients, who were considered deficit in life skills or abilities. Program participants' deficits or problems were discussed more than their strengths and problem-solving abilities. In fact, sometimes the clients' strengths were never even acknowledged. In the strengths model, the professional shifts from expert to facilitator and the client shifts from receiver of services to full participant.

Through **empowerment** strategies, the strengths model puts much of the control of the program in the hands of the participants. The program itself becomes a place where abilities can come to light, can be strengthened, and can be honored. Depending on the type of program, participants may need a safe environment in which to practice new skills and assert themselves. For example, a **court-mandated** parenting program for abusing parents might begin with the facilitator selecting the topics for discussion. Over time, the decisions about focus of the program might be transferred to the participants. Thus, the parents literally take ownership of their learning, and in selecting their discussion topics, they make decisions about the stock of knowledge that brought them into the program to start with. With guidance, the parents can set the rules for program participation, thus making standards such as confidentiality of information (shared within the group) more likely to be followed. When program participants or clients are empowered to direct their own learning and to maximize their strengths, the outcomes of the program or treatment are more meaningful, and more valuable, to the participants.

Displaying a deficit model is something that is easy to slip into. Even the most self-aware professional may have the thought, "If only they would just…" suggesting that if only the client would think like the professional, any problem could be addressed. This is not mistaken logic; helping professionals tend to be excellent problem solvers. But thinking of the client as being deficient may create new problems. First, the client is likely to sense disapproval and may even avoid returning for help. Second, the message that is communicated ("You cannot take care of yourself") may make the client believe that improvement is not possible. Psychologist Martin Seligman's (1975) early clinical work on helplessness even suggested that clients can learn to not improve.

Through self-monitoring as well as developing respect for the ways that other people address problems, professionals can avoid displaying a deficit model. As poverty expert Ruby Payne (2001) explains, professionals must come to the understanding that not everyone *wants* to adopt their ways, that middle-class values of success may have little meaning for others. An empowerment model respects the client's own determination of goals and does not assume that the client values what the helping professional values.

In the world of education, teachers have a special challenge in avoiding a deficit model as they work with children. This is because, in many ways, children *are* "deficit" in terms of stock of knowledge. And as strengths and weaknesses become apparent in schoolwork, a child may even be described as being deficient in one subject or another. Children with learning differences may be labeled as "learning disabled," which risks a deficit model. By looking for learners' strengths, a great deal of negativity can be avoided. By acknowledging the many styles in which children learn and the potential differences among children, teachers create a strengths model in the classroom.

Resilience

Resilience is a more formal theoretical framework than the family strengths model. Modern resilience theory grew out of crisis and stress theories. Researchers asked why some babies and young children thrived in homes where they were neglected and where perhaps their siblings did not even survive. In recent decades, research and literature on resilience have gradually dominated how we view humans of all ages and their response to adversity. The current thrust of the research and practice has gone beyond asking how some people survive crisis and now asks if resilience can be taught. Can professionals assist

---

deficit model
Approach by the family professional that assumes problems or client's lack of ability to resolve problems; reflects opinion that something is lacking in the person or family, especially when compared to the professional.

empowerment
Supply access or ability for a person to act on one's own.

court-mandated
Ordered by a judge or court.

resilience
Ability to bounce back from adversity.

people in becoming resilient? Can people learn to be resilient on their own? If so, how is this characteristic developed? Resilience is often the premise of preventive youth programs and also intervention programs for youth labeled as "at-risk." From a resilience perspective, should professionals even use the term *at-risk,* or should they avoid all labels?

The classic study that serves as the foundation for resilience theory is Emmy Werner's (1992), which focuses on the children of Kauai. Longitudinal research since 1955 has followed the children born on the Hawaiian island as they endured social ills as well as extreme challenges from climate. The researchers asked how does a community respond to a hurricane? How do individuals respond? Does a "naturally" resilient person just bounce back more easily after a storm? Or is that person more likely to have changed conditions in order to lessen the impact of a storm? For example, the resilient person is more likely to prepare for a storm by nailing boards over house windows. Thus, resilience may have as much to do with self-protection before a crisis as it does with bouncing back after a crisis.

Ecological Theory

ecological

Relating to the relationships and interdependence of humans and their environments (both physical and social).

Frameworks that focus on setting are called **ecological**. A well-known ecological theory is Urie Bronfenbrenner's (1977) model of concentric and nested circles representing environments (see Figure 4-2). Bronfenbrenner described the environment from near to far, from micro to macro. The inner circle, called the microsystem, commonly represents one person, one child, or one family. The next circle, the mesosystem, refers to interaction of that focus person with other individuals in the near environment. The next circle, exosystem, refers to community or neighborhood. The outer circle, or macrosystem, refers to the largest community, typically society or culture. Bronfenbrenner's interest was in studying humans, and especially children, in their natural environment instead of the laboratory, thus his focus on environmental levels. For professionals working with

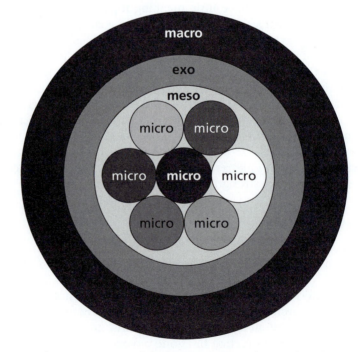

Figure 4-2 Bronfenbrenner's model of concentric and nested circles representing environments.

children and families, Bronfenbrenner's model provides an easy-to-understand approach to relationships and interaction across levels of environment. A picture of the interdependence of people and society emerges. Spheres of influence can be identified without focusing on causation. Thus, a problem can be viewed in terms of related factors without blame and without necessarily seeking out the why of a circumstance. Perspective on how outer environments impact families also emerges in an ecological view. An intern working with a family can use the model to see beyond the immediate concerns of the family and understand what other influences are impacting the family.

Adapting Urie Bronfenbrenner's ecological systems model, Figure 4-2 draws special attention to the meso level, the environment that reflects the micro unit's interaction with other micro units. The center micro circle represents the person or family under study. The three micro circles to the left of it represent three people with whom the center person interacts but at different times and with no overlap. To the right, are three people who interact with the center person and who also have interaction with at least one other person interacting with the center person.

An application for a child life specialist might be to trace the child's interactions with helping professionals and pinpoint potential stressors, for both the child and the family. Using Figure 4-2 for this application, imagine the center micro circle as the child being hospitalized for surgery. The micro circles to the left may represent a radiologist, an anesthesiologist, and a surgeon. The child is visited by each specialist singly. To the right of the child circle are circles that interact with each other as well as with the child: a child life specialist, a parent, and a pediatric nurse. If the child is anxious after visits with the left circles (the specialists) but not after visits with the right circles, the child life specialist can hypothesize possible reasons. Perhaps the visits from specialists are more goal-oriented (examinations and assessments); perhaps the specialists are not very communicative with the child. But the child life specialist rightly assumes that the specialists work in pediatric surgery because they like children; thus, we can assume that they *are* communicating appropriately with the child. A study of the micro circles allows another hypothesis to emerge: perhaps the child benefits when the adults around him communicate with each other (as would be the case for micro circles on the right), and perhaps the child feels anxious when he does not witness communication among his helping adults. Just witnessing *all* his helping adults in conversation may boost confidence in the child. Especially if he cannot understand the procedures to come, the child must place trust in something, and that something may be in the interaction among all the adults who are involved in his care.

The child life specialist may even sketch out the groups of micro circles to share with the child and the adults, too. Graphically representing the interaction can serve as motivation to the adults to schedule their visits to coincide with other professionals' and also assure the child when, occasionally, visits occur without interaction among the adults. The support network for the child becomes a concrete idea through the illustration and anxiety drops.

Systems Thinking

Systems thinking draws from traditional theory, which includes both family systems theory and general systems theory. Systems thinking refers to approaching an issue with the intention of looking at the whole and how a change for one part affects all parts. Modern theories such as chaos theory and the butterfly effect provide the example of interconnections that are not immediately noticed. The classic example of the butterfly effect says that a

systems thinking

Viewing the entirety of the situation, or the big picture. Acknowledges the interconnectedness of parts of a system.

butterfly flapping its wings on one continent creates movement that eventually produces a weather effect on another continent. On a program level, the intern might take a systems view and look for the connection between having refreshments available for a meeting and the successful accomplishment of program objectives.

Major concepts of **boundaries**, **subsystems**, and **feedback** are common to most systems theories. Boundaries can most simply be described as open and closed. When describing a family, *open boundaries* suggest that family members may freely interact with outsiders. Even young children are aware of the boundary between their family and a neighbor's family, but may name extra members of their family, such as pets and distant grandparents. *Closed boundary* describes the family that in some way severely restricts interaction with people outside the family system. The family may keep to themselves, to the point of isolation. Help from outsiders or even new ideas may be suspect and unwelcome. From the perspective of the professional, this may be the family that is "invisible." Even knowing their needs or issues may be difficult because contact is hard to establish.

Recognizing subsystems in families or other entities provides the helping professional with an understanding of a family's decision making and interaction processes. A family system may have subsystems of adults and children; of "his," "hers," and "our" children; of nuclear family and extended family. Power differentials may be evident among subsystems and influence how the family members interact. For example, a preschooler in a blended family may exhibit some confusion about who's in charge at home or whose rules to follow.

Feedback in a system can be labeled either *positive* or *negative*. These terms have nothing to do with goodness, but rather describe how change is acted upon by members of the system. Positive feedback promotes a change; negative feedback either slows or stops change. In applying the concept, a CASA family advocate who supervises parental visits may identify feedback mechanisms of a family. Regular visits serve as positive feedback, encouraging family members to continue with visits. Requirement of photo ID at the start of a visit could serve as negative feedback and discourage future visits. An agency thus benefits from thinking through even basic requirements and procedures that may act as a feedback loop. In school settings, teachers become expert at identifying and maximizing feedback loops that promote learning.

Biosocial Perspective

The interplay of nature and nurture has been recognized in the biosocial perspective. It avoids implying a choice of nature *or* nurture and, instead, stresses that the two are intertwined. The biosocial perspective has been driven by the advances in biological sciences since World War II. It acknowledges that some behaviors are genetically influenced while others are produced primarily by the environment. If a behavior is problematic, treatment may be designed to mediate effects of either the biological or the social factors. An example of a problematic behavior might be a child's inability to stay on task at school. A diagnosis might be **ADHD**, and strategies to help the child might be based on both physical and social aspects. Medication may be used in combination with changes in the environment. Over time, adjustments may be called for as the child grows or his social group changes.

In recent decades, research on infant brain development has heightened our awareness of how nature and nurture both contribute to how a person grows. The ZERO TO THREE initiative in the United States documents

boundaries

Borders or limits; in a family system, borders may indicate membership or activity in (or out of) the family unit.

subsystems

Smaller units within a larger unit or system; in a family system, common subsystems are parents, siblings (among children), extended family.

feedback

Information that is returned to the system; as a process, a loop of information that returns and changes the system, which produces more output, to be returned to the system, and so forth. In a family system, feedback is information that influences change and relationship dynamics.

ADHD

Attention deficit hyperactivity disorder.

the tremendous change in the young child's physical brain and cognitive development. While the child may be born with certain potential, the early environment can determine how that potential is realized. Early stimulation and a rich environment encourage brain development, making cognitive functioning a product of both nature and nurture. The role of caring adults during the child's early years is instrumental in shaping the child's development.

The role of caring adults during the child's early years is instrumental in shaping the child's development.

Child care providers, whose training includes brain development of children, birth to age three, are part of the nurture that many children experience. At the classroom level, a teacher must not only understand the training but must apply it in everyday activity. At the agency level, a child care center has to make a commitment to program practices that include maximizing interaction and stimulation during children's "windows of opportunity," or sensitive periods of development. At the community level, professionals must be ready to rate child care facilities on their attention to how children are stimulated as they develop. Thus, the single concept of brain development can be applied across all levels, exemplifying the interaction between this function of nature and the multiple levels of social environment, or nurture.

Stress Theory

Theories about crisis and stress make assumptions that humans will react to stressors in their environment. Most research and treatment of stress have centered on individuals' reactions. Americans' tendency to think of problems as an individual's responsibility may have influenced the theories, too. Taking a systems view of stress, though, invites us to look for the group response to stress. Reuben

Hill did that with the ABC-X theory of family crisis (Waller & Hill, 1951) (see Figure 4-3). Contracted as a researcher by the U.S. Army during World War II, Hill considered the question of how families would adjust if a member died in the war. His work on family dismemberment was the basis for his ABC-X theory.

Figure 4-3 outlines the parts of the theory, with letters from the theory name embedded in the drawing. A stands for the event or condition. B stands for the resources that are at hand. C stands for the family's perception, not just of the event, but also of the resources. X stands for the crisis that threatens family functioning. See Table 4-5 for an easy way to remember these elements.

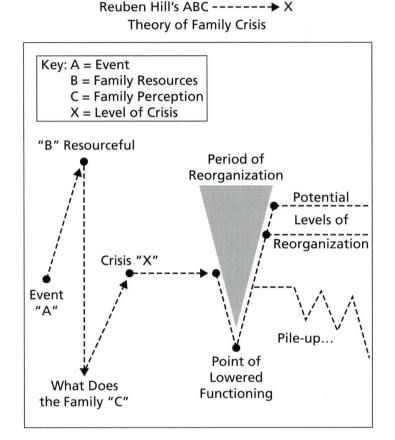

Figure 4-3 Reuben Hill's ABC-X Theory of Family Stress. (*Sources: LaRossa, R., & Reitzes, D. C. (1993). Symbolic interactionism and family studies. In P. G. Boss, W. J. Doherty, R. LaRossa, W. R. Schumm, & S. K. Steinmetz (Eds.). Sourcebook of family theories and methods: A contextual approach. New York: Plenum. Waller, W., & Hill, R. (1951). The family: A dynamic interpretation. New York: Dryden.)*

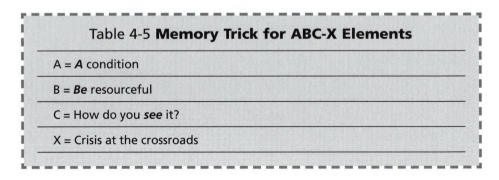

Table 4-5 **Memory Trick for ABC-X Elements**
A = *A* condition
B = *Be* resourceful
C = How do you *see* it?
X = Crisis at the crossroads

For professionals working with people facing crises, a key point of ABC-X theory is the C for perception. The theory predicts that people in crisis will recover only if they perceive that they can. This perception is called the **subjective definition** of the situation. It is important because sometimes it is not understood by the professional helpers viewing the same situation. A teacher may see all the resources a family has to support a child recently diagnosed with hearing loss. And the family may even acknowledge the presence of those resources. But if the family also perceives hearing loss as an overwhelming problem, *that* perception, and not the presence or lack of resources, will influence educational and even life outcomes for the child.

A career counselor objectively defines a pilot's loss of a job as a by-product of a changing economy, to be followed by gaining a job in the same or a related industry. By contrast, the unemployed pilot *subjectively* defines the loss of a job as a personal failure and the end of a career. Professionals who understand which definition is crucial to the client (the objective definition or the subjective definition) can potentially serve as change agents in their clients' perception of the crisis and eventual reemployment.

As indicated in Figure 4-3, people under stress have a decline in functioning. In most cases, we can describe lowered functioning in terms of daily life activities. Disrupted sleep, inability to concentrate, unhappiness, depression, and similar problems may indicate that stress is interfering with daily life. ABC-X theory predicts that after daily functioning hits bottom (a point that is understandably different for everyone), it is possible for the level of functioning to return to the precrisis level. In fact, a family's or individual's functioning can even exceed that level; after a period of reorganization, they may report that they are *better off* than they ever were before the crisis. When people do not return to a previous level of functioning, the cause is frequently a series of setbacks. Called *pileup*, the setbacks may be related to the original crisis or may be new problems, coincidental to the crisis. When setbacks come one after another, piling up, there is little opportunity to recover in between them. Pileup, then, is a series of ups and downs with a risk of daily functioning continuing to drop with each new crisis. As resources are depleted, the person may despair of ever seeing improvement.

The study of stress continues to be important, especially as the biological sciences and neuroscience can now track physical changes related to stress. For example, knowing the causes and effects of **cortisol levels** has influenced how we view and even define child abuse. With research into resilience occurring at the same time, we are learning much more about the interplay between nature (biological) aspects of stress and nurture (environmental) aspects of stress.

Feminist Perspective

Not to be confused with the feminist movement, feminist theory and perspective address the issues of all people who are ignored or marginalized by society. That general description may include women, who are the focus of the feminist movement, but the perspective presented here seeks to study, represent, and where appropriate, advocate for those populations that have no voice. Phrases such as "no voice" and "giving voice to" reflect the feminist perspective of honoring all segments of society. A basic assumption is that society does not hear all the voices, and so "having no voice" may also mean having no power in society or not being represented by the factions that do have power. Every subgroup of society (or subculture) has a collective voice of its members that is in addition to the individual voices of members. Feminist theory seeks to acknowledge the voices of all, from the individual level to the subculture level.

subjective definition
The family's or individual's own perception of the situation, including the magnitude of the crisis and the capacity of the family or individual to manage the crisis and emerge from it. Because of subjectivity, this perception may not match an onlooker's assessment.

cortisol level
Measured level of steroid hormone produced in the body when a person is under stress.

standpoint

Theoretical assumption that the viewpoint of the person under study has merit and authority, even though it is only one person's (or one group's) interpretation.

qualitative methodology

Nonnumerical data collection. Research procedures that seek to study through observation, interview, etc.

conflict resolution

Broad description of the study and practice of using skills for problem solving and ending conflict.

nonzero-sum conflict

The end of the conflict is not represented by the parties "canceling out" each other's position. Thus, resolution could be that both parties lose (lose-lose) or both parties win (win-win).

conflict mediation

The use of procedures, especially those based in communication, to resolve conflicts through intervention by a specially trained facilitator.

A key to understanding how feminist theory undergirds research is the concept of **standpoint**. The researcher considers and seeks to define the point of view (POV) of the person or group under study. Thus, research data include information *by* the person (or group) and not just *about* the person (or group). Feminist research relies heavily on **qualitative methodology** to involve participants in studies. Through techniques such as case study, ethnographic field research, and long interview, researchers identify standpoint and thus illustrate the variable under study from the perspective of the person most affected. Feminist theory is a helpful tool in communities where some people either have been ignored or have had decisions made for them.

Conflict Theory

Modern conflict theory in the United States arose in the 1960s when campuses and communities erupted with debates, sit-ins, and strikes. The issues ranged from peace to women's rights, and the strategies of all factions were broadcast nationally on television and chronicled in newspapers and books. Conflict was in the open and visible to all. Criticism of government and authority was articulated in a country that had no recent memory of such dissent, having supported World War II a generation earlier.

Researchers in the 1960s had a close-up view of nonmilitary conflict and identified the elements of conflict between those without authority (or power) and those with it, between younger people and older people, between ethnic groups, and between the sexes. Communication was key. Where factions found a way to listen to each other, problem solving was possible. Where factions competed to be the only speaker, conflict continued or escalated. Researchers dug deeper and the study of **conflict resolution** emerged. The concepts were expanded to address not only communication but also needs theory (to identify what needs of the parties were not being met) and perception of loss. When in conflict, each party may fear loss and resent the possibility that the other side will gain. Loss and gain, then, are frequently assumed to be the only possible outcomes ("my loss is your gain, but your loss is my gain") and are labeled *zero-sum* (summing the gain and the loss produces zero). With the perception that the conflict is win-lose, parties often stubbornly persist in their positions. With an assist, the situation can shift to **nonzero-sum conflict**, whereby satisfactory resolution is win-win.

Family conflict also came under study in the 1960s, a natural extension of the growing fields of conflict resolution and **conflict mediation**. Family conflict can be discussed on several levels: nonviolent daily conflict in the home, violent conflict between partners or among family members, and legal conflict at the dissolution of a marriage or other change in family composition. Outside of family legal matters (which may rely on conflict *mediation*), the term **conflict management** is commonly used to describe recommended strategies for families. What is important about family conflict theory is that it provides for conflict management instead of conflict avoidance.

As noted earlier in this chapter, a theory's assumptions are the foundation for its explanations and predictions. In the case of family conflict theory, the primary assumption is that conflict within the family is unavoidable (Sprey, 1969). As an expected by-product of familial relations, conflict is thus **normalized**. A family's goal is not to eliminate conflict but to reduce its negative consequences. Open and frequent communication serves not only to resolve conflict but also to strengthen the relationships of family members. Thus, a prediction of the theory is that conflict can produce improved family functioning. If conflict in the family is inevitable, family members can feel free to disagree and not risk harm to the family unit.

Solution-Focused Intervention

Solution-focused intervention is a technique and a perspective. Professionals who use solution-focused techniques generally aim for shorter-term treatment, such as counseling in a limited number of visits. At the start of counseling, professional and client discuss the anticipated outcomes and work on strategies that move toward those goals. With emphasis on the desired outcome, clients are motivated to make changes. A counselor may use such a technique to help a client change a behavior or habit, such as stopping smoking. A parent educator might suggest two to three techniques parents can use to help a child stay in bed through the night. A school professional might outline a focused short-term intervention to quickly change a classroom disruption.

A parent educator might suggest techniques parents can use to help a child stay in bed through the night.

Short-term therapies limit the cost of a treatment as well as the time required to achieve a solution. The trend toward shorter treatments is not new: hospital stays for surgery are shorter today than a generation ago, and day surgery has replaced overnight stays for many procedures. Insurance companies promote the trend for both medical and behavioral therapies, and professionals in both arenas report better outcomes for their clients.

Short, **solution-focused** intervention carries other benefits that align with the strengths model. First, such an intervention communicates confidence in the client's capacity for change. Second, it establishes a calendar for noting progress. Third, it offers a concrete plan of action. These three aspects of the intervention make it attractive to clients—and we can assume that some of those clients would have shied away from longer-term behavioral therapy.

Broken Window Thesis

The **broken window thesis** is a controversial theory that addresses how people react in their environment when there is distress or decline. Law enforcement and municipal authorities often rely on the premise of the theory, which predicts that if a community becomes rundown (for example, if broken windows are left unrepaired), the people living there will take less care of their neighborhood and allow crimes to be committed (Wilson & Kelling, 1982). Many cities have used the work of James Q. Wilson and George Kelling to plan community revitalization

conflict management

The use of skills, techniques, and attitudes to control the effects of conflict, even if the conflict is not resolved or ended.

normalized

Event or process changed to conform to an accepted standard or norm, sometimes by reducing stigma attached to it.

solution-focused

Short-term intervention or strategy emphasizing desired outcomes.

broken window thesis

Idea that the condition of specific environmental elements (such as broken windows in a deserted building) reflects overall health of a community or residents' commitment to it; idea that untended elements in a community influence the processes of the community.

initiatives that take the complementary position: by repairing and cleaning structures, neighborhood residents take pride in their environment and become energized, productive citizens. Research has not always confirmed the results of such initiatives, making the theory debated by academics. Within a workplace, you may observe the broken window thesis. Employee restrooms, by the end of the workday, may reflect lack of cooperative spirit at a worksite. Litter on the floor or sink area may depict lack of caring. Even your desk or cubicle may be seen as a reflection of your caring or commitment to the organization. Whether the state of your desk actually reflects your commitment is debatable, of course. Whether the state of your desk influences people around you is the central point of the broken window thesis.

✳ UNDERSTANDING AUDIENCES THROUGH THEORY

In the helping professions, the journey of knowledge to practice is well charted in terms of how to work with clients and audiences of all ages. Indeed, in the education world, much of the academic preparation centers on methodology of working with learners. For most professionals, interaction with children or clients is integral to their theoretical lens. For example, if a parenting educator subscribes to the family strengths model, the educator is likely also to subscribe to empowerment of parents and that principle will guide the interactions with parents. Beyond integration with theory, interaction with clients or students deserves planning and practice. The internship may permit observation of how professionals work with their audiences. Some aspects and theories of interaction are covered here: facilitating the learning of adults, leading youth audiences, and honoring diverse learners. Chapter 5, "Communication and Networking," covers specific techniques for working with diverse audiences.

Facilitating the Learning of Adults

Most of the adult audiences or groups encountered in internships form for an educational reason, but the education processes and purposes are likely to be very different from school-based education as interns know it. Certain

Interaction with clients or students deserves planning and practice.

learning theories are applicable across all settings, but the focus for adult learning utilizes theory and practices that are new to most interns.

Andragogy is the study of adult learners. Contrast it with the more familiar term, **pedagogy**. Pedagogy is commonly used to refer to all teaching matters (even classroom technique at the college and graduate school level), but andragogy is specific to its focus on adults—it does not address learning by children at all. By definition, then, andragogy is concerned with adults. Some of the established principles of andragogy describe how adult learners are different from child learners: adults are more self-directed and self-motivated. Adults have identified what they need or want to learn and are therefore more aware of the scope of learning that is possible than children are.

Andragogy can apply to any setting, formal (such as university) or informal. A term specific to informal learning is **community education**, and it may be created for either adults or children. Community education can include semester-organized classes such as those offered by universities as continuing education or lifelong learning. They are contrasted with for-credit offerings by colleges and universities. Another community-based offering is **family life education**, which focuses on topics pertinent to families but may be delivered to either adults or children. Table 4-6 charts the characteristics of these styles of education; the overlap of the characteristics helps explain why the terms frequently are used interchangeably by some professionals.

Malcolm Knowles (1990) is generally credited with formalizing andragogical theory, although he was not the first scholar to address the unique characteristics of adults as learners. Andragogy's main point is a simple one: adults learn in ways different from children. Adults are goal-directed and seek information that has meaning for them. (Contrast the goal-directedness with children's experience in school, where the child's goal may be one of any number of objectives other than acquisition of knowledge.) When adults seek

andragogy
Study of learning by adults.

pedagogy
Study of learning by children; also frequently used to refer to learning, teaching, or art of instruction without specifying the age of learners.

community education
Informal education or instruction, typically taking place outside of schools.

family life education
Instruction in or facilitation of knowledge, practice, and skills that individuals and families can use to enrich their lives.

Table 4-6 Characteristics of Styles of Education

	Andragogy	Pedagogy	Community Education	Family Life Education
Adults as audience	X	X	X	X
Children as audience		X	X	X
Whole families as audience		X	X	X
Curriculum may be credit-bearing for a college degree	X	X		
Curriculum may be career-oriented in the form of continuing education units (CEU) that can be counted toward license	X	X	X	
Curriculum is for use in personal life, with no career or college application	X	X	X	X

facilitator

Discussion or activity group leader (rather than teacher or lecturer).

The Adult Learner . . .

is independent

wants efficiency

seeks new knowledge

needs interaction for optimal learning

wants a facilitator, not a teacher

---

experiential

Hands-on learning activity involving participants.

abstract thinking

Cognition that uses concepts to form generalizations; typically contrasted with concrete thinking, which focuses on actual objects or things at hand.

fluid intelligence

Reasoning ability that does not depend on what has been learned in a culture; often associated with the nonverbal mental processing in solving puzzles or adapting to a new condition.

education, they expect to move quickly through a curriculum, and they may even expect to help design the curriculum. Because adults can articulate their wants and needs, a **facilitator** has the opportunity to include materials that will be relevant to the learners. Thus, the curriculum can be customized to their needs. Curriculum materials and educational outcomes must be tied to real-world experience. When those items incorporate the experience of the adults in the room, they are especially meaningful and well received.

Adult learners seek an efficient means to acquire new knowledge, sometimes for employment purposes and sometimes just for the sake of learning. Expecting to be independent and self-directed in the learning task, the adult learner is nevertheless stimulated by the company of peers in the learning setting. This may even surprise the adult learner, who rarely enters an educational setting with the goal of learning with others. This profile of learner suggests clearly that the adult learner is not in search of a teacher. The adult learner does want a guide to the learning and may express that as turning to the expert, the facilitator with academic training or degrees in the subject being learned.

Leading Youth Audiences

Youth audiences may include young children as well as adolescents, but the emphasis here is on youth in early and midadolescence, roughly ages 12 to 17. This age range is challenging both programmatically and in facilitation. Teenaged learners may have other things on their mind besides attending a program on "Readiness for College Testing," for example. They even may need sleep more than they need another program! Too, youth audiences may resist programs that are too much like "schoolwork." Using **experiential** curricula helps to counter that resistance.

Through an understanding of adolescent development, professionals can plan appropriate programs and approaches for teenaged audiences. For example, an educational program must be complex enough to capture the audience's attention, but also allow for easy answers or quick insights. The adolescent's capacity for **abstract thinking** is in place, but that doesn't mean the adolescent wants every issue to require it. In fact, the adolescent may demand that answers be concrete and conclusive. This need for sure answers seems to contradict the adolescent's tendency to question authority and facts, but it may actually reflect a desire for clarity, something that emerges when we question authority and facts.

Related to adolescents' capacity for abstract thinking is their **fluid intelligence**. The model of cognition that describes fluid or **crystallized intelligence** suggests that adolescents and young adults' thinking is fluid, allowing intuitive leaps and high creativity. Some of the most innovative work in the

---

Characteristics of Adolescent Learners

1. They question authority and facts and yet want a simple answer that they do not have to analyze.

2. They value spontaneity.

3. They value peer interaction and peer opinion.

4. They begin to select activities on preferred interests and focus on just one or two.

5. Their brains undergo change and growth, affecting everything from sleep to reasoning.

A thorough understanding of adolescent development will enable a professional to plan appropriate programs and approaches for teenaged audiences.

disciplines of physics and mathematics has been created by young people. By contrast, crystallized intelligence relies on fewer leaps of intuition and builds on more structured stocks of knowledge and experience. Crystallized intelligence is no less creative than fluid intelligence; it is simply different. In some disciplines, the crystallized intelligence of older scholars produces the outstanding work of the field. Certainly, experts are not limited by being in one mode or the other, but new theories typically emerge from scholars who are relatively new to a field, regardless of the age of the scholar. In working with adolescents, facilitators can apply principles of fluid intelligence to engage learners: pose problems that are solved by creative thinking rather than by experience, invite imaginative responses that differ from conventional thinking, and generate discussion about issues beyond learners' immediate experience.

Brain development in adolescence also helps to explain teens' behaviors. The decade of the 1990s was named Decade of the Brain and marked a turning point in the biological and behavioral sciences. So much more is known about the human brain that we can reasonably theorize that some of adolescents' issues have more to do with brain chemistry than conscious desire to confound their parents and teachers. Sleep is one such issue. Long observed but little understood was the adolescent's propensity to stay up half the night and then sleep past noon the next day. Many adults spent time and energy trying to readjust their teenagers' hours so that everyone in the house slept and ate at the same time. Research has documented that the teen's sleeping preference is actually the result of brain development. The internal clock is adjusted so that the adolescent's peak hours are late in the day. This shift appears to be a

crystallized intelligence

Learned abilities or stores of knowledge gained through exposure to a culture; often associated with facts and experiences.

delayed sleep phase syndrome

Chronic disorder in which a person delays the start of sleep, but is able to then sleep soundly into daytime hours. Probably related to circadian rhythm and also associated with adolescence, the syndrome may change over the life course.

normal change at or following puberty. When the shift is exaggerated, it may fall into the category of **delayed sleep phase syndrome**. For some people, this requires treatment as a sleep disorder. Most adolescents do not continue in the delayed phase pattern, obviously, or all adults would also display it.

Brain growth slows in early adolescence and then has a spurt by midadolescence. This is most notably marked by new growth in the frontal lobe (prefrontal cortex), the center for planning, reasoning, and judgment. Growth for this center takes about a decade; it is complete when the young adult is about 25 years old. The fact that the frontal lobe is just beginning in adolescence helps explain why teenagers are often poor planners and sometimes show poor judgment, at least by adult standards. Teens are literally unable to reason through all the contingencies of a situation and make a sound judgment for a plan of action. This doesn't mean that they are not cognitively able to create a list of contingencies and even chart them on a timeline. But the integration of that information and the decision making that produces what we call judgment is not likely to emerge for years.

The role of the professional has been described as supervisory and supportive. It can also be interpreted as influential in youth's development of adult personality. This interpretation comes from group socialization theory, which predicts that the adults who have the most direct impact on children's personality development are those adults who have access to the child peer group (Harris, 1995). In short, the adult serving as the youth leader may have more influence than parents at home. This theory, articulated by Judith Rich Harris in the 1990s, is not widely cited in child and family studies. The theory challenges much of our traditional wisdom about the importance of parents as primary influence on children. Educators who work daily with child peer groups are more open to the idea because they witness the power of peers in both school and play. Group socialization theory names the elementary school peer group (roughly ages 6 to 12) as the primary group influence on personality development and the adolescent peer group as the secondary influence. As the theory is tested and (probably) refined, it may provide more clues on how to help young people in school and in community. In the meantime, it serves us as a check on our assumptions about child development, and it encourages us to scrutinize all research and theory.

Honoring Diverse Learners

One of the most positive contributions to the study of intelligence has been Howard Gardner's (1993) theory of multiple intelligences. Embraced by educators, especially in kindergarten through 12th grade, the theory maintains that intelligence, or ways of knowing, can vary, and that any one person may have multiple ways of processing information and learning. In short, Gardner's theory has provided a framework for diverse learning styles. In planning educational programs, Gardner's nine intelligences, listed in Table 4-7, can be applied in order to honor diverse learners and their needs.

Verbal/Linguistic Intelligence. The learner is probably an effective and expressive writer or speaker. Language comes easily to this learner, who is also frequently a heavy reader. Of course, not all of these linguistic abilities may be equal: reading, writing, and speaking may have developed at the same pace, but not necessarily. The best reader in the room may have a fear of public speaking, for example. Even though both activities are based in language, they are different abilities, and they are expressed in different settings. Applications in education include report writing, oral presentations, storytelling or other narrative performance (such as plays), and reading.

Table 4-7 Gardner's Multiple Intelligences

Verbal/Linguistic
Logical/Mathematical
Musical/Rhythmic
Visual/Spatial
Bodily/Kinesthetic
Interpersonal
Intrapersonal
Naturalist
Existential

Logical/Mathematical. Liking numbers, this learner may excel in math and related areas, such as data analysis. Pattern seeing and pattern making may follow. This learner may also have similarity with the verbal learner, displayed through a high ability to understand metaphors and analogies. And many logical-mathematical learners are also musical learners. Applications in education include quizzes, tests, and analysis opportunities.

Musical/Rhythmic. Through music and rhythm, this learner not only takes in knowledge but also shares it. Especially through performance, the learner shares this orientation toward music. In learning situations, the person is sensitive to all sounds. Applications in education include song, dance, listening, music making.

Visual/Spatial. This orientation to learning means that the person "maps" ideas with mental representations. The learner may even think in pictures. Applications in education include graphics of all kinds (both prepared *for* the learner and prepared by the learner), photography, art, sculpture.

Bodily/Kinesthetic. This person learns best by doing. Activity is important for this learner and may even be necessary in order to attend to a lesson. Activity does not have to be whole body movement but a mix of large and small motor activity is valuable. Applications in education include movement in the environment (which might include walking outside the learning setting), role-play that allows physical action, manipulation of learning materials (which might be tied to music or art activities and thus blended with other intelligences).

Interpersonal. The learner who has high interpersonal abilities is able to work well with other people, both one-on-one and in groups. Sometimes referred to as people skills, interpersonal intelligence involves understanding how others think and picking up on subtle clues about other people's feelings. Applications in education include group projects, interviewing, team building, mentoring, peer editing.

A learner with strong interpersonal skills is able to work well with others.

Intrapersonal. This learner is highly attuned to self-knowledge and self-understanding. In a group setting, this learner may be quiet and introspective but certainly capable of contributing to a learning community. Applications in education include individual projects, journal writing and other essay writing, critical thinking that requires reflection.

Naturalist. The naturalist is well suited to study of the natural world and may well like to do all learning *in* the natural world, as is common for people who love the outdoors. Applications in education include environmental study, translating other concepts to environmental considerations, studying animals and plants, drawing analogies between human behavior and animal behavior, locating lessons in various physical settings and outdoors, when possible.

Existential. This intelligence was added to the basic list when Gardner revisited his theory almost two decades after he first proposed it. The existential learner considers the meaning of essential questions about life, death, and existence. This requires thinking or philosophizing on a different level than we typically use in everyday functioning. Applications in education include questioning what is known about the universe, studying philosophy, taking a global perspective, and making self-review.

◉ SUMMARY OF CHAPTER CONTENTS

Transition from Preparation to Application: The transition from campus to workplace is essentially a shift from preparatory studies to application of content knowledge in the real world.

Readiness for the Real World: Readiness must be an individual assessment reflecting both attitude and awareness.

Intervention and Prevention: Much of the work in the helping professions can be classified as being either intervention or prevention. Overlap occurs, and professionals may be trained in both types of service.

Theory and Perspective: Theory is a framework of ideas that describes or predicts behavior. The scope of theories in the child and family professionals' repertoire reflects a wide variety of uses; a measure of a theory's validity is its usefulness.

> *Family Strengths Model:* The family is described in terms of its strengths and abilities, making an assumption that the family sometimes needs support in order to find solutions for challenging circumstances. Professionals assist through an empowerment model.

> *Resilience:* Individuals and families can bounce back from adversity.

> *Ecological Theory:* Highlighting interdependence, interaction, and context of people and their surroundings, ecological theory is easily understood by lay people.

> *Systems Thinking:* Human systems are described in terms of boundaries, information feedback, and interconnections. Wholistic systems thinking is derived from a number of systems theories, including family systems theory and general systems theory.

> *Biosocial Perspective:* These theories detail the interplay of biology and environment in producing human behavior.

> *Stress Theory:* Family functioning after a crisis depends upon the stressor, family resources, and the family's perception of the crisis.

> *Feminist Perspective:* Drawing from feminist and critical theories, this perspective seeks to give voice to marginalized populations.

> *Conflict Theory:* Modern conflict theory, focusing on families, assumes that conflict is normal and serves a function.

> *Solution-Focused Intervention:* This recent movement in therapy brings focus to a specific problem or challenge and assumes that it can be resolved quickly.

> *Broken Window Thesis:* The theory maintains that a disintegrating element of an environment (such as a broken window) signals that residents do not care and that the neighborhood is vulnerable to negative forces.

Understanding Audiences through Theory: Theory informs how audiences learn information. Professionals make conscious selection of methods and content in light of the ages or backgrounds of their students, clients, and other audiences.

> *Facilitating the Learning of Adults:* Andragogy and community education principles guide professionals as they prepare programs for adult learners.

> *Leading Youth Audiences:* Science and theory provide understanding of young learners, especially adolescents.

> *Honoring Diverse Learners:* Style of learning and the theory of multiple intelligences describe the variety of learners that professionals must be able to communicate with.

DISCUSSION QUESTIONS

1. In reference to the case study at the start of this chapter, when would it be appropriate for Matthew to discuss theories learned in college course work at an internship? With his colleagues? With his clients or students?

2. What is an advantage of having a late adopter or laggard in a workplace?

3. Could there be a social theory of everything addressing universal behaviors?

4. A theory of everything would be valid for all time; how have theories of human development changed over the last 10, 20, or 100 years?

5. Why might theories learned in school "fail" according to observations at your internship site, and yet still be valid theories?

6. Give an example of your personal resilience or of someone you know. What helped you? (Sense of humor, a neighbor's interest, etc.)

7. Describe how perspective through different theoretical lenses influences your observations of normative and nonnormative events.

8. For the following types of internships, which theories will be most applicable?

   Student teacher

   Veterans Adminstration hospital outreach

   Parent educator

   Head Start coordinator

   Financial services coordinator

9. What overlap is there between intervention and prevention services? Describe benefits and disadvantages of combining resources for intervention and prevention services.

10. As a future professional, do you identify more with intervention or prevention?

GUIDED PRACTICES

Guided Practices offer structured exercises in critical thinking, observation (including self-observation), synthesis, and self-expression. The title of Guided Practice sums up the purpose of providing a guide: an opportunity that permits practice and does not require a final, ultimate effort.

All of the guided practices can be used by one person or by a group of people. The practices are designed as self-report instruments, meaning that answers are reported by the respondent and not collected by an interviewer or by another person who may speak with or observe the respondent.

There is not a standard amount of time to spend on the exercises. One person may use a guided practice for making a quick check while the next person may choose to spend hours on the same practice. Individual interest in a topic makes a difference in use, as does current need for the topic.

The greatest value is derived when the guided practice is completed with honest answers and observations. Any instrument may generate socially desirable answers, the kind of responses that a person thinks will be acceptable or expected. Especially when related to academic study, an instrument that calls for self-disclosure or self-evaluation risks being answered this way.

Guided Practice:
Personal Change Model

Your response to change in your environment can be described as low tolerance or high tolerance—with many possible values in between. You can identify your tolerance for change by placing a checkmark along the continuum to reflect your reaction to the Change Statement. Use the bottom half of this guided practice to write your own Change Statements. Try to write some that you must score low, and some that you must score high.

Change Statement	I Resist a Change Like This	I Don't Have Strong Feelings about a Change Like This	I Embrace a Change Like This
1. New hours at work or campus	Low_____	_____	_____High
2. New furniture	Low_____	_____	_____High
3. New room arrangement	Low_____	_____	_____High
4. New hairstyle	Low_____	_____	_____High
5. New people in a campus or work group	Low_____	_____	_____High
6. _____	Low_____	_____	_____High
7. _____	Low_____	_____	_____High
8. _____	Low_____	_____	_____High
9. _____	Low_____	_____	_____High
10. _____	Low_____	_____	_____High

Guided Practice:
Intervention and Prevention

In the child and family professions, you will find many opportunities to serve as an interventionist and also as a preventionist. Use this chart to consider your preference at this time. You may find your preference will change with experience or as a function of your own development. You may also find employment that draws from both columns.

Frequent Condition or Setting	Prevention Orientation	Intervention Orientation
Number of people/clients	☐ Groups	☐ Individuals
Timing	☐ Before a crisis	☐ After a crisis
Role	☐ Educator	☐ Counselor
Relationship with child/client	☐ Reserved	☐ Personal, in-depth
Duration of relationship	☐ May be shorter	☐ May be longer
Focus on problem type (often)	☐ Normative event	☐ Nonnormative
Collaborating	☐ With copresenter	☐ In consultation only

Guided Practice:
Theory Conceptualization

Conceptualizing a theory on your own is a creative application of your knowledge and a good way to cement a theory's elements in your memory. Use a blank space such as this or create a drawing space on a larger paper or electronic background (using PowerPoint, for example). Create a poster about your theory, as if it were a movie or song to be advertised and promoted. A poster display communicates the relationship of elements, illustrates meanings with easy-to-understand graphics, and uses words sparingly.

Guided Practice:
Articulating Andragogy

As an adult learner yourself, you probably have thought some of the same things in campus classes as adults think in community classes. Add to this list of typical complaints that adult learners have expressed about classroom environments. Then write in a strategy that a community educator could use to quell the complaint.

1. When I arrive at class on time, I don't like to wait for latecomers.

   Educator's strategy: _____

2. When I arrive for class late, I am embarrassed to have to walk up to the front row of the room.

   Educator's strategy: _____

3. I don't like a pop quiz that puts me on the spot.

   Educator's strategy: _____

4. I like the convenience of holding class at the neighborhood school, but I hate sitting in child-sized chairs.

   Educator's strategy: _____

5. Complaint: _____

   Educator's strategy: _____

6. Complaint: _____

   Educator's strategy: _____

Guided Practice forms are also included on the accompanying CD-ROM.

ADDITIONAL RESOURCES

Helpful Web Sites

National Family Resiliency Center, Inc., http://www.divorceabc.com

Harvard Family Research Project, http://www.gse.harvard.edu/hfrp/projects
.html

Bowen Family Systems Theory, http://www.thebowencenter.org/pages/theory
.html

Building Family Strengths, http://www.clemson.edu/fyd/bfs.htm

REFERENCES

Bronfenbrenner, U. (1977). Toward an experimental ecology of human
development. *American Psychologist, 32,* 513-531.

Burr, W. R. (1995). Using theories in family science. In R. D. Day, K. R. Gilbert,
B. H. Settles, & W. R. Burr (Eds.), *Research and theory in family science*
(pp. 73-90). Pacific Grove, CA: Brooks/Cole.

Doherty, W. J. (1999). The levels of family involvement model. In *Tools for ethical
thinking and practice in family life education* (pp.14-19). National Council
on Family Relations.

Gardner, H. (1993). *Multiple intelligences: The theory in practice*. New York:
Basic Books.

Harris, J. R. (1995). Where is the child's environment? A group socialization
theory of development. *Psychological Review, 102*(3), 458-489.

Johnson, S. (1998). *Who moved my cheese?* New York: Putnam.

Knowles, M. S. (1990) *The adult learner: A neglected species*. Houston, TX: Gulf
Publishing.

Payne, R. (2001). *Framework for understanding poverty*. Houston, TX: Aha
Process.

Rogers, E. M. (2003). *Diffusion of innovations*. New York: The Free Press.

Seligman, M. E. P. (1975). *Helplessness: On depression, development, and
death*. San Francisco: W. H. Freeman.

Sprey, J. (1969). The family as a system in conflict. *Journal of Marriage and the
Family, 31,* 699-706.

Waller, W., & Hill, R. (1951). *The family: A dynamic interpretation*. New York:
Dryden.

Werner, E. E. (1992). The children of Kauai: Resiliency and recovery in
adolescence and adulthood. *Journal of Adolescent Health, 13,* 262-268.

Wilson, J. Q., & Kelling, G. (1982, March). The police and neighborhood safety:
Broken windows. *Atlantic Monthly,* 29-36.

For additional material and resources to complement this
chapter, the Online Companion Web site can be accessed at
http://www.earlychilded.delmar.com.

CHAPTER 5

Communication and Networking

CASE STUDY: Like many students, Tamara held back from announcing her future plans for her career after college. Her family all knew she would land a job as a teacher of some kind; her closest friends knew she longed for a kindergarten classroom of her own. Her natural ability with children was obvious, as she could drop all adult pretense and join a child in play. Through college and her internship, she had developed the needed skills to assure that her natural ability was maximized.

Speaking to people outside her personal sphere, however, was not so easy. She felt self-conscious about stating her teaching goals and was unsure that many people would be as interested in children's literacy initiatives as she was. But with newfound confidence as an intern at Head Start, Tamara learned to speak of children's early education at a societal level, describing how her work with children affects the whole of a community and, therefore, is properly of interest to anyone.

At social events as well as career events, Tamara now feels ready to explain her own goals as well as describe her internship to others. With an appreciation for the power of networking, Tamara actively looks for opportunities to introduce herself and describe her hopes for a career working with young children.

✳ COMMUNICATION SKILLS OF A PROFESSIONAL

The professional in the field uses skills in different modes of communication, including writing and speaking in multiple channels such as print, e-mail, transmitted voice, and in-person speaking. Skill building is a process for everyone: so-called natural writers and speakers are not very common. Practice, which includes practice on the job, is the most common means of improvement. New professionals benefit from critique of their communications, and the internship is an opportunity for that exchange.

Table 5-1 demonstrates a simple model of communication, which considers the modes of verbal, nonverbal, and written communications. You may have studied communication in course work, especially interpersonal communication. In the workplace, you will have the opportunity to put your studies to work for you. Your training in writing, for example, will permit you to write reports and gauge your vocabulary for multiple audiences. Your awareness of nonverbal communication will allow you to conduct yourself professionally in meetings and in working with clients. Verbal communication skills will allow you to adopt a workplace vocabulary and address the population you work with respectfully.

Communication with clients should be free of jargon that is specific to the agency or organization. An important first step is to refer to clients by name instead of labels, such as "John" instead of "the ADD case." Similarly, educators strive to use child-first language, such as "children with autism" instead of "autistic children." In referring to agency processes with clients, speak plainly about what is needed, such as "Your signature is needed on the permission form," instead of technical references such as "Form 5843 needs your compliance." The technical reference, which is more formal and more specific, may still be used in communication with colleagues. The technical language serves an important purpose in record keeping and auditing. The professional is knowledgeable about appropriate word choice for the professional and lay person.

Just as you hold back from using familiar forms of address with clients, reserve use of first names and nicknames with colleagues until you are invited. You might ask your supervisor directly about how people are addressed ("Mrs. Smith, how should I address the director?"). Observe or ask about when and where the business of the agency is discussed. Some break rooms are appropriate settings for talking shop, and others are strictly for social conversation. Your site supervisor may also guide you about discussing

Table 5-1 **Modes of Communication**

Verbal *Voice*	Nonverbal *Body*	Written *Recorded*
Heard in person or through phone, videotape, etc.	Observable, in person or through videotape, etc.	Fixed on paper or computer; retrievable; editable

cases. Most agencies expect you to not discuss the organization outside of that setting.

Interns sometimes worry that they will be asked to speak to large groups. Many people have a fear of public speaking, and in fact, it is routinely identified as the leading phobia among adults in the U.S. An intern position, like a professional position, can have a requirement of public speaking, but the intern will have more support than most people in meeting this challenge. A quiet person who dislikes public speaking may find it helpful to distinguish an improvement in that skill rather than a change in personality. Quiet people may speak in public only for professional reasons, and yet, their skill may be as strong as the person who loves public speaking. In short, personality does not have to change in order to be effective as a communicator. Practice and desire can produce the skill needed for the professional. At the end of this chapter, you will find a Guided Practice to make a "Self-Assessment of Communication Skills." You may be surprised at the number of skills you already possess. Many more skills than just public speaking comprise professional communication, including:

- maintaining interest in other people's words
- asking appropriate questions (at the appropriate time)
- making a self-introduction and introducing other people
- determining the appropriateness of a handshake
- welcoming newcomers

✳ SELF-PRESENTATION

Through written, verbal, and nonverbal communication, people send intentional and unintentional messages. Through self-awareness and a technique called **self-monitoring**, the professional seeks to reduce unintentional messages that may interfere with effective communication with peers and clients (see Table 5-2).

Self-monitoring is the conscious evaluation of one's own language, including body language. Students self-monitor when they decide to hold back in a class after speaking at length or several times. (The same technique is at work when students wish a fellow student would hold back instead of dominating

self-monitoring

Conscious evaluation of one's own communication and language, including body language.

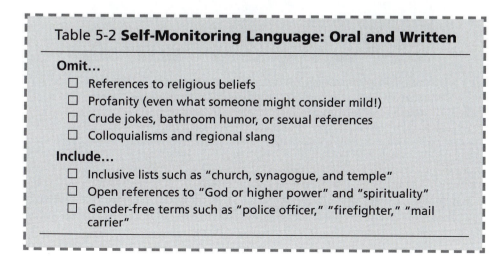

Table 5-2 **Self-Monitoring Language: Oral and Written**

Omit...
- ☐ References to religious beliefs
- ☐ Profanity (even what someone might consider mild!)
- ☐ Crude jokes, bathroom humor, or sexual references
- ☐ Colloquialisms and regional slang

Include...
- ☐ Inclusive lists such as "church, synagogue, and temple"
- ☐ Open references to "God or higher power" and "spirituality"
- ☐ Gender-free terms such as "police officer," "firefighter," "mail carrier"

the class discussion!) Realizing such a need depends on your ability to see and understand the dynamic of the entire group. By taking a bird's-eye view of the room, you can observe the needs of people besides yourself, and act or speak accordingly. Observation is the key skill involved in self-monitoring.

In the workplace, self-monitoring practices include:

- avoiding the correction of a supervisor's error or misstatement
- not assuming that anyone wants to hear how things were done at your prior school or workplace
- not calling attention to people arriving late
- maintaining the appearance of being interested, even in long meetings

In working with adult clients, self-monitoring includes awareness of silences and your reaction to messages, both spoken and unspoken. A simplified feedback loop for interaction might look like this: client speaks, you nod; client speaks, you nod; client speaks, you speak; client does not speak again. Through self-monitoring, you would realize that the client continued speaking as long as you responded with nods. You would also realize that when you responded with words, the client stopped speaking. Assuming your purpose was to engage the client in conversation, you would adjust your responses and only nod to the client's comments. Careful observation is thus the hallmark of self-monitoring: you must observe yourself, the other person, and the other person's response to your behavior.

In working with adult clients, self-monitoring includes awareness of silences and one's reaction to messages, both spoken and unspoken.

In school settings or early childhood education facilities, self-monitoring must extend to interactions with children, of course. Observation is more productive if you also know about children's developmental stages. For example, when interacting with a child putting together a puzzle, an adult may start making suggestions about where to place the pieces. Self-monitoring on your part assures that you will not rush to complete the puzzle or even coach verbally.

"Hi, I'm Melanie Berry from the intern pool. I work with nine-year-old girls in the Theatre Club. You're welcome to stop by the stage any time we're rehearsing. At four o'clock, we take a break for snacks and you might like to join us. In fact, we're looking for a sponsor for our next pizza party."

Figure 5-1 Sample elevator speech.

Self-Introduction

In a field experience, you may be called upon to introduce yourself without prior warning. You may have very little time to present yourself or tell someone about your program. This challenge of the self-introduction presents an excellent opportunity to build communication skills. In fact, the best practice in speechmaking is based on the circumstance of having limited time to communicate a message. Sometimes called an **elevator speech**, a self-introduction of about 30 seconds is thus the building block for successful speechmaking in professional settings (see Figure 5-1). Even though you may never be in the position of introducing yourself to someone in an elevator, by imagining that setting, you can construct a concise self-introduction that does more than state your name and job title or student status. In the space of the time of an elevator ride, you can introduce yourself, explain your program, or invite a dignitary to an event. With practice, you will find it easy to transfer your elevator speech to any setting.

A lot of information can be communicated in 30 seconds. Think about how much a half-minute advertisement costs during a Super Bowl half-time show! Marketers obviously consider that half minute adequate to convey a powerful message. Radio advertising also demonstrates how much can be communicated in seconds. The length of 30 seconds is adequate for all of these speechmaking events.

- welcoming an audience, large or small
- introducing a speaker or guest
- announcing an event or meeting
- explaining the agenda for a workshop
- teaching a short safety lesson
- demonstrating how to burp a baby
- giving three tips for stress-free holidays

Begin with a clear focus: What are the key points about your role or activity in your internship? How might you introduce yourself in the terms of your internship? Skill at writing and delivering 30-second speeches provides confidence for the public speaking that is required of professionals. Not every professional delivers speeches to national audiences, but most professionals have reason to address groups of five to 500, even if only for 30 seconds to thank an audience for attending a forum. A Guided Practice appears at the end of the chapter to assist with "30-Second Speaking."

✳ **elevator speech**

Concise and practiced speech that can be delivered in a short time span of 30 seconds to three minutes; typically delivered as a self-introduction, the speech can be used in any setting but was named "Elevator" to draw attention to the requirement for a short presentation (as if in an elevator traveling between floors in a building).

Handshake and Touch

Observation of culture and self-monitoring will inform your decision about how to approach meeting people and introducing yourself and others. In some cultures, handshakes are welcomed, and in others, they are avoided. Observe for customs and adapt accordingly. In some settings, handshakes are avoided because of concern for health. For example, in the Centers for Disease Control and Prevention (CDC), handshakes are frequently replaced by nods. The World Health Organization (WHO) recommends the use of a gentle elbow bump to replace handshakes. The substitutions are intended to cut down on the transfer of germs and viruses—and they are effective.

You may visit settings such as hospitals, clinics, child care facilities, and schools, where handshakes are unhealthy greetings. You may find that a broad smile or a short bow adequately communicates a greeting. Some people raise a hand for a quick wave, both when entering and leaving a room. If you try raising your hand near your head and saying, "Hi, I'm Janice," you may forestall a person's attempt to shake your hand. Of course, sometimes the person you are meeting will consider a handshake mandatory. Your awareness of the needs of people around you will guide you to know what to do. Assuming that you may need to shake hands, your responsibility would be to wash your hands thoroughly before entering such a setting to minimize the risk of transfer of a virus from your hand. To avoid being on the receiving end of unwanted germs or viruses, you can plan to clean your hands after leaving the setting, conscious about not touching your own face before having a chance to wash.

Helping professionals have an opportunity to model the behaviors that cut down the spread of contagious ailments, such as washing hands or using a tissue for a sneeze.

Helping professionals, especially those who work with children, have an opportunity to model the behaviors that cut down the spread of contagious ailments. Using a tissue for sneezing and turning to the crook of your arm for a cough instead of covering your mouth with your palm are sound moves to contain germs. A child will mimic these behaviors, especially if adults encourage them by noting the child's consideration for others. When adults comment about an illness, they also can serve as models for consideration: "Excuse me if I sit a little further away from you than usual. I am recovering from a cold and I do not want to accidentally give you a virus." You can also promote a healthy distance from babies by saying things like, "My hands may not be clean, so I won't ask to hold your baby today." Or, upon greeting a baby or small child in a stroller, you can offer a "footshake" by gently touching the child's stockinged foot. Parents of babies will be much relieved by your holding back, and other people in the room (especially children) will have an example to follow.

Touch, in general, is a "touchy" subject when working with children. Hugs and pats can be misinterpreted, and so many teachers and child care assistants use discretion in both initiating and receiving such contact. Men who work with children are typically more concerned than women about physical gestures being misconstrued as inappropriate touching. But all professionals should be alert to the possibility that a hug can be interpreted as inappropriate. Some workplaces, including schools and child care facilities, have guidelines about physical contact or being in a room alone with a child. These guidelines are meant to protect children and also to protect adult employees.

Conference-Style Speaking

Have you ever been in a large group setting and been frustrated when you couldn't hear an audience member's question? Or have you been curious about the identity of the person with the question? Your own frustration as an audience member should guide you in planning your own conference-style speaking for such events. Professionals routinely attend meetings and conferences, and they must know how to communicate in them, both as podium speakers and as audience members.

At workplace meetings, just as at professional conferences, questions and comments are often invited from the audience. The opportunity to contribute to a meeting carries responsibilities: identifying yourself and making yourself understood. It may help to think of your participation as simply joining a conversation. Your question or comment can be to clarify just one element of the presentation. By asking a focused question, you are almost always serving someone else in the audience too, just as in your campus classroom. Some basic behaviors lead to your input being valued: stand up, speak up, identify yourself, and contribute.

Stand up. If you stand in a large room, your words will be better understood. One reason is that your voice will carry better when it's above the crowd. Another reason is that listeners will benefit from the nonverbal communication of your face and body. As you may have noted in your own experience, it is easier to hear a voice when you can see where it is coming from. If a sign language interpreter is present, your face should be pointed in the direction of that person so that your words can be heard clearly.

Speak up. Sometimes a microphone is available for audience speakers, but more often, it is not. Be prepared to project your voice across the room. Shallow, fast breathing cannot support the big voice you need for public speaking; in fact, it makes your voice higher and also promotes nervousness. Concentrate on breathing deeply and evenly to relax before you speak.

Table 5-3 Contributions Can Be Large or Small

Ask a question.

Offer an alternative view.

Contribute additional information.

Suggest a role you can play.

Tell a speaker you enjoyed a session.

Volunteer for the next assignment.

Offer to help plan the next meeting.

Identify yourself. Communicate with as few words as possible, getting to the heart of your question or your comment quickly. Do not assume that intern or student status makes you a less important contributor. State your name and intern site, then ask your question, as the example below shows.

> "Melanie Berry; Youth Center Intern Program. Can you tell us more about the funding program for preteens? I'm especially interested in the deadlines for the grant applications. Thank you."

Contribute. Interns, as well as new professionals, are sometimes reluctant to participate in organizations and conferences. As one of the newest members of a profession, you can bring fresh insights and new ideas. Table 5-3 illustrates some of the ways you can contribute.

Speaking from the Podium

The best way to speak from the podium is to speak *away from the podium.* As quickly as possible, move toward your audience and let them know who you are. The only time a speaker is really tethered to the podium is when a microphone cannot be moved or when the speech is very formal and requires the heavy use of speaking notes or a script. To gain the confidence to speak away from the podium, speechmakers practice public speaking and even study formally in classes or informally in associations such as Toastmasters. While only practice can build skill, there are other strategies that can support a new speaker while skill builds.

Forget the ice water. Fix your own glass of warm (not too hot) water to take to the stage with you. Warm water will keep your throat relaxed. Audiences are highly tolerant of a speaker's need to sip water during a talk. Don't be a bit self-conscious about drinking from a cup on stage. (Do strategize your logistics: cup of water near your hand, tissue in your pocket, eyeglasses within reach, etc.)

Prepare minimal notes. A single index card should be your goal for notes (if you need any notes at all). Use a large eight-by-five-inch index card, but do not fill it with many words; print key words in a large enough size to see them easily. Try to limit your main points to just three or five items, and don't be afraid to number them for your audience. In fact, your audience will like knowing your agenda! But don't start with the most complex point, or your audience may fear a very long and complicated presentation.

Table 5-4 **Creating an Effective PowerPoint Presentation**

Use font sizes of at least 32 points.
Create a few good slides, not a long slideshow.
Original art or charts are stronger graphics than clip art.
Use key words as text on slides.
Limit animation and sound effects.
Test colors and text for readability from a distance.

Use visuals to make your points. Through large props or computer display or overhead transparencies, give your audience something to focus on as you speak. If you use a PowerPoint slideshow for this purpose, design it so as not to overwhelm *or* bore your audience (see Table 5-4). Audiences have seen just about all the novel PowerPoint slides they care to, so plan your presentation accordingly. Some experts warn that typical PowerPoint choices actually decrease the quality and amount of information delivered. All information displays deserve planning and proofreading. Critique your own displays before putting them before an audience, and ask peers to help you in that exercise.

Rehearse and revise. While some experts advise speakers to practice in front of a mirror, this is not a good strategy for everyone. Other methods of checking yourself in rehearsal are practicing in front of a small pilot group and videotaping/audiotaping. An iPod in your pocket can substitute for a lapel microphone for recording and can provide nearly as good a quality. Another recording option is to use a desktop videocam directed at your head and upper body. (Saving a file to your computer hard drive allows repeated viewing.) Even a short taping segment can be helpful to review: you can capture a short video of yourself with some digital cameras and cell phones. If you expect to speak with a microphone, make that one of your rehearsal props (even if it means holding a flashlight as a substitute mike). Rehearsals, especially recorded rehearsals, allow you to review content, stifle "ums," and check for unintended utterances like "you know."

Make and maintain eye contact. Select two or three people in the audience to make periodic eye contact with. No one can really make eye contact with every audience member.

Restate audience questions. To entertain questions from your audience, develop the habit of repeating or rephrasing the question before you begin to answer. You may want to ask the audience member to clarify the question.

Keep an eye on copresenters. Actually, the best advice is to keep both of your eyes on your copresenter. Whether sharing the stage with one person or several (on a panel, for example), you can help keep the audience on task by always turning your head to watch the current speaker. Your obvious listening (through nods and smiles, but not so many that you distract attention from the speaker) is important to the dynamic of the room.

Enjoy talking with your audience. Relax and enjoy this public conversation with an audience. You have the opportunity to share your expertise. A smile can help establish rapport and connection with your audience.

Clothes Make the Professional

Communication is verbal, nonverbal, and textile. Your attire will make a statement . . . make it a professional one! Spaghetti straps, tank tops, halters, shorts, sandals, and any amount of cleavage are almost always mistakes in the workplace. Even if invited to dress for Casual Fridays, hold back the first Friday or two to see just how casual the clothing becomes. Sandals, athletic shoes, and baseball caps may be too casual. Planning your appearance can include all of these possibilities as follows:

- Ask about clothing in the interview. For example, "Do you have a preference about what I wear on the job?"

- Observe clothing of the supervisors you meet in your placement interview.

- Observe clothing of the people you will work with as well as the dress of clients.

- Learn about customs of the neighborhood or the culture you are entering. For example, some communities expect women and men to dress differently, and so women may never wear pants in public.

- Makeup may be another consideration.

- If you work with young children, think through every item. For example, most teachers in early childhood education avoid jewelry or chains, high heels, and long nails.

- Track what you wear over time if your clients care about your clothing. For example, if you work with teenagers, you may discover that they notice everything about your appearance. They may even comment on how often you wear certain clothes!

An intern's attire will make a statement
. . . it should be a professional one!

Table 5-5 **Meanings of Casual Friday**	
Informal: Jeans and T-shirt Sandals or flip-flops	**Relaxed:** Khakis and a cotton shirt Loafers or sandals
Dress casual: Dress slacks and jacket Low-heeled shoes	**Comfort uniform:** Short-sleeved or summer version of standard uniform

Like it or not, we humans do judge books by their covers, children in restaurants by their behavior, and adults by first impressions. Clothing is an important part of that first meeting. That first impression may be made in as few as three seconds. The people you meet will take in your appearance, demeanor, and perhaps even your level of vocabulary in that short span of time. Should we depend on these snapshot impressions, sometimes called snap judgments? Research tells us that most of the time, most people can rely on their first impressions of strangers. The more people you meet, the better you are at sizing up a person. Presumably, this is why adults make better snap judgments than children do. On the receiving end of a snap judgment, you may feel as though you don't have a fair chance at making a good impression if someone is judging you in three seconds. Fair or not, impressions and judgments are made just this quickly. You can prepare for some of those initial meetings, at least, by planning an appropriate wardrobe. Use the Guided Practice, "The Mirror Check," at the end of this chapter to begin planning.

Take a mental snapshot of yourself or, even better, study a color snapshot of yourself, dressed for the workplace. What does your appearance say? If you can sum up your appearance as clean, well groomed, and appropriately dressed, then you are ready to go make a first impression. Maximize your appearance by wearing colors that suit you, selecting clothing styles that flatter you, and paying attention to details. The details that deserve conscious decisions are shoes, hairstyle, bag (purse, backpack, computer bag, etc.), jewelry, and the amount and style of makeup, if you wear it. An important variation in dress that you should consider at the same time is what you will wear to the workplace on a Casual Friday, if that opportunity is offered. As Table 5-5 illustrates, attire for Casual Fridays can mean different things in different workplaces.

Appropriately Dressed

Sometimes it means dressing conservatively.

Usually it means dressing consistently (day after day).

Always it means fitting in.

✳ COMMUNICATING WITH DIVERSE AUDIENCES

Contextual responsiveness in communication means that you are highly aware of the setting or environment and are able to adjust your own language or mode of communication in order to adapt to that setting. The first step toward this standard is simply being aware that people in a particular setting may have expectations (and assumptions) that are different from your own, and each audience you encounter will vary. The next step typically requires study and keen observation: acknowledging the current audience's needs, use of language, and unwritten rules of verbal and nonverbal communication. Professionals cannot always be prepared with thorough and detailed knowledge about every population. Therefore, they develop general standards for their own communication, expecting to customize communication as they continue to work with a specific population. These standards address communicating with a variety of audiences, restraint in gathering information, and the handling of disclosures of sensitive information.

The Adult Audience

Interns are sometimes startled when they realize that *they* are the experts in the adult learning classroom. In some settings, interns are invited to facilitate group learning after as little as one demonstration by a professional. Your expert status in a topic may bring you to such a position. Perhaps your college course work has included in-depth study of children's literacy. A practicum site supervisor sees you as a valued resource on this topic and might ask you not only to address a parent group about the value of reading to babies, but also to conduct an in-service training for the preschool teachers at the site.

After all, as your mentor might casually mention, your recent course work in literacy is up to date and research-based. A mentor may have two more reasons for asking you to lead such a training: first, you will be a new face for the teachers, a sound educational strategy for presenting to an audience who routinely attends trainings, and second, you will gain experience in facilitating a training—with a friendly audience.

In the setting of an in-service training, the challenges you would face are easily anticipated. You may expect to worry over having too much material, or not enough. You may anguish over the choices of technological display or the lack of any choices. You may fear that the audience will ask questions that you cannot answer. These healthy worries will make you a good presenter! If you flounder at one or even all of them, you will still benefit overall by having had the opportunity to facilitate a training. Key to the benefit you will enjoy: the friendly audience that the site's staff comprises. A staff that knows you as an intern expects to overlook your nervousness, inexperience, and even errors in the presentation. More important, the staff will give you feedback that you need in order to self-evaluate your own performance and preparedness. And the staff benefits, too: they gain the knowledge about literacy that you brought to the training. Thus, the challenges are balanced by the benefits of leading an in-service training.

Challenges in a community setting are higher stakes. In addition to the natural worries as described above, you will face adult audiences that may not be thinking kindly of you as an intern or new professional. In fact, these audiences may not be thinking about you at all. Some challenges of communication with adult audiences are briefly described here with response strategies. Additional facilitation strategies appear later in this section. As a novice presenter, you may choose to observe many professionals before tackling your own community group facilitation.

court-ordered or **-mandated**

Required participation by a judge or court. Common examples: required educational program for hot check writers; parenting education for divorcing parents; parenting education for parents at risk of losing custody of their children.

The Hostile Audience. Audience members may not be in attendance by choice. For example, they may be **court-ordered** to attend parenting classes due to charges of abuse or neglect. Less severe legally, but no less resented by at least some parents, are **divorce education** classes, required by family law courts in virtually all U.S. counties. One more step down in severity, a hostile audience may be employees who are required to attend an unwelcome training, especially if on a weekend without compensation. All of these audiences challenge even the most experienced speaker or facilitator. Most professionals do not even try to engage such an audience in an activity at the start; some hostile audiences resist such involvement throughout all sessions. Direct, to the point, and focused communication is called for. The facilitator can at least indicate respect for the audience's time (if nothing else) and present material at a steady pace, not rushing but also not including tangential topics that would typically arise with a more relaxed audience. The mature facilitator understands that the hostility directly or indirectly expressed is complex and reflects more issues than the curriculum addresses. By proceeding in a businesslike fashion, some facilitators will earn a hostile audience's appreciation, and occasionally, the audience will come to terms with the requirement of attendance and shift to a cooperative manner.

The Restless Audience. An audience that cannot settle in for a session gives a clue that other interests or commitments are distracting audience members. They may have their minds on commitments at home, on children in the next room, or on a session that comes after the current one. The facilitator may have to ignore the distraction if the material to be communicated is crucial. But if the session agenda can be flexible, the facilitator may choose to face the distraction head-on. Audience members will almost always say what is on their minds, if asked. The purpose of the session may shift to that topic, making good use of the distraction that is clearly more interesting at that time. If appropriate, the facilitator may cut short the session in honor of the event that the audience is thinking about and perhaps heading off to next.

Unplanned events may also distract an audience's attention and the facilitator may need to think on his or her feet. When September 11 events in 2001 became known, teachers at all levels had to make decisions about how to address the issue of incoming news, worry, and fear among their audiences and the schedule of classes. Depending on location, the responsibility extended to safety concerns. Whether the audience is adult or young, the facilitator influences the group's response in a national emergency. Similarly, severe weather reports can distract an audience. Professional facilitators think through how they will handle such events, even if they have no prior experience. What they *do* have is memory of how they felt when in an audience distracted by extreme events. Such memories can help in the planning of a confident response for future events.

The Overwhelmed Audience. When a facilitator attempts too much material, or material on the wrong level, the audience may feel overwhelmed. If the facilitator is lucky, the audience will speak up and express their frustration. Unfortunately, not all adult audiences will be so forthright. Out of politeness or embarrassment, many adults will not volunteer that they are not following or not understanding. One way to invite audiences to speak up is to share with them the concept of the **teachable moment**, a well-respected measure for making material relevant to the audience. For example, a parenting educator might open the discussion in the following way.

divorce education

Instruction on effects of divorce (especially on effects on children) directed to parents who are divorcing or divorced. Typically, sessions are short (half day or less) and number just a few.

teachable moment

Time during which a learner is ready to absorb new knowledge about a topic of high relevance.

"As we learn about infant brain development this month, you may find some sessions especially interesting and others not so much. Chances are, the interesting sessions will be the ones that match your baby's growth right now. So, you'll be in your *teachable moment,* as they say in the trade. Teachers have always known that the best time to teach a subject is when the learner is ready for it—in this case, you will be ready to learn exactly that part of the curriculum because it matches your baby's *development moment* and it is, therefore, your *teachable moment.* Of course, we have a lot to cover in our four sessions this month, and it won't all match your immediate need for information. When that happens, you may find the material overwhelming or too detailed or just not your cup of tea. Let me know and I'll pace our sessions accordingly."

That advisory doesn't promise to skip over the so-called boring parts for the learners who are not interested, nor the parts that are difficult to grasp, but it does establish that some of the material will be more relevant than others. There is also warning that some of the material may be overwhelming with too much detail. The facilitator has invited the audience to give feedback on their teachable moments and has accomplished **concomitant learning** about the concept of teachable moments, a good thing for every parent to be aware of.

The Reactive Audience. Much like the hostile audience, the reactive audience challenges the facilitator's poise. A difference is that the reactive audience does not arrive angry; indeed, the reactive audience is attentive and typically cooperative. It is in being attentive that reactivity occurs. In most cases, emotional reaction is in response to the session content. Perhaps a case study on abuse prompts a personal disclosure by an audience member, or an issue under discussion stimulates an argument between two audience members. As facilitators learn quickly, the entire audience does not have to react to produce a reactive audience! A single person can influence the mood of the audience; if several people react, a session may be so altered that the facilitator cannot get it back on track. In some cases, the facilitator will choose to follow the audience's emotional reaction. In all cases, the facilitator will have to draw on skills in influencing group dynamics as well as skills in maintaining composure amid high emotion.

The Reluctant or Fearful Audience. Many facilitators (and classroom teachers) were good students in school, as young children and as adult college students. Consequently, they may be unaware of the reluctance or fear that an audience member (or an entire audience) may feel upon entering a classroom or meeting room. For some people, any learning setting is threatening or a place of sad memories. Seasoned facilitators tap into their own memories of school in order to relate to what their audiences may be feeling. Recalling what it was like to "feel stupid" or "be embarrassed" in a classroom identifies the very real emotion that many adults experience at crossing into a learning room. Note that an adult may feel such emotions even when entering his or her child's classroom for a short visit.

While some adult learners may be open to discussing their insecurities about school, most are not. Presentations and activities should quickly communicate to the audience that the learning session will be enjoyable, nonthreatening, and productive. In fact, the adult's desire for productive knowledge gain

concomitant learning

A gain in knowledge that is ancillary to the primary and intended learning. For example, in learning to drive, an adolescent gains knowledge about the main task (driving) and concomitantly learns about car maintenance (adding fuel, checking oil, checking air pressure).

is the facilitator's single best ally in setting the tone. Experienced facilitators deliver lecture material in many formats and design learning activities that do not put adults on the spot. For example, the wise facilitator does not ask adult learners to read aloud or answer questions, two potentially embarrassing tasks for nonreaders or vulnerable participants. Even if the program is one that requires testing, the curriculum can be designed so that the assessment does not evoke unhappy school memories.

The Adolescent Audience

The style of communication and programs for adolescents should take advantage of three things teens value in their leisure: spontaneity, peer interaction, and a sense of independence. Successful youth coaches and youth ministers capitalize on these elements and sometimes enjoy loyal followings across middle school, junior high, and high school. Why don't all adults take advantage of these distinct preferences when planning programs? Probably because most adults do not value spontaneity (instead they tend to like events that involve advanced planning) or peer interaction (at least not in large numbers) and are uneasy with balancing adolescent independence. Often, adults are irritated when teens make spur-of-the-moment decisions, especially if adult-provided transportation is required. A frequent complaint among parents is, "Why can't they plan their outings the week before or even the day before?" But for the adolescent, the planned event would not carry the same import or excitement. In short, the spontaneous event is more highly valued. Adolescent program directors do not live quite as much in the moment as their participants, of course. They simply make it appear that they do. Thus, a youth director may keep a number of activities and trips at the ready—and therefore is able to announce a "spontaneous" decision that actually has a lot of planning behind it. In addition, youth programs offer adolescents plenty of opportunity to perceive as though they are making their own decisions (even if, truth be told, the adult facilitator is quietly guiding).

Peer groups (which may overlap with friend groups) form around specific interests by the time of adolescence. While 6th grade girls may be eager to sign up for theatre classes, softball camp, music lessons, and cotillion, by 9th grade their activities probably will not be so diverse. By middle adolescence, teens start to focus on their highest interest areas. Thus, high schools are represented by the band kids and the athletes, the theatre club and the scholastic decathlon team. An area of specialty may bring intense pleasure and pride to the adolescent as well as to family and friends. But the youth program director is aware of the transition that made this possible: the sometimes difficult stage of dropping out of activities. Between 8th and 10th grades, hard decisions are typically made about what to give up. The athlete who played softball, soccer, and basketball had to give up two sports in order to focus on basketball. Perhaps the athlete's parents were disappointed she quit softball and soccer; perhaps the coaches of those teams were dismayed at their sports being rejected; and perhaps the athlete anguished over the decision. The adults who work with teenagers in this transition stage see it as a typical part of development and can help everyone understand the processes and pressures. Through sensitive communication techniques, the professional can help the teen normalize and take ownership of his or her experiences, which gives the teen a sense of independence, a highly sought trait in adolescence.

Chapter 4, "Knowledge to Practice," discussed how adolescents' brains are just beginning to develop the center responsible for reasoning and planning. They cannot mentally work through ideas and arrive at a sound decision, recognizing all possible consequences. As with most behaviors tied to brain development, these abilities probably cannot be developed ahead of schedule. Of course, under supervision and with support, adolescents can reason and plan, but they still desire the opportunity to feel as though they are independent and able to make their own decisions. The professional working with teens, then, will involve them in planning but knows that follow through may be up to the adult.

The Child Audience

Children may be an audience in an elementary school classroom, a kindergarten or pre-K classroom, or a less structured environment such as a recreational group. Education and Child Development majors are well-versed in the standards of DAP, or developmentally appropriate practice, which translate what is known about children's development to the design and delivery of programs for children. Other college majors that include working with children should become familiar with DAP in order to recognize strong curricula and to have a shared vocabulary when working with educators and developmentalists. The Web site of the National Association for the Education of Young Children (http://www.naeyc.org) is a good source for this information.

An intern working in an elementary school classroom will have children as her audience.

DAP addresses foundational issues about children's programs and services and identifies shared goals of programs and families. Safe and nurturing environments are emphasized, as are caring communities of classroom learners and reciprocal relationships with families. Although based on generally accepted principles of child development, DAP does undergo scrutiny by professionals in early childhood education. DAP authors, such as NAEYC, responsibly reexamine the relevance of their positions on DAP. As Chapter 4 addressed usefulness as a valid measure of a theory, so might it be a good measure of DAP. As long as educators and developmentalists find DAP a useful framework for creating, running, and assessing programs, it is a valid basis for standards.

Using DAP to plan for communicating with child audiences, you would seek to understand how the child is developing in terms of language but also recognize the variability in development among a group of children. You would also seek to learn how the physical environment impacts children. Theory and practice work together to inform a DAP setting, and it may be that a consultant is the fastest route to designing a program. Consultants may be professors and graduate students of child development and early childhood education, as well as advanced undergraduates who have observed or worked in exemplary programs for children. When we take this level of care in preparing for an audience of children, we avoid the too-common errors of reliance on television and video as time fillers and of employing one set of books or toys for children across multiple ages and interests.

Language and Demographic Sensitivity

Identifying participants' demographic and cultural placement should not be taken for granted or assumed an easy task. The intern will want to develop a sense of the typical clients at a site and that will govern the type of language that is used. The use of the word *typical* is intentional in this discussion. Describing clients as *average* or *normal* is rarely accurate and may suggest deviance from an ideal standard. More likely, programs serve a wide range of clientele and do not aim to make people fit into an average mold. For example, the stereotypical nuclear family often depicted on television was never an accurate reflection of American family composition. In 1960, 43% of American families matched the model of husband working, mother at home, and two children born inside a one-time marriage; and that was the highest proportion ever in the U.S. since records were kept (Hernandez, 1993).

Thus, using appropriate language begins with self-monitoring of your vocabulary. Basic rules of polite society govern some usage across most of society. Cursing is inappropriate in workplace settings, as is sexist humor. Unkind humor is also inappropriate, and, as an old saying goes, "Don't say anything that would upset your grandmother." (Of course, not all grandmothers have the same standards!) As professionals self-monitor their speech and manners, they find that "polite society" does not go far enough in insuring that language will not discriminate and that vulnerable populations, especially, have needs that demand careful attention to language.

You may already use inclusive language in terms of gender because public media have made certain phrases common in society. For example, *police officer* has very nearly replaced the older term, *policeman* and accurately reflects a workforce made up of men and women. Some male-oriented terms have persisted, such as *manpower,* but the trend toward nonsexist language is a strong one.

Inclusive language is especially valued in the helping professions, where the objective is to include all parts of a community. Thus, professionals make intentional references to *church and temple,* not just *church,* even if that is the predominant place of worship. Religious events or initiatives themselves may be inclusive, often indicated by the term **ecumenical**. Ethnic descriptors are also important to signify respect and inclusion in community. Professionals take time to learn what terms are accepted in a locale. For example, in one community an identifier of *Mexican American* may be appropriate. In another community, the preferred term may be *Hispanic.* In another, no term at all may be used. Similarly, the professional does not assume that *African American* is a preferred descriptor. Comparable terms are *Black* and *Black*

ecumenical

Nondenominational; representing many different faiths.

American in some communities. And, again, in some communities no descriptor is used at all. *Asian American* is too broad a descriptor; whenever possible, professionals ascertain the person's country of origin and use more specific descriptors, such as *Korean American, Japanese American, Vietnamese American.* In the U.S., multiple descriptors refer to the majority population also: *White, Caucasian,* and *European American.* With so much variety in language in one society, the professional is wise to use observation skills and to ask guidance from community gatekeepers in order to select terms that are inclusive and appropriate.

Working one-on-one with community members, the respectful professional can ask what ethnicity description the person prefers. You can ask, "Do you wish to be referred to as 'Latino', or 'Hispanic'? 'Mexican American'? Or 'American'?" Similarly, the form of address should be chosen by the individual. One woman may say that she likes to be called "Ms.," which does not denote marital status. Another prefers "Mrs." as her title. And another may ask that you use her first name.

In working within a program, know and follow the policies and standards for language that must be adhered to. For example, in some school settings, selected terms and topics (such as *birth control, abstinence, condom*) are avoided. In parenting education, some practices (such as spanking) are open for discussion depending on the curriculum. As an intern, you must follow program standards even if your personal opinion differs.

Other descriptions of populations served include demographic terms such as majority and minority. Statistically speaking, these terms refer to more than 50% (majority) and any fraction less than half (minority). In other words, a minority could be a small group of 5% of the population or a sizable group of 45%. When an ethnic group represents more than 50% of the population, it may still be referred to as a minority group (sometimes being described as the *majority minority*). Thus, the cultural meaning is that the group has less power and less access to resources.

In working with multiple populations, professionals also learn how to adapt language so that labels are avoided and comments about people are

General Guidelines for Cross-Cultural Communication	
Language interpreter	If you do not speak the same language as the client family, arrange for an interpreter rather than expect a family member to be able to interpret conversations. Children, especially, should not be expected to serve as interpreters for their parents.
Language preference	Ask about language preference. Don't make assumptions about language based on physical appearance or surname.
Prescribed roles	Cultural customs may prescribe roles and expectations for how information is communicated. One person in the family may be the spokesperson; other family members may hold back from speaking with the professional.

nonjudgmental. In a school setting, a teacher or parenting educator is likely to meet families of diverse composition. Finding the language to describe families can be difficult. In the long-running children's television show *Mister Roger's Neighborhood,* the issue of what to call a child's caregiver was solved by referring to the adult(s) in a child's life as "your grown-up." The consistent use of the term created meaning so that "your grown-up" was clearly the person providing parenting to the child viewer. Parenting education in the U.S. has similarly addressed the potential of many types of people serving as parents by stressing the word *parenting.* Thus, the process of parenting is the focus, not the people who may or may not be the parents, by traditional definition.

Consider what meanings are communicated by the common terms used to describe family (see Table 5-6). What you may consider descriptive or neutral

Table 5-6 Common Terms Used to Describe Family

Average family—suggests a norm, which is probably not known

Blended family—describes a family with at least one step member

Broken family—offensive, outdated term for a family that experienced divorce

Co-parented family—suggests two divorced parents actively parenting their children

Deviant family—offensive and outdated term with vague meanings of wrongdoing

Dysfunctional family—offensive and outdated term with nonspecific meanings

Extended family—describes family members beyond the small nuclear unit

GLBT *family*—indicates parents are gay, lesbian, bisexual, or transgender

Good family—outdated term that carries loaded meanings such as *normal*

Healthy family—describes a family that is flexible and has a positive environment

Ideal family—suggests a deficit model for any family that differs

Normal family—suggests a deficit model for any family that differs

Nuclear family—refers to parent(s) and offspring; sometimes a loaded term

Standard family—outdated term that referred to nuclear family

Step-family—still accepted term for a family with at least one step member

Typical family—describes a statistically common family (not necessarily a norm)

GLBT

Gay, lesbian, bisexual, and transgender people, referring to parents of a family; sometimes reordered as LGBT.

terminology may carry a different meaning to someone else. Some phrases may be considered code words or loaded terms by another listener. Some carry implied meanings. Some terms may be offensive if used in the workplace; many may offend client families. What are more appropriate terms? As example, an outdated term such as *broken family* still makes its way into conversations; more neutral terms are *single-parent family* and *blended family*. However, as you will soon read, neutral terms are still not appropriate descriptors at all times. The professional self-monitors and replaces offensive, noninclusive terms with neutral and positive terms, while keeping in mind that some terms may still carry negative undertones.

Sometimes, the language of research provides professionals with vocabulary that helps both school personnel and families identify their unique circumstances. For example, the grandparent-headed household can be described neutrally with the language of research: *grandparents raising grandchildren*. (Most grandparents in this circumstance do not use any phrase at all to describe their household.) Within that growing subculture, another term from research helps to identify the family in which the grandchild's parent is absent: *skipped generation household*. These clear descriptions help identify the family composition without creating a stigmatizing label.

Not all descriptive terms avoid negative connotations. While the now common phrase *single-parent family* improved on the term *broken family,* it is not necessarily accurate. Children may live primarily with one parent who is single, but they may have another parent in their lives, also. Further, society attaches extra meaning to *single-parent family*. Common connotations are that children will have negative outcomes and that neither the parent nor children are thriving.

Some labels persist because a replacement term is not flexible enough. *Blended family* is a popular substitute for the former *step-family,* but it does not provide new names for the roles of individuals: stepmother, stepfather, stepsibling, and so forth. (It is an example of being superior to the research term, however, which was, for some time, *reconstituted marriage/family*.) When language emerges from families themselves, it is almost always positive, and family professionals therefore highlight a child's invention of a term, such as *my bonus mom* (referring to a stepmother).

Families may also present professionals with new uses of words without providing definition. A teacher may hear a parent use the term *co-parent,* which can mean the child's biological or adoptive other parent who may live in the same household or a different household. But *co-parent* may also refer to a same-sex partner in a GLBT (gay, lesbian, bisexual, transgender) family. *Co-parent* may also have a legal implication if custody is shared with an ex-partner or with another relative. A teacher or parenting educator must decide whether to ask for clarification or wait until the parent discloses more information later. An important question for all professionals to ask themselves is, "Do I need to know?"

Restraint and Response

Restraint in gathering information is not often discussed because most of the time the professional's goal is to gather *more* data. Part of dealing with people, though, is to recognize when seeking information, or just being a caring observer, becomes intrusive and counterproductive. The context may help decide the answer. Working with children, working with clients in community, working with other professionals—all would have different thresholds for what constitutes invasion of privacy. The intern or new professional can self-monitor and adjust information-seeking by asking the following questions.

1. Am I asking because I need to know in order to provide appropriate service? Or am I asking because I am curious?

2. Has my prior relationship with this person engendered trust? Or might this person resent my question?

3. Will my question make this person feel cared for, acknowledged? Or will my question make this person feel "picked on"?

4. Will my question allow us to set aside a matter and get on with the purpose of the visit? Or will my question cause discomfort or self-consciousness, either of which could distract us from our purpose?

5. If my question addresses a chronic condition, will it demonstrate my continued interest or will it irritate the person?

An intern must learn to recognize when seeking information becomes intrusive and counter-productive.

In all walks of life, we may react to a bruise or injury with concern: "How did you do that? I hope it's not painful." A physical injury may be an indicator of violence that deserves exploring or documenting, especially in the context of the helping professions. But even in the setting of a domestic violence shelter, physical signs may be intentionally ignored in conversation (at least initially). An intern in such a setting would expect to learn how to handle such situations through training and mentoring.

Of course, not all injuries are pertinent to the services of the professional. The person whose arm is in a cast, due to a fall or automobile accident, has no need to explain that injury. Considering the number of weeks that cast may be worn, you can imagine the number of times the person may be asked about it. A good self-monitoring strategy is to remind oneself that an injury may not be new and, therefore, not the primary focus of the person. A chronic condition similarly may be left unmentioned. A client or coworker with a chronic cough or long-term skin rash, for example, will appreciate when the condition is ignored and does not require continued comment. The principle of restraint is also appropriate for most daily or trivial matters that do little but make people self-conscious. Questions such as "Aren't you hot in that?" and "Are you wearing makeup today?" are unnecessary.

Responding to disclosures of sensitive information is another concern for professionals. Sometimes disclosure is part of the client-professional relationship. But even when that is not the case, helping professionals are frequent receivers of information because they tend to be good listeners and relate well to people. Knowing how to respond does not come automatically. Most professionals develop their own manner of responding over time, gradually learning what words they are most comfortable using. A simple phrase such as "I'm sorry to hear that" may be a sound start to developing a professional demeanor for handling disclosure of serious illness, a death, or similar sadness. The impulse may be to offer sympathy or suggestions in response. In many cases, the person who has made the disclosure is not seeking such feedback. By saying little, the professional gives the person a chance to articulate what is being sought. Sometimes, the person merely wants the professional to know the information and any further discussion may become awkward. In future meetings, the professional may need to refrain from asking questions about the matter, instead allowing the person to be in control of future discussion of it.

Confidentiality

confidentiality

Protection of personal information and identity, sometimes utilizing anonymous or pseudonymous references.

In all cases of personal information, **confidentiality** is expected. If a disclosure is not pertinent to services being delivered or the professional is not bound by ethics and law to report the information, then the professional should maintain the confidence. When a professional feels a need to consult with a peer or mentor about the information, the identity of the person should still be protected. When the intern has that need to consult with a mentor, the identity should be protected in discussion with a university instructor but a site supervisor may need to know who the source of information was. If the information or some part of it is appropriate to share in an intern's journal or internship class, the identity of the person should be masked, and if necessary, the information should be altered slightly in order to shield identity. For example, in relating an encounter with a youth during an intake interview at a correctional facility, an intern might intentionally describe the situation with pseudonyms. Thus, no one would be able to trace the information to a real person or real circumstance. Such masking is based on a research principle called *data injection,* whereby details are altered in order to protect privacy of research participants.

Preparing for Successful Learning Events

Especially in an internship, learning strategies to interact with an audience is an exciting opportunity. Whether the audience is comprised of adults seeking to learn about fly-fishing or 10th graders required to learn about safety rules, the facilitator can prepare to make the session as successful as possible. Not all strategies will be appropriate for all events, of course. And some strategies require practice. But the observant facilitator will experiment with several strategies, note what worked and what didn't, and thus be able to improve for the next event. Even the least experienced speaker or facilitator can quickly become an effective group leader by employing selected strategies listed below.

1. Engage learners in the first three minutes of the session. This means that introductions must be very short and that starting on time is a must. Consider your opening words carefully: some learners will judge your entire presentation on the first few seconds of it. (When learners are not engaged, they "vote with their feet," meaning they leave.)

2. Prepare physical materials or props to serve as your speaking notes, if you must deliver a lot of information. A stack of books, visuals, household objects, and gadgets can guide you through all your points. If you forget what your third example was going to be, just look down at your stack of props: it will be waiting for you to pick it up and explain it (as representing that third example in your talk). Some props, such as books, may turn into items to pass around the group. Share your props!

To ensure a successful learning event, a presenter should prepare physical materials or props to serve as speaking notes.

3. Speaking points can also be put on posters and given to audience members to hold for you. Thus, an audience participates in some way even if your material is basically a lecture. Having posters or props around the room also helps to keep your audience focused. They must turn their heads and even bodies to follow the progression of your talk, and these simple movements help to keep the audience engaged.

4. Provide for diverse learning styles among your audience members. If you cannot provide for all nine styles represented by Gardner's theory of multiple intelligences, at least prepare graphics, sounds, activities, and manipulatives that address the basic three types of learning: visual, auditory, and kinesthetic.

5. Break up the agenda by type of activity, alternating a high-visual activity with a high-kinesthetic activity.

6. Plan so that no agenda segment is longer than 18 minutes. This is the maximum length of time that adults can attend to one subject. (Compare to the length of a television show: of a 30-minute episode, only about 22 minutes is devoted to the show and the remaining time is punctuated by commercials.)

7. Look after your audience's physical needs, such as comfortable seating. This is especially important in school settings where adult-sized chairs may be at a premium.

8. In most communities, it is appropriate to start on time, every time, to honor those who came early. In order to be polite to late arrivals, arrange the room

so that they can enter without feeling self-conscious or embarrassed. Have handouts at the ready so that latecomers can catch up by reading about what has already been covered. Be aware that in some locales, starting late is not only acceptable but also expected. You should be flexible to meet their expectation. Open acknowledgment of the different attitudes about promptness will benefit you and your audience.

9. Invite audience members to take breaks at their own convenience by assuring them that they may come and go as they please. At the same time, announce where restrooms, water fountain, and snack machines are located.

10. When scheduling a stretch break for everyone, make it long enough to allow conversation among participants.

11. Treat adults like adults and, whenever possible, offer the same treatment to younger audiences. Don't tell them where to sit; assume they have a good reason for sitting near the door (it may be to step into the hallway to answer a cell phone and does not represent an antisocial attitude). If someone sits apart from the group, assume there is a reason for that, also. Perhaps the person feels ill or has a contagious cold. Letting people sit where they want to sit may place a burden on you, the facilitator. You may have to move around the room a lot in order to make eye contact, or you may have to speak louder than you would otherwise. If someone who is sitting apart is clearly uncomfortable (evident through coughing or sneezing, for example), you may do the person a favor by *not* trying to make eye contact and by *not* including the person in the discussion. In short, try to determine what facilitation style will be most helpful to the person and act accordingly.

12. Provide for attendees' children to the greatest extent possible. Breaks may be needed for checking on children in the movie room or infant babysitting room. Lunch or dinner may be needed for the whole family. Your adult audience will be grateful if you have provided such services and will also be able to concentrate more fully on the program.

13. Identify barriers to learning early in the process. Take what measures you can to reduce the barriers. They may include weariness after a long workday, conflicts with family, learning differences, physical layout of the room, discomfort in a group setting, and so forth.

14. Learn how to guide a group (especially in discussion) without directing. Observe master teachers and group facilitators. You will see that they rarely lecture and they place learners at the center of the activity.

15. Respond to learners' questions immediately, even if they are out of the order of topics you planned. Occasionally, you may need to ask the questioner to "Hold that thought." But have a good reason for making someone wait—otherwise, adjust your presentation so that questions are honored right away.

16. Don't assume that everyone is a strong reader and adjust your planned activities so that only volunteers will be public speakers, public readers, and so forth.

17. Role-play is the number one teaching tool for cementing ideas in people's minds. It is also the number one most disliked group activity among adults. Use it as a learning strategy only after gaining the respect and cooperation of your audience.

18. Handouts can be helpful tools for extending the learning material. Don't be afraid to hand them out early. Some speakers make the mistake of holding the materials until the end, thinking that the paper will distract the audience. On the contrary, a good handout is a support to your main

points, a place for the audience member to make notes, and a polite guide to the length of the session.

19. Visual display is especially helpful to create a sense of togetherness among an audience. Looking at a computer display or overhead together implies that everyone is on the same page and comprehending the material. Especially if the group is invited to discuss topics as they are presented, a display helps everyone with the shared vocabulary being used.

20. Displays often rely on software such as PowerPoint or having live Internet access. Always have backup and contingency plans in case of technical glitches. Backup might include different equipment or media. So, a PowerPoint slideshow should be printed off as color transparencies, as well. An Internet Web site should also be copied as a canned Web site on fixed media, such as a CD-ROM, or saved to a USB drive.

21. Rewards and gifts are appreciated by audiences. Examples are door prizes of groceries, laundry detergent, fast food restaurant gift certificates, movie theatre passes, children's books. They also help everyone leave on a positive note.

22. Ask learners to provide feedback on your presentation. A very short evaluation form can be offered (five or fewer items), or if all participants have e-mail addresses, you can send them a hyperlink to an online survey.

23. Address participants respectfully and use their first names only in the most informal groups or if they ask you to. Use name badges to good advantage, which includes wearing one yourself.

24. Refrain from using too-familiar language or physical touch with participants. Especially when working with young people, limit physical contact that could be misinterpreted.

25. Enjoy your audience! With confidence and practice, you may find that facilitating groups will become a favorite professional activity.

✳ JOURNALING

As introduced in Chapter 3, "On the Job as an Intern," journaling helps interns process their feelings experienced on the job (see Table 5-7). **Reflexivity**, or self-analysis, is a characteristic of journaling, especially when the daily or weekly writing includes reflection. Making an observation influences one's behavior, which is what is next observed. Thus, this type of reflection starts a

reflexivity

Self-analysis that creates change in self simply by virtue of the process of analysis.

Table 5-7 **Features of the Internship Journal**

Provides synthesis of observation
Reflects on the activity, the people, and the purposes
Reflects on the agency's mission statement and site standards
Progresses over time in terms of learning and articulation of observations
Becomes increasingly more critical, more complex, more analytical
Strengthens the ability to take the view of the other

```
┌─────────────────────────────────────────────────────────────┐
│              Specialized Segments for a Journal               │
├─────────────────────────────────────────────────────────────┤
│ Chronological Checkpoints: At 25% of Internship, at 50%, at 75% │
│ Accountability Report: How Did I Spend My Time?               │
│ Reflection on Professional Growth                             │
│ A Day from Open to Close                                      │
│ Verbal Snapshot: Description of the Environment               │
│ From the View of the Other: My Supervisor's Perspective       │
│ From the View of the Other: My Client's Perspective           │
│ From the View of the Other: My Student's Perspective          │
└─────────────────────────────────────────────────────────────┘
```

cycle of change. The deliberate self-consciousness can also be described this way: the position you are in influences the position you observe. Physical scientists rely on the Heisenberg uncertainty principle for a similar explanation of observation. Heisenberg concluded that the observer cannot be wholly objective because the observer's presence in the environment *influences* the environment. Thus, the observer can never see the environment as it would exist without the observer; even the most unobtrusive observation method has an effect on the environment.

Type of Writing

The deliberative and conscious writing about a field experience allows understanding of the relationship between the academic knowledge and the field application. This relationship is not always obvious. It may not be intuitive even to an observer. As the actor in the process, you must think differently about describing it. Just listing a set of tasks does not get to the meaning. The deliberative process is one of being aware of the present and the future. For example, awareness allows seeing a connection between a task of today with long-range career goals. Just as important as that forward view is a backward view to see how far you have come. Within the internship period, revisiting your journal entries can produce an appreciation of the change not only in your activity but also in your thinking.

The style of writing in a journal may vary, as suggested by the categories in Table 5-8. The order of styles reflects progression to complex and abstract thought, using the terminology of Bloom's taxonomy (1956). Because journal writing and reflection are individualistic, internship journals are very different from one intern to the next. Rather than seek comparison with other students' work, you may want to try self-evaluation using Bloom's level. Even before your internship begins, you can write a trial journal entry based on your interview visit at a potential practicum site. It should be easy to write an initial entry:

> "I met with two supervisors for 15 minutes and then toured the facility. No clients were in the center, but I was able to view a dorm unit and the cafeteria. My guide then took me to the staff conference room, where I met a current intern. He told me about his favorite assignment (intake interview), and I asked about the hours, cell phone rules, etc."

Table 5-8

Journal Terms	Bloom's Level	Ways to Demonstrate
Log, Diary	**Knowledge**	Describe, label, recognize, identify, reproduce, list, recall Examples: Can I name my coworkers? Can I list my daily tasks?
Report	**Comprehension**	Explain, exemplify, paraphrase, summarize, classify, generalize Example: Can I explain the mission of the organization?
Praxis	**Application**	Apply, modify, predict, produce, solve, use, schedule, change Example: Can I use age-appropriate guidance techniques?
Reflection	**Analysis**	Compare, contrast, diagram, examine, discriminate, infer Example: Can I draw a model of clients' access to services?
Integration	**Synthesis**	Critique, evaluate, interpret, conclude, defend, justify, design Example: Can I interpret the policy about agency liability?
Self-Evaluation	**Evaluation**	Appraise, judge, predict, value, evaluate, rate, measure, assess Example: Can I rate the effectiveness of my contribution?

As Table 5-8 indicates, this entry is at the knowledge level. It related facts and details about the visit; described some aspects of the site; identified a specific intern function (intake interview) that might be available; listed some of the concerns discussed, such as hours. In short, the entry logged basic knowledge about the site.

Technology of Journaling

The journal remains a primarily written document, even though other media can be added, especially when in digital format. A compilation of mixed media is likely to take the form of an electronic portfolio, perhaps bringing together written entries, photographs, audio files from the intern site, and a video of the intern either on the job or articulating a philosophy about the experience. The basic text could be presented in a word processing file or a Web page. All files could be affixed to CD-ROM, or submitted via e-mail, or posted to a Web-based course in a learning management system. Less frequently, the journal may be presented as a blog on the Internet; in that setting, the journal is likely to be password protected.

When created in digital formats, journals have obvious security requirements. But actually a print version of an internship journal has many of the same concerns: If a notebook is used for handwritten or typewritten journal entries, don't consider it private or secure. Because an internship journal appropriately includes detailed descriptions of people and places, its readership should be a small circle. Sometimes, that circle may be just you and your academic instructor. Even with limited readership and even when protected with passwords, descriptions in journals should not include addresses, full names, or distinguishing features of locations.

Ethics of Journaling

The journal provides for personal reporting in a safe environment. The academic instructor who reads it comes to the exercise with respect for the intern's experience and also for the other people reflected in the journal. The challenge is to maintain confidentiality throughout the internship and afterward, as well. The internship site's business is confidential, as is any client information. The academic instructor adds another expectation: that the student's reflection on these matters is also confidential. Essentially, the internship generates an additional ethical concern for the intern in requiring a journal.

In the great majority of cases, the journal is a private document between intern and instructor. But a site supervisor or mentor in the field may feel concern about a record being made by a student. If a site supervisor requests that record, the university instructor will follow academic policies in guiding the intern in making a response.

✳ ELECTRONIC COMMUNICATION IN THE WORKPLACE

Increasingly, electronic communication impacts how business and education are conducted; therefore, most workplaces—and internship sites—have both formal policies and informal practices about communication technologies. As an intern, you will need to be able to comply with policy as you use technologies; as a new professional, you will likely help formulate policies and practices. Your recent tenure on a campus almost assures that you have up-to-date experience or training, whether or not you consider yourself a technical person. In terms of spread of technology, campuses have led the U.S., starting with the first public uses of e-mail in the 1990s. Understanding and use of Internet Web sites has increased dramatically in just a couple of decades, due to the combined influence of college students and business people transferring their Internet skills and knowledge from campus or business to home.

In the child and family professions, recent college graduates are often the catalysts for technical change in schools and agencies. This is in large part due to their exposure to technology during college, even in programs that are not technology-driven. While interns may not directly influence adoption of new technologies, they may, nevertheless, have an impact on a site's use of technology, or they may simply come to view their own use of communication technology differently. This section addresses the possible uses of technology at internship sites, both for personal communication and for internship-related communication.

Being on the job may mean that you will have to be out of touch with friends and family. Workplace rules and customs may tolerate your cell phone . . . or may not. Your internship may involve changes in e-mail, texting, and cell phone habits. A review of your communication tools, along with typical concerns of work settings, is in order. How many of these communication technologies do you use daily?

- cell phone and **texting**
- e-mail and **IM**
- PDA, or personal digital assistant
- pager
- Internet

On the job of the internship, how might the people around you view your use of these technologies? Consider not just your supervisor and co-workers, but also clients and visitors. Self-monitoring your own use of your communication tools is wise, even if the agency does not limit your use of them. First, observe whether there are unwritten rules about making personal calls, sending e-mail, or other means of personal communication. Next, notice what times of day (and what locations) best tolerate your taking a break for a call. Let your friends or family know about this best time to reach you. Self-monitoring also means controlling the volume of phone rings and pager beeps. If your use of computers for e-mail is not restricted, you should still think about potential impact of your e-mail screen if it were to be viewed by a passerby.

Restrictions on communication technologies in the workplace typically involve two issues: confidentiality and time use. Confidential records of an agency or business may include budgets, **proprietary information**, personnel information, and student or client files. Time use refers to how employees' time is spent during work hours. If personal communication is part of the workday, then productivity is compromised. Even if the number of minutes spent on personal communication is few, the activity may still be a distraction that causes a problem. Consider the potential distraction for an employee in a child care center: in this case, the cost to productivity might be compromised safety of children because supervision is lacking. Even in solo work pursuits, personal communication can interrupt attention to tasks and interfere with the total day's work.

Equipment

Use of the agency's equipment for personal purposes may not be allowed at all. In some settings, restrictions may be tied to the source of the funds that purchased the equipment (such as state funding at a school or university). Security concerns may include hardware or software theft, inappropriate access to or use of files stored in the computer, and accidental loss of information. When the agency issues equipment to the employee or intern, it is important to clarify how the equipment may be used. For example, a desktop computer is logically confined to desk use; is a laptop computer similarly confined to use in the office? If it is to be used elsewhere, is there a system of recordkeeping to track the whereabouts of the laptop? Is either style of computer dedicated solely to work purposes, or can the individual also conduct personal business such as maintaining personal files, checking e-mail, and surfing the Internet?

Settings on computer equipment may be controlled by the agency or school. Privacy levels of Web sites, cookies (which identify a computer when

texting

Alphanumeric messaging through cell phone, PDA, and e-mail.

IM

Instant messaging through services such as Google and Yahoo!™.

proprietary information

Material that is owned or controlled.

It is important to clarify how agency-issued equipment may be used. May it be used for agency business only?

filter

Software that blocks a computer's access of certain Web sites or certain content, according to settings that are amendable by the computer owner.

firewall

Hardware or software that protects gateways (entry points) between the Internet and a network or computer system and prevents an unauthorized outsider from accessing the files and computers.

a user revisits a particular Web site), **filters** (routinely set by sites such as schools), and **firewalls** (routinely employed by virtually all sites that have multiple computers) are all pertinent in terms of work-related use and personal use. Other equipment, such as PDAs and cell phones, also may have controls or restrictions. Required use of passwords is typical, and the agency may issue rules about sharing of passwords. The agency may also issue rules about the use of personal equipment on the job: is a personal cell phone even allowed in the facility, and can an employee use an MP3 player with earphones?

Internet Access

Use of, and even access to, the Internet may be limited to agency or school business or not allowed at all. Restrictions are typically geared to avoid viruses, inadvertent installation of spyware and cookies, spam and pop-up ads, illegal downloads (e.g., of music), inappropriate downloads (e.g., of pornography), and pirated software downloads. If Internet use *is* allowed, interns should familiarize themselves with agency policies, as well as common standards, such as these:

History: Will a list of your Web site visits be stored on the computer? How would you feel if your supervisor saw the list of your most recent sites visited? You will need to self-monitor and not visit some Web sites from work computers. Even an innocuous Web site may sound suspicious; avoid creating doubt about your surfing.

Screen Views: What would a passerby glimpse of your computer screen? Popular culture sites may give the wrong impression. The same issue exists for your wallpaper, screensavers, e-mail messages, and instant messages.

Pop-Ups: If pop-ups are not blocked automatically, limit the number you leave on the desktop. Consider other users who would have to clean up the desktop.

Sounds: Control speaker volume so that you are the only listener. If a computer's sound is muted when you begin using it, return it to that setting when you finish.

Browser Windows: Be cautious about leaving windows open after you have entered passwords or any personal information. Even when no private information is communicated, be aware that other users may be irritated at finding a computer with many windows left open.

User Profiles: On shared computers, limit your use of features such as saved passwords that are remembered by the browser, fill-in-the-blank options on forms, etc. Always log off and close all applications. If a computer has multiple users, log out of your user profile every time you finish.

Passwords: Know the policy at your workplace for recording and sharing passwords. Your private passwords should remain confidential, of course.

E-mail

Workplace e-mail is necessarily different from your personal e-mail. The tone is more formal and should demonstrate correct grammar, few abbreviations and contractions, and standard spelling and punctuation. Frequency of messages should also be self-monitored. Do not expect immediate replies; use a calendar to track the need for prompts or repeated e-mails.

Your professional identity is reflected through your e-mail appearance and choice of decoration. Unless the agency uses a standard stationery design or color, use plain formatting and background. Emoticons, animations, and sound effects are not appropriate elements of business e-mail. Quotations at the bottom of your e-mail or motivational sayings are typically not used in business correspondence.

Identity is also maintained through your e-mail name or address. An agency may have a naming convention whereby a pattern is evident in all employees' e-mail names. If a naming convention is not in place, you will have the opportunity to create your own e-mail name. Use your name or initials in an intuitive pattern such as "JDoe@" or "Jane.Doe@" (or similar format) so that other people will be able to identify you in their Inboxes and also easily call up your e-mail address when sending a message to you.

Use multiple e-mail addresses in order to categorize incoming e-mail, but limit the number to just two or three. Maintaining more than a few e-mail accounts is time-consuming and may result in some accounts rarely being checked.

Conventions of "carbon copy" (CC: or cc:) and "blind carbon copy" (BCC: or bcc:) allow you to include (or exclude) other people in an e-mail. Only the CC option, where all parties' names are visible, is appropriate in professional e-mail communication. Blind copying violates ethics in most settings. Caution is also needed to protect against making a Reply to All when your response is appropriate to only select persons.

Group e-mail is often handled by using premade distribution lists, either provided by the agency or of your own making. Distribution lists may or may not display the actual e-mail addresses of the people on the list. To hide e-mail addresses, one strategy is to place the multiple addresses on the BCC line, and address the To line with your own e-mail address. This is especially important if you have compiled a list of e-mail addresses of people who do not know each other and, presumably, would prefer that their e-mail address not be shared with other people.

Listservs are a convenient means of mass communication sometimes utilized by agencies and organizations. Understand the methods of replying to a Listservs' message and know who will be receiving your comments. The convenience of Listervs is undermined when an error generates multiple copies, or inexperienced users send replies to everyone on the listserv.

All e-mail messages are improved when they carry a relevant and meaningful subject line. When the subject is entered as "help" or "please help me," be aware that some recipients will fail to open it, assuming it is spam. If your recipient may not recognize your address or name when it appears in the Inbox, you may want to use the subject line to provide an assurance of identity. For example, an intern on a large school campus may well have an address that will not be recognized in the office, so a good subject line might read, "Doe, Building C intern: Need photocopies." Especially if the e-mail includes an attachment, such an identifier is appropriate.

E-mail messages, even when deleted by you or a recipient, reside on network servers. Thus, they make a permanent record. Write only what you would wish someone to see and keep—or forward to other people. Be considerate and ethical in how you handle messages to and from others.

Voice Mail

Follow agency rules and guidelines about voice mail on the job. Depending on the type of work and clients, privacy and confidentiality may be issues in telephone communication. For example, messages left on voice mail should not reference personal details, clients' status, or even clients' names. A rule of thumb is that if you wouldn't want to repeat the message in a legal proceeding, don't leave it as a voice mail message.

Be aware that the person who retrieves a message may not be the person you intended to contact. A good strategy is to simply refer to the day and time of an appointment, without mentioning the topic (especially a sensitive or private topic). When you leave a message on someone else's voice mail system, speak slowly and distinctly. Repeat your name and contact information at the start and the finish of the message. Make a brief generic statement of your reason for calling and indicate the day and time. See Figure 5-2 for a sample voice mail script.

Cell Phone

Cell phone communication has become ubiquitous in the U.S., but that does not mean that it is fully integrated in our lives or does not cause disruption. At the basic level of daily life, cell phones provide a level of convenience and connection that cannot be rivaled by any other current technology. But like any other technology, cell phone communication requires strategies to deal with its intrusion into public spaces and its disruption of human processes.

Many people complain of the rudeness of loud voices that accompany cell phone use, frequently pointing out that private conversations should not be conducted in public. Preliminary research in this area has suggested that the irritation to others is actually caused by a human need (or at least preference) to hear two sides of a conversation. Thus, if we heard two people talking we would not be as irritated as we are when we hear only one of the voices. Just knowing this about human preferences helps to plan the time and place for a

> "My name is _____. My number is _____ and I will repeat that at the end. I need to speak with you about _____. Again, my name is _____ and my number is _____. My e-mail contact is _____."

Figure 5-2 Sample voice mail script.

Table 5-9 Tips for Cell Phone and Personal Communication

Establish habits for turning off phones and pagers at the start of meetings.

Select the least obtrusive ringtones for workplace use.

Consider the effect of your conversation on everyone in your listening range.

Avoid texting during meetings.

If you must respond to a call (from the Vibrate mode), quietly step out of the meeting.

If your assigned work is completed, do not use personal communication as a time filler.

cell phone conversation. (Being quiet in a cell conversation would help, but it may not avoid irritating others, anyway.)

In terms of disruption of a person's life, it may be that cell phones cause more spillover effect (between work and home life) than laptop computers and e-mail cause. All technologies potentially create spillover from the work sphere to the home sphere; in most research, spillover is identified as the negative effects that arise when tasks cross the boundaries between time on the job and time off the job. The cell phone appears to demand more immediate reaction by employees when they are away from work. By contrast, e-mail may follow an employee home, but the employee is better able to manage it. Spillover effects can occur in the opposite direction: home issues spilling over into work hours. Cell phone technology has increased the access family members have to reach people in their workplaces.

The intrusion of noise, in general, in the workplace is a problem. And the emergence of personal phone rings has caused many companies to ban rings during the workday. The variety of rings, musical interludes, and sound effects can distract coworkers and also create confusion as people check to see if their own phone is ringing.

The portability of cell phones also creates a problem because of potential security lapses. In phoning or texting someone (either professional colleague or client), you cannot be certain that the person will be alone when receiving the information. Add to that issue the concern about digital communication's inherent lack of privacy, and the risks are high for confidential information. See Table 5-9 for a list of cell phone and personal communication tips.

Fax Communication

Use of fax (facsimile) technology carries responsibility in terms of confidential information, just as telephone and e-mail technology do. Before you send a fax, especially with identifying or personal information, ensure that the intended person will be in place to receive it. Clearly identify documents to be faxed with "TO:" and "FROM:" entries. Cover sheets help with this function and also typically announce the number of pages in the fax. Signatures may be adequate for some purchasing or legal purposes. Clarify with vendors and agencies whether an original signature is also needed through snail mail. (Because a fax is a scanned reproduction of a document, it may or may not be accepted as a legal document.)

Conducting personal business on an agency fax machine presents an ethical dilemma. Because of the ease of transmitting dense information quickly, the temptation may be great to send a fax regarding nonagency business. To avoid being in this position, be familiar with other options in your work or internship neighborhood: office supply stores typically offer fax services and so do shipping and mailing centers. From your home, you can also use fax software on your computer to act as a fax receiver. With a scanner, you can create your own scanned image of a document to either send through fax software or as an attachment to e-mail.

Electronic Image and Identity

In your personal Internet use, you may have created alternate identities for specific uses. Such practice is appropriate for some settings and for self-protection. In the workplace, the display of alternate identities or names may cause problems and confusion. You should create a username or standard e-mail name reserved for your professional identity.

A common error of new professionals is to use an electronic username or moniker that was created years previous for social purposes and is not appropriate to the workplace. For example, an e-mail name of "cheeseball@chickmail.com" may have been admired by your friends in younger years, but it is likely not the image you want to project now. Unfortunately, you may not even notice "cheeseball" anymore because it is just part of your everyday screen view.

Electronic identity may include membership or display pages at social media or social networking sites. While a display on MySpace or a similar Web site is generally viewed as personal expression, the mere existence of such a Web page may be problematic on the job. Increasingly, employers search for such Web-based displays as added information about a job applicant. Words and photographs created in adolescence or in an informal social setting may not be representation the job applicant would like a potential employee to view, but there may be little chance of avoiding the Web page being seen. Even when an individual removes a personal Web page, it may continue to be displayed through servers not controlled by the individual, archived Web page data maintained by search engines, and also by Internet indexing and preservation initiatives. In short, just as an e-mail message can persist, so, too, can a Web page.

Regarding employees who maintain an Internet persona, some companies issue explicit directives that personal Web pages cannot reflect anything about the company. (And this may also apply to interns; see next section.)

Blogging

blog

Shortened form of *Weblog*, which is an online journal or diary, typically posted in reverse chronological order.

A new issue has arisen in terms of Internet blogging: personal freedom on and off the job may be important to you, but keeping a **blog** on the Internet is forbidden by some companies. Even where policies are not written, blogging may be discouraged or lead to dismissal. The question of oversight or control of personal expression is not an easy one. The Internet has moved the debate beyond the simpler questions of not violating a company's policies on confidentiality, trade secrets, and the like. The informal reporting power of the Internet can overstate one person's opinion or concern about a matter and turn that opinion into a lawsuit. Public perception can be impacted so that a company's image and reputation are damaged. False allegation or rumor distorting one fact can cause lack of confidence in a company, and this is often the argument for forbidding even seemingly innocuous blogs by employees. Blogging is not the only Internet source for such problems, of course. Any Web site or Listserv can do the same, but because blogs are often used for personal expression, they are more often named as the source for negative information.

An Internet search for online intern blogs can produce samples of blogs across multiple disciplines and settings. They can be a good source of insider opinions about internships, but, like all Internet sites, they may also contain inaccuracies. Some bloggers have begun to print a disclaimer about their sites in order to identify their words as their own and not representing an agency or company.

✳ MENTORING AND NETWORKING

A common theme among internships is the opportunity to work with a mentor and to network with professionals. This opportunity depends on both the professional's willingness to serve as mentor and guide and the preprofessional's openness to learning. For all parties, the opportunity can be rewarding but must be based on realistic expectations. The intern's perspective should take into account the constraints of time and individual attention.

A common theme among internships is the opportunity to work with a mentor.

Mentoring

Some internships feature a formal and explicit mentor-intern match. A matching process might begin in your interview before placement. The mentor could be based on your long-term career goals or current need for exposure to a particular expertise. At other sites, no formal process is used, but you may find a person who fulfills this role.

Mentoring may include making suggestions about your intern activities, providing new learning experiences, introducing you to professional meetings and organizations, providing feedback about your work performance, offering guidance on handling problems, answering questions as they arise, and listening and reacting to your ideas. The relationship is one of mutual trust.

✳ **mentor**
Experienced professional who serves as guide, advocate, and facilitator for a new professional in the workplace.

Mentoring may not be one-on-one; if you must share the mentor resource (with other interns, for example) you may have to wait for an appointment. Some internship sites address mentoring through a shared resource such as an intern coordinator. This person may be your starting point, your initial trainer, and your check-in point for logging hours. The intern coordinator knows a little bit about every department in the agency, but specializes in the legal and paperwork aspects of your internship. In many cases, the intern coordinator is also a good safety net for elementary questions about the agency. (While the intern coordinator may also be of help when problems arise, your first point of contact should still be your Instructor at school.)

The intern coordinator may make the match between you and a mentor, but some agencies have an automatic match simply because of the way their programs are structured. This means you may have no choice at all in who your mentor is. Your responsibility as a mentee is to make that match work. Working in your favor is the fact that your mentor also takes seriously the responsibility to make it work. Table 5-10 outlines guides for sound mentoring relationships, considering both sides of the relationship with complementary positions for mentor and student.

What about bad mentoring? Not every mentor match is a good one. When possible, discuss your expectations with your mentor *and* your campus instructor. Clear communication can salvage a relationship. Often, the real culprit is lack of time on the mentor's part, and the student may feel ignored or overlooked. In this situation, the student must respond with maturity and

Table 5-10 **Guides for Sound Mentoring Relationships**

Mentor: Respect the student's desire to learn and support exploration of the practicum site.

Student: Respect the mentor's experience and accept guidance about the best way to explore the practicum site.

Mentor: Understand the student's caution in entering a new environment and create a welcoming experience.

Student: Understand the mentor's time priorities and be prepared to sometimes introduce yourself to staff members.

Mentor: Expect the student to need advice from time to time.

Student: Expect the mentor to provide advice, realizing that you must articulate your need for information or guidance.

Mentor: Help the student learn the culture of the site, including unwritten/unspoken rules about conduct.

Student: Help the mentor understand your previous experience (or lack of experience) in the field.

Mentor: Anticipate the student's need to discuss difficulties and, when possible, hold in confidence what the student may disclose to you.

Student: Understand the limits of your mentor's responsibility to meet your needs. Rely, too, on your academic supervisor or instructor to help with difficulties.

seek alternate means for gaining experience and information at the site. For example, the student can forge relationships with several staff members, in effect breaking up the mentor tasks among several mentors.

Networking

Mentors are often the intern's first guide to networking opportunities. Professional networking can take place in the workplace, at conferences, at trainings, and in community meetings. Opportunities for networking may come during sporting events, lunches, social events, or other occasions. You will want to be prepared to introduce yourself and present your business card. There are different cultural expectations about the use of business cards. In some countries, it is considered rude to write on the back of a card you have been handed. Consult with a mentor or research on the Internet about etiquette in networking.

Your business card should reflect your professional image. The information should be easily read and understood. Typically, this means limiting elements to the pertinent contact information and no illustration. Proofread carefully to ensure that your correct and current e-mail and telephone contact information is printed. Print just a few cards at a time for different events, using perforated card stock designed for use in laser printers and inkjet printers. Restraint in short print runs will pay off for you: you will be able to edit the information frequently without wasting cards.

Networking produces friendships, business contacts, program collaborations, and even job prospects. But it does not always come easily to students and new professionals. The communication skills introduced in this chapter can be put to use to ease any tension felt in meeting professionals at their gatherings. Additionally, these tips may help to make sense of the business of networking.

- *Small talk* is light, informal conversation that paves the way for later recognition. Recommended for interns: plan which aspects of your life/internship to share. This means being ready to disclose your major at school, but not sharing the details of your home life or relationships.

- *Talking shop* is almost always limited to brief discussions of agency or program business and can be thought of as one more version of "small talk." [Interns should engage in this practice with caution.]

- *Glad-handing* is the real or virtual handshaking that indicates that you are ready and willing to meet everyone in the room. [Interns should engage in this practice with caution.]

- *Wheeling and dealing* is the negotiation or exchange of services. [Interns should not engage in this practice.]

⊙ SUMMARY OF CHAPTER CONTENTS

Communication Skills of a Professional: The professional is prepared to communicate with children, clients, and audiences in multiple ways and intentionally builds skills to assure that communication is effective.

Self-Presentation: Interns send intentional and unintentional messages through written, verbal, and nonverbal communication; through self-monitoring, the intern becomes aware of the impact of his or her messages.

> ***Self-Introduction:*** By practicing strategies such as the 30-second elevator speech, interns can become comfortable introducing themselves to members of the community.

Handshake and Touch: Understanding the cultural and health aspects of physical contact assists in making sound choices in using handshakes and touch with children and clients.

Conference-Style Speaking: Adopting several standards for speaking in groups lends credibility (and audibility) to your message.

Speaking from the Podium: While public speaking is frequently cited as a major fear, it is nevertheless a skill that professionals must master on some level. Using specific techniques, speakers can communicate effectively, whether or not they enjoy the process.

Clothes Make the Professional: Appropriate attire in the workplace may depend on a person's willingness to ask about what kind of dress is expected or careful observation of colleagues' choices in clothing and accessories.

Communicating with Diverse Audiences: Professional communication encompasses learning about and practicing delivery to a variety of audiences.

The Adult Audience: While many adult audiences are cooperative and eager participants, the professional also is prepared to work with audiences that are hostile, restless, overwhelmed, reactive, reluctant, or fearful.

The Adolescent Audience: Knowledge of adolescent development enhances one's ability to connect with adolescents.

The Child Audience: Working successfully and responsibly with children demands learning about or consulting an expert about developmentally appropriate practice (DAP), which represents widely accepted standards for programs and environments designed for children.

Language and Demographic Sensitivity: Language and sensitivity about demographic descriptions is an essential consideration for effective communication in the child and family professions.

Restraint and Response: Developing appropriate communication skills includes knowing when to restrain from comment and how to respond to disclosures of personal information.

Confidentiality: Protection of children and clients extends to not sharing their personal information outside of the workplace.

Preparing for Successful Learning Events: To facilitate a group or teach a workshop, special communication strategies can be employed to engage the audience and assure an enjoyable learning experience.

Journaling: Many internships require that a journal or log be maintained as a record of activities and also as a reflexive account of experiences.

Type of Writing: Interns may adopt a new style of writing for the journal that is deliberative, conscious, analytical, and subjective.

Technology of Journaling: Increasingly, internship journals rely on electronic communication to document the experience.

Ethics of Journaling: Intern, site supervisor, and university instructor typically share expectations for confidentiality of the intern's journal.

Electronic Communication in the Workplace: Increasingly, workplaces rely on communication technologies and, therefore, adopt formal policies and informal practices about their uses.

Equipment: Intern sites are likely to have strict regulations about use of equipment, which is typically owned and controlled solely by the site.

Internet Access: Permitted use of the Internet should be understood with respect to protection against viruses, downloads of software and music, user profiles, and etiquette for shared computers.

E-mail: Workplace and personal e-mail standards differ; self-monitoring should include awareness of professional identity, the permanency of remarks in e-mail, ethical uses of e-mail, and practical considerations such as descriptive subject lines.

Voice Mail: While often taken for granted, messages left on telephones should be considered in terms of ethics (especially concerning the possibility of retrieval by someone other than the intended recipient) and pragmatics (how effective the message is).

Cell Phone: The ubiquitous cell phone can create disruption in the workplace; conscious use of the convenience can minimize the negative aspects.

Fax Communication: Confidentiality may be compromised by use of fax documents; care should be taken to avoid such problems.

Electronic Image and Identity: One's identity on the Internet may enhance or destroy a reputation. Cached Web sites may extend a youthful personal expression long after intended.

Blogging: Keeping a personal blog may conflict with an internship or workplace policy; at the same time, intern blogs on the Internet provide a wealth of information about potential internships (with the proviso that accuracy may not be assured).

Mentoring and Networking: A common theme of internships is the opportunity to work with mentors and network with professionals.

Mentoring: A mentor offers guidance to a newcomer or intern; whether formal or informal, the mentor-mentee relationship has the potential for benefiting both of the people, the workplace, and the profession at large.

Networking: Networking with professionals produces friendships, business contacts, program collaborations, and even job prospects.

⊙ DISCUSSION QUESTIONS

1. Use the opening case study of this chapter to compare your own level of skill and comfort in self-introduction, networking, and public presentation. What specific communication skills did Tamara develop? What role did time play in skill development? How does this compare with your own stage of development? Like Tamara, how will you overcome fears of self-disclosure or speaking about your strengths and your own expertise?

2. Over the next week, every time you see someone speak publicly, note one aspect that you find effective and one thing you would do differently. Examples: professors lecturing, officers speaking at a campus organization meeting, sports coach addressing a team, Oscar/Emmy Award acceptance speeches.

3. If asked to give a five-minute presentation during the second week of your internship, what would you be comfortable presenting on? Examples: infant brain development drawing from your course work, report on a current book, critique of a Web site designed for either professionals or parents.

4. When speaking to a group, is it better to cover the material as prepared or be flexible to audience background and interests? Give examples of settings in which each strategy is appropriate.

5. In the following internships, how could e-mail or other forms of electronic communication be used effectively with the clientele?

   Youth minister working with teenagers

   Middle school classroom aide

   YMCA soccer coordinator

6. What is a technique you are comfortable using to refocus a lecture for a restless audience? An overwhelmed audience? A reactive audience? A fearful audience? Can some techniques be used with more than one type of audience?

7. Brainstorm multiple ways to describe or introduce family relationships, including biological sibling, half-sibling, stepsibling, foster sibling, adopted sibling, fictive kin, extended family members. Descriptions might include words, graphics, photographs.

8. If working with a teenage population, how could you talk with them about appropriate attire for school?

9. What aspects of nonverbal communication engender trust in a speaker? Create doubt about a speaker? (Politicians think about these aspects around election time.)

10. What are advantages and disadvantages of being able to keep a personal cell phone at the internship site? To check personal e-mail?

◉ GUIDED PRACTICES

Guided Practices offer structured exercises in critical thinking, observation (including self-observation), synthesis, and self-expression. The title of Guided Practice sums up the purpose of providing a guide: an opportunity that permits practice and does not require a final, ultimate effort.

All of the guided practices can be used by one person or by a group of people. The practices are designed as self-report instruments, meaning that answers are reported by the respondent and not collected by an interviewer or by another person who may speak with or observe the respondent.

There is not a standard amount of time to spend on the exercises. One person may use a guided practice for making a quick check while the next person may choose to spend hours on the same practice. Individual interest in a topic makes a difference in use, as does current need for the topic.

The greatest value is derived when the guided practice is completed with honest answers and observations. Any instrument may generate socially desirable answers, the kind of responses that a person thinks will be acceptable or expected. Especially when related to academic study, an instrument that calls for self-disclosure or self-evaluation risks being answered this way.

Guided Practice:
Self-Assessment of Communication Skills

Communication skills are often developed during an internship. Use this grid to assess your starting point. Repeat the assessment at the end of the internship.

	Expert	Developing	Novice
I can look interested during a meeting.			
I can ask appropriate questions that reflect my listening.			
I can introduce myself confidently one-on-one.			
I can introduce myself confidently in a small group.			
I can introduce myself confidently in a large group or conference setting.			
I can describe my internship.			
I can describe the mission/purpose of my workplace or internship site.			
I can answer questions about my background/future.			
I can determine when to offer my hand for a handshake.			
I can determine when NOT to offer my hand for a handshake.			
I can approach and begin to converse with someone I would like to know professionally.			
I know how and when to offer my business card.			
I know how to express thanks to a colleague.			

Guided Practice:
30-Second Speaking

Use each block to construct a concise 75-word speech, which typically translates to 30 seconds. With each block, add more information in order of priority.

Your goal for a three-minute presentation will be 450 to 500 words.

30 seconds	
30 seconds	
30 seconds	
30 seconds	
30 seconds	
30 seconds	

Guided Practice:
The Mirror Check

Imagine your first meeting with your supervisor at your internship site.

What message would this supervisor receive about you?

How would the supervisor assess your appearance?

	Appropriate for Worksite	Needs Improvement	Not Appropriate for Worksite
Hair			
Makeup			
Shoes			
Style of attire			
Fit of attire			
Hygiene			
Accessories (purses, backpacks, bags)			
Jewelry			
Body piercings or tattoos			
Overall appearance			

What adjectives would be used to describe your appearance?

_____

What do you need to change?

_____

 Guided Practice forms are also included on the accompanying CD-ROM.

⦿ ADDITIONAL RESOURCES

Search Terms: Communication, especially computer-mediated communication (CMC), is the subject of both scholarly and popular Internet Web sites. Search terms to continue your own exploration of professional communication are: *CMC, Deborah Tannen, John Gottman, nonverbal communication, self-disclosure*.

⦿ REFERENCES

Bloom, B. S. (Ed.). (1956). *Taxonomy of educational objectives: The classification of educational goals, by a committee of college and university examiners*. New York: D. McKay.

Hernandez, D. (1993). *America's children: Resources from government, family and the economy*. New York: Russell Sage Foundation.

For additional material and resources to complement this chapter, the Online Companion Web site can be accessed at http://www.earlychilded.delmar.com.

CHAPTER 6

Ethics and Public Policy

Major Points in This Chapter:

Introduction to Ethics
Themes of Professional Standards
Elements of Ethical Codes
Articulating a Personal Code of Ethics
Workplace Ethics
Impact on Clients, Children, and Families
Ethics and Decision Making
Research Ethics
Application of Ethical Thinking to Public Policy
Ethical Dilemmas

CASE STUDY: Lynn was thrilled to have an internship as a child life specialist. The position involved applying far in advance and completing many hours of observation prior to being placed. The hospital had an excellent reputation for helping children with disabilities, exactly what Lynn wanted to do after school.

After being on the job for a week and learning more than ever expected, Lynn was invited to join several coworkers for lunch. As they enjoyed their meal at a small restaurant close to the hospital, a recent patient and her family entered the same area. To Lynn's surprise, no one in her group greeted the family by name. The coworkers acknowledged the family with a warm smile but did not engage in conversation with them. Lynn wanted to hug the child but held back after noting the group's response.

During the meal, the conversation focused on personal activities and hobbies. A main topic of conversation was an upcoming seminar on play therapy, sponsored by a professional organization. Several people at the table were planning to attend, and Lynn was included in the invitation to carpool to the nearby university for the seminar. Lynn noted that no current cases were discussed or compared during the lunch. Each member of the group paid for his or her own meal, and they returned to the hospital. Lynn thanked the supervisor for allowing an intern to join them.

✳ INTRODUCTION TO ETHICS

ethics

Personal principles leading to critical reasoning and reflection on conduct.

Critical reasoning or reflection about responsibility to self and others is the basis for **ethics** and the new professional. In the helping professions, ethics, duty, and responsibility are often overlapping concepts. New professionals may face decisions involving all of these areas. This chapter addresses ethics at the professional and personal levels and outlines ways you can identify your own sense of duty and responsibility to your work. The chapter also identifies some key elements of codes of ethics and how they can be used to guide your decision making in the workplace. The chapter ends with describing the process of articulating your personal code of ethics representing your personal commitment to your profession.

People describe ethics with different terms. You may have heard any number of these terms: *ethical guidelines, doing the right thing, values, morals, morality, right and wrong, honorable acts, fairness, principled, conscientious, honesty, upright, virtuous, following a compass, exercising judgment without external controls.* All these phrases suggest the importance of ethics in daily life. While values are your basic beliefs and attitudes, ethics are a little different. Ethics relate more specifically to conduct—what you believe is the right way to behave.

When ethics are lacking, they are easy to identify. We call that, among other things: *wrong, unethical, unprincipled, unscrupulous, false, out of kilter, unfair.* It's not always appropriate to judge behavior from external appearances only or an outsider's opinion; ethical guidelines provide standards for distinguishing what is ethical and what is not.

Institutional ethics may also rely on phrases. This plain-speaking phrase from the University of Southern California (n.d.) is immediately understood by readers:"We try to do what is right even if no one is watching us or compelling us to do the right thing." It is the essence of personal responsibility, expressed as we might explain the concept to a young person. Children develop awareness of right from wrong in stages, one of them being, "I'll do what is right because the grown-ups are watching." A sign of maturation for all of us is commitment to doing the right thing, even with no observer.

Ethics always begin as personal commitment. An institutional statement of ethics (as USC's above) represents the decision by individuals to carry personal commitment into their professional lives. For some interns, the field experience is their first exposure to having to think beyond what's right for the individual. The challenge is to not only learn how to take the view of the "other," meaning other people, but also to learn how to preserve one's own view.

Research into undergraduate students' development charts stages across nine changes (Perry, 1981). Initially, students look for absolute answers from authorities and rely on experts' guidance. For example, students may initially rely on the rules or want to consult a supervisor for answers or advice. Through exposure to new ideas and diverse people, both in the classroom and out of the classroom, students begin to acknowledge that there are multiple answers and sources. This acknowledgment may lead to the student realizing that an external expert cannot provide every answer. The student must gain confidence in his or her own ability to form solutions rather than to search for mythical absolute right answers. Students learn to back up a first opinion by gathering information for sound decision making on their own. With further experiences, one of which may be the internship, students come to appreciate the differences and challenges of multiple truths and realize their own responsibility to commit to their values. There is no end point to the responsibility. Professionals constantly evaluate and reevaluate their positions and the bases for those positions. In short, for an ethical person, experience leads to more questions than answers.

This ongoing process extends beyond graduation and an internship. In your career, you are likely to participate in research-based, continuing professional development. Through working with professional colleagues and in making your own contributions to your field, you will maintain currency in knowledge (not just building on your knowledge base, but able to adopt new perspectives). The lifelong learner stays open to new ideas.

✳ THEMES OF PROFESSIONAL STANDARDS

Across professions, rules of conduct may be similar. Published standards reflect **professionalism** and commitment to ethics. All of the organizations reflected in Table 6-1 have created codes of ethics and conduct to which their members subscribe. In fact, most professional organizations provide similar guidance to their members. You can find the complete codes on their Web sites, accessible to members and nonmembers. An Internet search will display a wide range of codes of ethics, from the informal to the formal. International comparisons can also be made.

✳ **professionalism**
Possessing special knowledge and skillfulness.

✳ ELEMENTS OF ETHICAL CODES

As similar as organizations may be in general themes, they can differ greatly in their elements. Depending on setting, detailed provisions include legal concerns, confidentiality, conflict of interest, and dozens of more specifics. In one code, a provision may spell out clear expectations that serve as requirements for membership or licensure. In another code, provisions may be written generally and rely on the individual professional to interpret how to apply them. Some professional associations also have specialty guidelines to cover areas such as providing services for culturally diverse populations or record-keeping guidelines.

New professionals may feel a bit overwhelmed at the scope of the guidelines to be learned and applied. Even seasoned professionals must continue learning, as more attention is focused on ethics in our society. It is not unusual today for certifications and professional licenses to require continuing education in ethics. Your own evolving skills will help you translate broad, general guidelines into your own professional code of conduct. The codes are a good foundation rather than a specific set of blueprints for you to follow.

AAFCS	NAEYC	NCFR	Table 6-1 **Themes of Professional Standards**
✓	✓	✓	**Ethics and Professional Conduct** Legal requirements, honesty, confidentiality, responsibility
✓	✓	✓	**Application of Academic Learning** Classroom, independent study, certification, advanced degrees
✓	✓	✓	**Working with Diverse Populations** Immigrants, first-generation citizens, diverse family compositions, age groups
✓	✓	✓	**Effectiveness of Practice** Evaluation, self-assessment
✓	✓	✓	**Professional and Personal Development** Continuing education, personal growth
✓	✓	✓	**Bridge of Theory, Research, and Practice** Synthesis of classroom, lab, and field

AAFCS – American Association of Family and Consumer Sciences

NAEYC – National Association for the Education of Young Children

NCFR – National Council on Family Relations

Legal Requirements

Ethical issues are regulated by both laws and professional codes of ethics. Laws usually define the minimum standards, enforced by government. Licensed professionals are trained in their legal obligations and typically take examinations to demonstrate their understanding. Licensure may include regular updating of skills, making credentials available to clients and the public, displaying credentials and self-identification such as titles.

One example of a legal obligation is the reporting of suspected abuse. As a professional, you will need to know how to recognize and report potential abuse, of both children and adults. If children or dependent adults disclose abuse to you, you are obligated to report the situation to appropriate authorities. Most

Licensure may include making credentials available to clients and displaying them for the public.

states provide legal immunity for reporting suspected abuse or neglect if such a report is made in good faith—if you suspect abuse exists. Be aware of the different types of abuse and the mandatory reporting laws in effect in your state. If you have any doubts about determining whether or not a situation represents abuse, or a different cultural approach to disciplining a child, for example, ask your site supervisor for guidance.

New professionals should make it a point to be regularly updated on any changes in federal, state, and local laws. Don't hesitate to ask questions of co-workers at the field experience site; ask about their interpretation of laws and policies that impact their clients.

Laws often establish the minimum standards acceptable to society and enforced by government. Occasionally the law and ethics overlap. While you always know and are in compliance with the legal requirements, ethics extend beyond the law. Focus on developing a broad overview that encompasses both legal requirements and ethical standards.

Confidentiality

Confidentiality is addressed in most professional codes of ethics and is typically included in agency guidelines, as well. The number of government regulations has increased to dictate how confidential records must be handled. For example, **HIPAA** (Health Insurance Portability and Accountability Act) regulations now require special training for health professionals. The regulations specify how to protect the privacy of personal health information. Agencies have guidelines about how long to hold records and whether shredding is the appropriate way to destroy records.

Respecting clients' privacy and personal information may range from not identifying them by name to not reading their file folders without cause. Interns are sometimes startled by the level of detail of information they learn about clients' personal lives. The agency may have guidelines for what belongs in files—and what may be discussed about what is in the files. The procedures to maintain security of files are usually well known to staff members, and the intern should learn them quickly. For example, some files may not be carried around the building; others can be taken home at night for

✳ confidentiality

Protection of personal information and identity, sometimes utilizing anonymous or pseudonymous references.

✳ HIPAA

Health Information Portability and Accountability Act, passed by Congress in 1996 to regulate patient access and control over their health records; designed to safeguard security and confidentiality of records.

easier access. Interns may be granted access to client files at one site and denied access at another site. Even if the reasons for different policies are not explained, interns and new professionals must respect the standards and honor them.

An intern must learn and follow the guidelines regarding maintaining file security. For example, some client files may be carried around the building; others may not.

Confidentiality standards extend to safety issues, child endangerment, health issues such as HIV/AIDS, and other circumstances that require consultation with agency professionals. Knowing when to break a confidence may be a judgment call. Sometimes the ethically responsible action is to warn and protect third parties about their danger. The duty to warn to protect innocent victims may arise from issues such as clients or students who are HIV positive and are continuing to have unprotected sex with unsuspecting third parties. The intern should rely on mentors and instructors if the matter arises. One way to consult with an advisor is to ask the question without naming the client. The safety of the client is always the first consideration, and the situation may demand that you immediately interrupt a professional for assistance.

Conflict of Interest

Conflicts of interest may include dual or multiple roles, possession of inside information, and potential personal gain. Multiple relationships emerge when professionals know a client in two or more settings. For example, a program facilitator may know clients through parenting education for parents who have abused their children and then may meet those parents in a volunteer capacity at their community center. The program facilitator may have to choose between activities, perhaps withdrawing from the volunteer activity. Thus, the professional role and the needs of the client are made the priority.

Having inside information may create a conflict for the professional who then must decide whether to act on that information. For example, a program director may be aware of the home locations of accused child molesters. Should that information be shared with friends who are considering moving to that neighborhood? Ethical dilemmas of this sort may not be spelled out in ethical codes, but are nevertheless the subject of codes. How professionals apply ethics to such dilemmas can influence personal, as well as professional attitudes.

Personal gain is probably the best known and understood of the conflicts of interest. Federal government regulations specify what may constitute violations in stock trading, employment, and lobbying. Agencies may also specify policies about political participation. Professionals are expected to recognize situations in which they might have a gain and then either disclose the potential gain or remove themselves from the situation.

Gifts and gratuities also create conflicts of interest. In the helping professions, clients sometimes want to make gifts of gratitude. Agencies may have guidelines about how to receive such gifts in a way that does not create obligation. If no written guidelines exist, interns should discuss the matter with a supervisor or mentor.

Some ethics guides make distinction between gifts of appreciation and gifts that promote special treatment or favors. For example, a parent's gift of a loaf of banana nut bread may signify a thank-you or sincere appreciation for your help with a child on a difficult day. By contrast, a parent's presentation of season tickets to a professional sports team may come with the expectation that you put a child at the top of the waiting list for a new program. Ask yourself what the gift-giver's motivation is; also, question your own motivation for accepting or declining the gift.

The level of gift or monetary value may also cause concern. A client's presentation of a box of candy to share with the staff is a comfortable and acceptable gift. On the other hand, a gift certificate in a large dollar amount might raise questions. If such a gift cannot be graciously declined, the professional may suggest a way to redeem the certificate that benefits not just an individual staff member, but program participants as well. An example might be the parents in a parenting support group who pool money for a large gift certificate at a restaurant, intending for the professional leading the group to use it for personal pleasure. The professional could use the certificate to purchase a tray of appetizers from the restaurant to share with program participants at the next meeting.

The gift that intends to garner favor must be returned or reported within the agency or school. The familiar expression "quid pro quo" means "you scratch my back and I'll scratch yours." If intended to gain advantage, such arrangements are unethical. Similarly, any condition that makes people feel they must reciprocate (in any manner) borders on the unethical. Intentionally or unintentionally, actions can generate a sense of obligation that is inappropriate.

Consider that there are sometimes cultural implications of offering gifts. It may be common practice for persons in some cultures to give presents as a sign of respect or gratitude. Sometimes refusing such a gift might be an insult. Think through your own code, as well as that of the agency.

Accountability

Ethical behavior is synonymous with personal accountability: the professional must be willing and able to take responsibility for all actions. The mandate "do no harm" is a basic guide for decision making. It acknowledges that the professional has the capacity to do harm, either intentionally or unintentionally. The professional makes a conscious decision to put the interest of the client first.

Accountability requires awareness of the potential consequences of actions, although controlling consequences may be impossible. Thinking ahead is especially difficult without experience. The beginning professional may not be able to imagine outcomes (for example, how a classroom practice will play out at the end of the school year). For the intern, this may mean awareness of long-term results after having left the site. Also, through noticing short-term consequences, interns can begin to envision long-term consequences. The intern can also ask mentors about likely consequences. While no one can predict the future perfectly, professionals on the job can usually predict a typical outcome.

The professional is also responsible for what does not get done. The omissions of service may need to be accounted for. Frequently during an internship, goals are revised or task lists prove to be too ambitious. If discussed with the site supervisor, unfinished or unattended items do not have to be considered a failure. Ethically, the intern assists in identifying tasks that need to be reassigned. But simply not mentioning such needs is not appropriate. An unaccomplished task, such as contacting the persons on a waiting list, could result in clients not receiving services. A lesson plan for the classroom not executed (and that fact not reported) may result in a false record being generated inadvertently by the classroom teacher. In the great majority of cases, omissions create little harm if they are reported; their damage is in the consequence of not being reported.

Goals or task lists are frequently revised during the internship.

Accountability also extends to knowing the limits of expertise. For example, the professional knows when to ask for help or refer clients to other sources. Referrals do not reflect a failure to serve the client; a referral may be in their best interest. The intern may need to consult with colleagues about a course of action, especially if he or she is not a trained counselor or if no training has been offered on dealing with serious situations. For example, during a home visit, an intern may learn of a client's depression or need for medical attention. Rather than giving advice or attempting to help, the intern needs to acknowledge that a trained professional is needed. The intern's contribution is to make a good referral and help the client in understanding how assistance can come from another direction. By approaching an intern, the client may be expressing trust in that intern or comfort level to disclose a need. The intern can help in transferring that trust to the professional who can provide more than advice. The intern's role is to make the appropriate referral and support the client in following through. The Guided Practice at the end of this chapter called "Making a Great Referral" provides a framework for referral strategies.

Conduct

Professional conduct refers to behavior on the job but may also involve behavior in personal life. Interns frequently interact with people at different levels of hierarchy in the organization. Differences in hierarchy may be reflected in power, control, or access. Thus, a client may be the person with the least resources in the organization (on the receiving end). Professionals are in a position to grant resources or withhold them. Interns may also be in the position or place to influence distribution of resources. For example, even in scheduling an appointment for a client, you may be the one in control of agency resources. Your professional conduct would be fair and impartial treatment of all clients seeking appointments. You might be the first contact person within an organization and, thus, become the gatekeeper to those in authority. Your responsibility is to assist all clients in gaining access or resources.

As an intern, you may be the one seeking a resource. Thus, you are reliant on people in that hierarchy. For example, you need client contact hours to meet your practicum goals. An agency professional has the power to facilitate or limit your access to clients. Your supervisor's professional conduct would be facilitating all interns' access to clients.

Professional conduct means not exploiting position and not taking advantage of anyone. Clients may be reluctant to complain about apparent unfair treatment, or coworkers may be reluctant to complain about their supervisors. Unprofessional conduct may not be obvious when there are no complaints. On the other hand, agencies do not want to be seen as promoting complaints. Some agencies establish monitoring procedures so that clients are not in a position to have to complain. Evaluations may also be made available so that clients can make anonymous complaints. Interns are usually familiar with such evaluations in the form of instructor and course evaluations: they are typically anonymous forms that are not viewed by the instructor until after grades are filed. This type of protection of student or client is considered an important element of evaluation.

You will want to pay attention to especially vulnerable populations, or groups that are marginalized by organizations or mainstream culture. Groups could include those with impaired decision making skills, naive understanding of the system, or differences that make them targets. Such groups could be vulnerable to discrimination, lack of social supports, exclusion from society, over-complex regulations, gaps in the system, or being targeted for attack, insults, or belittlement. They are frequently "without voice," meaning that advocates may be needed to speak up for them. Use the Guided Practice called "Vulnerable Populations" to identify such populations at your worksite or in your community. Many social service agencies focus primarily on such populations—the young, elderly, homeless, runaway youth, mentally ill, immigrants, critically ill, prisoners, or persons who have already been victimized in some way.

Another aspect of ethical conduct at the workplace is avoiding even the perception or appearance of sexual misconduct. As an intern in a school, you might be only slightly older than some of the students. The students may look up to you or want to know you better. To avoid violating ethical standards—or legal guidelines—you will want to maintain your professional distance, requesting students to call you by your surname rather than the more familiar address of your first name. Avoid responding to inappropriate questions about your personal life or relationships. Know what the specific policy is on inappropriate touch for children (or other adults). Many school districts or agencies will have specific policies requiring two or more adults to be present at all times when youth younger than age 18 are present. You will want to ask your site supervisor for specific guidelines appropriate for your workplace.

Many school districts or agencies have specific policies requiring two or more adults to be present at all times when youth younger than age 18 are present.

Maintaining your distance includes situations outside the workplace. Dating clients or students is usually strictly prohibited. Even if there are no written policies, the intern would be well advised to avoid socializing with clients during the internship. You might want to avoid parties or social situations that could be awkward for all involved.

Responsibility to the Profession

Organizations promote professionalism through a climate of shared standards of excellence. Most professions rely on organizations for standards and ethical guidelines that can span many work settings. Members of the organization set and enforce the standards for themselves, often with entry requirements as well as continuing or recertification of credentials. Working with preprofessionals or serving as mentor to interns or new professionals represents a contribution to the profession, as well.

Public trust in the profession often resides in individual's experiences with professionals. Thus, you are a representative of your profession—you may be the only caseworker or child life specialist that the public will encounter. Qualifications are adhered to in order to maintain that public trust, and each professional's maintenance of credentials adds to the reputation of the profession as a whole.

Ethical standards provide guidelines for personal behavior but, also, help professionals to monitor ethical decision making by their colleagues. Sometimes professionals or clients must voice official complaints against other professionals. Usually the code of ethics for the specific profession, such as social workers or counselors or teachers, will provide guidance on how to proceed. Sanctions may be spelled out in the codes, ranging from reprimands to probation to suspension from professional memberships. Occasionally, practitioners may lose their license or certification.

As an intern, be aware that there are specific procedures to follow if you believe that there have been ethical violations at your worksite. Usually, the first step is to attempt to resolve the issue informally by talking with your co-worker or supervisor. Before reporting perceived unethical behavior, discuss the situation with your university instructor and your mentor.

Professionals also have the responsibility to maintain their expertise and keep their knowledge current. Most professionals engage in continuing education, with standards or number of hours set by a professional organization. This education could include reading current research in professional journals, attending a training on a specific topic (such as HIV/AIDS-related issues), participating in conferences—online or in person. Usually the professional organization requires some documentation of ongoing education. You might be asked to show a certificate of participation from a training or a program from a conference attended.

Collegiality

Collegiality is the sense of rapport and mutual respect that emerges among a group of coworkers. Collegiality may be in one work setting, and it can also span a profession (across many worksites). A collegial group is marked by compatibility of opinion and action, which does not imply constant or consistent agreement. Disagreements are handled with respect and in a collegial manner. Gossip about colleagues cannot be tolerated.

Sometimes collegiality involves setting aside personal interest for the good of the organization. For example, colleagues are willing to change work schedules in order to meet the needs of clients. Collegiality means meeting each other's and the group's needs without keeping score or tally of who owes whom. Relationships are reciprocal, involving give and take. Over time the goal is a perceived balance of individual needs and organizational goals.

Another integral aspect of collegiality is that colleagues are open to each other's ideas and perspectives. Coworkers respect each other as trained

An integral aspect of collegiality is that colleagues are open to each other's ideas and perspectives.

professionals and acknowledge that each possesses special knowledge and skills. Even though coworkers may approach a problem differently—and have unique solutions—each is willing to listen and accept different ideas.

Many organizations or worksites have unwritten rules regarding what is involved in being a collegial team member. You might ask your mentor or supervisor what it takes to be considered a team player. For example, at some sites, that could be as straightforward as eating lunch with the group or volunteering for committee membership. At other sites, collegiality could involve playing on the department softball team or going to the annual company picnic. When the event is away from the workplace, some groups share costs equally (for example, splitting the check at a restaurant), and others may automatically ask for separate checks.

Social expectations can be a factor in collegiality. In some work groups and school settings, holidays and personal celebrations (birthdays, weddings, showers) become shared social events. Sometimes interns are included; new professionals are almost certainly included. Learning the unwritten rules of participation can be challenging. A mentor or friend may be willing to advise on when gifts are expected, typical dollar amounts, and whether guests are included at gatherings.

Don't assume that your own rules of social life will match in a new setting. For example, an intern could be caught by surprise by accepting an invitation to lunch with staff members, thinking that the invitation meant the intern's lunch would be paid for. Instead (and in most cases), the staff members expect everyone to pay separately.

Cultural Competence

cultural competence

Acceptance of and appreciation for other cultures.

Developing **cultural competence** is a lifelong process that also involves your ethics and impacts your behavior on the job. One of the first steps in this process is being aware of your own beliefs and biases. What stereotypes do you have about others? How will these ideas influence your treatment of students or clients or families who might be different from you? A purposeful self-examination of your own cultural influences helps you appreciate the complexities of interaction with other cultures.

Expanding your knowledge of others and their worlds or their culture is another step toward cultural competence. You could intentionally read about different places and peoples, listen to music from other cultures, or sample food from outside your own upbringing. Focus on commonalities between you and others, rather than the differences. What are your common goals for your family or for getting along in the world? This intentionality of learning about others will help you become a more ethical person in your treatment of others.

One crucial aspect of being a culturally competent person is learning to value and see people as they are. It is important to acknowledge each person for their uniqueness rather than wanting to pretend they are all alike or ignoring the aspect that makes them special. For example, some persons pride themselves on being "colorblind," claiming that they see all people as the same. The disadvantage to such a perspective is that it denies the specialness of being Black or White or Asian or any other ethnicity. While the objective at your workplace might be to treat all people fairly, each might need to be seen differently and valued for their uniqueness.

You will want to strive to understand a client's behavior within the context of his or her own culture. Assess the behavior based on the norms in that culture, rather than automatically assuming that your own culture is the appropriate benchmark. You want to avoid misjudging or misinterpreting other's actions based on your own learned expectations. Assume that the differences between you and others are not necessarily deficits.

Assumptions

On-the-job decisions involve ethics and choosing appropriate actions, being aware of the influence of your assumptions. At first glance, a simple answer may be assumed. But most social issues are multifaceted and represent different value systems. Many factors are involved and few solutions can address all factors. Few answers are absolute. Interns often make decisions based on personal opinion, then progress to informed opinion. New professionals have a responsibility to know more about the dilemma or decision. Often there is no completely right or completely wrong answer to an ethical dilemma. The professional is willing to bring an approach to a question that invites exploring or debating without judging and condemning. Assess your own responsibilities and the risks involved.

You may be working in subject matter areas or on topics that the general public and lay persons feel qualified to give advice and have strong opinions. For example, many lay persons have experienced divorce or single-parenting and believe that experience qualifies them as experts on the topic. Your professional training might result in different conclusions or informed opinions. Also, it is important to separate your own personal knowledge and experience and be aware of how your background could color your perception of a situation or a group of people. It's important to maintain respect for the autonomy of the families you work with; sometimes their choices will not match your own.

Opinions frequently reflect assumptions about circumstances. Especially today, with greater variety in family compositions, these assumptions are likely to be misconceptions. Don't assume your language of family will match others'—use terms that people can answer without explanation and insert their own information. While your household might have consisted of parents and children, someone else's family might consist of a grandparent and a child or a stepmother and father. The term *family* is a more inclusive term than *parents*. So, when asking a child about his or her family composition, the best question is "Who's in your family?" The child can answer fully, without having to explain, "I don't have parents at home." This type of open-ended question also permits a child to tell you that a dog or a cat or a bird is part of the family, a common construction for young children.

Children are not the only people who benefit from open-ended questions. An example of a sensitive situation might be a grandparent who does not like to disclose the absence of the grown daughter whose children the grandparent is taking care of. That parent in the middle generation may be incarcerated or unfit to parent, but the grandparent is probably not prepared to share that information with authorities. Grandparents raising grandchildren in the U.S. are in a difficult legal status; few pursue the needed custody or parental rights to meet all the needs of the children. Many live in a month-to-month or year-to-year pattern, hoping the parent will return, or simply not taking any legal action. Although some grandparents would qualify for government assistance in rearing grandchildren, many avoid such arrangements. How family professionals gather information about a child's home life can be influential in grandparents' willingness to participate in helpful programs.

For some interns, one of the most difficult tasks of the field experience is to learn to accept others where they are. For the first time, you might be seeing living conditions different from your own—customs and standards that may not be mainstream in your community or culture. Examine your own attitude for assumptions about which situations are better or worse than what you have grown up with. Be aware of your own stereotypical beliefs and bias.

Humans cannot help but make comparisons (sometimes called *social comparisons*) between their own experiences and other people's. People who grew up in rural areas sometimes claim that the country setting is superior for rearing children; similarly, city residents sometimes claim that the urban setting is superior for rearing children. Obviously, good people can be reared in both settings, but this example reminds us that we tend to prefer the settings most familiar to us. When those preferences begin to influence professional attitudes and decision making, discrimination may result.

Discrimination is often associated with unfair treatment or denying privileges. The professional is on guard against letting personal values lead to discrimination. For example, a caseworker who interviews potential adoptive families must be aware of his or her personal lens. The student caseworker may believe that two parents who share religion, ethnicity, and similar education are requirements for a good home life for a child. That personal lens may not match the criteria for the agency and does not match today's appreciation for potential for success by other family types. Awareness of personal lens is a crucial step in learning to avoid discriminating.

However, you will want to question the assumption that all discrimination is bad or negative. Some individuals or groups of people require or deserve special, different treatment. Fair treatment isn't necessarily the same as equal treatment. A child who uses a wheelchair may require extra time to travel to

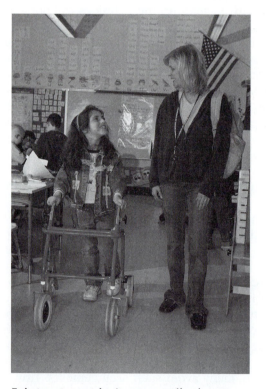

Fair treatment isn't necessarily the same as equal treatment. A child who uses a walker may require extra time to travel to classrooms and may require an aide in certain settings.

classrooms and may require an aide in certain settings. Use the Guided Practice, "Equal Treatment?" at chapter's end to stimulate your own discernment between fair and unfair discrimination.

In school settings, learning differences may result in unequal treatment among students. Extra time on tests, copies of lecture notes, or different formats for assignments are routinely offered, and this style of discrimination is positive for the student. The effect on other students in the class is not negative because the accommodation has simply leveled the playing field for the student with a learning difference.

Program practices also may accommodate for clients with unique needs. To protect against calling attention to different reading abilities, conduct intake interviews instead of assuming that written forms can be completed by all. In a group meeting, the same protection can be assured by not asking individuals to read aloud from printed material. To promote communication with all participants, provide a human translator or print materials in more than one language. Professionals anticipate needs, such as translation, to avoid asking children to translate for parents.

The ultimate goal of your work is to promote the good of others, as they define *good*. Sometimes, how families or a client view their own well-being will differ from your definition. Your role is to contribute to their growth and development without asserting your own values or goals. A guideline to remember is to treat others as they would like to be treated—even if different from your own preferences or desires. Professionals call this principle **beneficence.**

Plagiarism

Professionals often wish to replicate work or materials created by others. It is important to give credit to the creators for their work, which you may be copying or adapting for a new environment. It's easier to cite facts with references; students usually get a lot of practice in writing school papers. What may be more difficult is providing attribution for abstract concepts. When care is not taken to give credit, a charge of **plagiarism** may be made. Even if copying is accidental, the act is still plagiarism, and professionals go to great efforts to avoid such error.

Know the guidelines for copying and distributing material. For example, student teachers cannot copy consumable material such as workbooks or worksheets unless given permission by the publisher or author. However, some materials are created with the intent to be distributed freely. Look for advisories, such as "This material may be used in education or classroom settings." Many such advisories disallow electronic distribution, so a handout in a class is legal but a posting to a Web site is not. **Copyright** holders have the right to determine how their works can be used. In most cases, a copyright notice is the symbol for protected materials; however, copyright law protects all works, even if a notice is not apparent. When a copyright expires, it enters public domain, but this status can be difficult to check.

As the intern creates materials for a classroom or agency, the agency's rules about ownership and sharing should apply. Know and follow the rules for taping and showing videos or downloading music. In teaching settings, **fair use** of movie clips and other video are common. Electronic copying or distribution is typically not allowed, however. Downloading music for a presentation, such as a PowerPoint slideshow, can be problematic. Use of any commercially produced music is likely to be a violation of copyright. Downloading public domain music segments is an alternative but requires research into the Web sites that offer them. *Public domain* refers to material that is copyright-free, a status that is often hard to prove.

beneficence

Helping others achieve their goals, as they understand them.

plagiarism

Using someone else's ideas, words, program, or information without proper acknowledgment and credit.

copyright

Legal right granted to an author, composer, or publisher to exclusive publication, sale, or distribution of an artistic work or program.

fair use

Allows limited use of copyrighted work for educational purposes without the written permission of the author.

Making video and audio recordings of clients or students deserves similar caution. A standard permission form should be on file for every person who is represented in the recording. Children's participation must be approved by guardians and also reflected in permissions on file. Another ethical consideration is the risk of coercion: a client or child may agree to be recorded out of concern about a grade or program participation. Professionals typically either schedule such events so that coercion is not a risk or find a way to stress the volunteer aspect of the project, by assuring that participation does not produce any special reward (or nonparticipation does not result in negative consequence). When possible, the professional should also provide a copy of the recording for the individual or family.

In creating materials, follow appropriate procedures to cite authors, agencies, or programs for their works. Even if the program material is not copyrighted and is freely shared, give credit to the authors or sources. For newly created and original materials, add a copyright notice consistent with agency policy. If there is no published policy, ask the site supervisor and your instructor for guidance. In most workplaces, the work of interns will be considered the property of the agency. In school settings, traditions vary, although student works are almost always designated as copyrighted by the student. Works by K–12 teachers and university professors are also frequently considered to be the property of the individual. School districts and universities are likely to have intellectual property (IP) policies that explain copyrights and employees' sharing or ownership of them.

✳ ARTICULATING A PERSONAL CODE OF ETHICS

The internship is often a time to consider one's personal code of ethics. Ethics develop over a lifetime but may not be articulated formally. Entering a profession is often the impetus for assessing and clarifying ethics. In articulating your code of ethics, you are not required to compromise a moral or ethical stance or to sacrifice self, but to think through your personal principles. It's important to have a clear view of what is important to you and how your code matches the environment and profession you are choosing. Awareness of the profession's code and willingness to compare your own code are necessary steps. While the ethics codes offered by most professional organizations are usually broad and general rather than specific, you will want to think through how the general guidelines relate to your specific roles. Articulating your own set of guidelines prepares you for your professional decisions. Codes provided by an organization are a necessary beginning point but are not sufficient for resolving all issues.

While researchers disagree about whether or not males and females differ in their development of ethics, there does seem to be support for the concept of stages of development of an ethic of caring. Carol Gilligan (1982) describes the process of evolving from a focus on individual survival ("What's best for me?), to respect for others, then a stage of self-sacrifice, finally transitioning to a stage of doing no harm to self or others. If we assume that we all progress through stages, one conclusion is that change is possible across the lifespan. Thus, the first articulation of a personal code is only that: the first draft. You may revisit your personal code on a regular basis throughout your life.

The following questions serve as a starting point for self-assessment. Not all of them will apply to you; select the ones that best fit your current situation.

While researchers disagree about whether or not males and females differ in their development of ethics, there does seem to be support for the concept of stages of development of an ethic of caring.

General Points and Readiness

1. Do I know myself well enough to express a value in situations I will face in my profession?
2. Do I have a realistic knowledge of ethics concerns in my intended profession?
3. What does my professional organization publish on ethics and ethical standards?
4. What elements of my course work apply to the ethics concerns that I will face?
5. What are the limits of my current knowledge or my ability to access research-based sources for use in my profession?
6. How will I discern the unwritten rules of the workplace that will influence my conduct?
7. How will I know who to trust on matters of ethical issues?
8. How do I relate to authority figures?
9. How do I respond to rules and regulations?
10. How do I disagree respectfully with colleagues? With authority? With clients?

Professional Conduct

1. Do I know the basic legal points influencing my professional conduct?
2. How do I handle confidential information in my own life?

3. Can I be trusted?

4. How do I handle gossip? Rumors?

5. Do I know my own personal boundaries? How do I share information about my life?

Application of Academic Learning

1. Can I assess my own knowledge base or competency?

2. Do I need additional training? Certification? Formal course work?

3. How current is my knowledge base?

4. Am I reading appropriate professional sources and journals?

5. Do I have a plan for continuing to learn?

Working with Diverse Populations

1. Am I aware of my own biases? Stereotypes?

2. What is my comfort level in working with people different from me? What value do I place on diversity?

3. Do I have experience working with people of different ages? Ethnicity? Economic level? Education level? Immigration status?

4. Do I know how to self-monitor to adjust to needs of a group or individual?

5. Can I accept the environment without judging? Without negatively comparing it to my other work experiences?

Effectiveness of Practice

1. Do I know how to self-assess my performance or activity?

2. Can I respond to constructive criticism in a productive manner?

3. Do I know how to offer suggestions to other people to help them improve?

4. Do I understand the limits of my role as an intern or new professional in terms of revising standards or programs?

5. Do I understand the standards of evaluation used in my profession?

Self-Care

1. Do I recognize my own needs?

2. Do I acknowledge that I cannot solve all problems?

3. Do I rely on external rewards or an intrinsic reward system?

4. What are my strategies for stress relief or balancing home and work?

5. Do I model self-care for others (e.g., colleagues, children, client families)?

✳ WORKPLACE ETHICS

From the start, workplace ethics are reflected in your job application (or possibly even in your internship application). A common standard among employers is to consider the accuracy of your self-presentation on the application. For example, an omission is considered a lie, a reflection of your honesty. In listing previous employment, you may have forgotten or decided not to include a minor job as a tutor on a campus. But even minor short-term jobs are expected to be included on an application. On a more negative note, a job applicant might prefer to omit reference to a job firing. However, the omission would almost certainly be discovered and then serve as the reason for the applicant not being considered for the current job. The honest approach is to include the complete job history.

Letters of recommendation and references also require an ethical approach. How you handle requesting a reference letter, as well as the choice of relevant references, is part of the picture of your overall honesty. Your policy should be to ask permission before listing someone's name as reference—each time you use his or her name. You can easily e-mail or call and update your references on how your application process is going and politely request listing their name for specific positions.

Once on the job, ethics enters into how you represent your skill level. Accurately reflecting your skills, training, or current status in education is crucial to your success. The internship is the environment in which it is safe to say, "I do not know how to do that; I welcome the opportunity to learn it here." When such disclosure is not made, the trust level drops and is hard to rebuild. Especially where harm may result for a client, child, or participant, the professional must not consciously misrepresent skills or abilities.

Personal gain is typically described as unethical use of materials or funds at the workplace. This can include a wide range of behaviors: pilfering (stealing) office supplies, embezzlement of funds, padding expense accounts, "borrowing" petty cash, taking personal time on the job (running personal errands, napping/sleeping, making personal telephone calls, texting, or e-mailing), personal use of equipment such as office laptops, copying software programs in violation of the agency's site licenses.

Cheating in the workplace includes the unethical misreporting of hours on timesheets or overcharging on mileage reports. For the intern, the equivalent is fabricating journal dates representing days not worked. Fabricating content in reports might involve embellishing one's own role or tasks or exaggerating the work done. An equivalent by students is turning in someone else's work as your own (in the practicum as well as at school). Another example of cheating is covering for a coworker, a fellow intern, even a supervisor. Covering could mean doing their work for them, giving a false reason for an absence, pretending the coworker was present when not, or otherwise misrepresenting someone else's attendance or participation.

On a program level, one aspect of workplace ethics is maintaining records. The ethical professional avoids padding attendance at a workshop, filling out an evaluation form more than once, and so forth. The integrity of program records is just as important as the individual professional's integrity. If you observe professionals who are making up names on a membership roster or changing the ethnicity of attendees, consider your responsibility for reporting such unethical behavior to a supervisor.

Favoritism in the workplace may also be a violation of ethics. Recognizing favoritism is difficult; when we are on the receiving end, we tend to overlook the unfairness that others might feel. (When we are the "others," we are quick to accuse authority figures of playing favorites.) Favoritism might be exhibited in some employees being assigned better hours, better shifts, better territory, better tasks. One person might be repeatedly chosen as team leader, group leader, or recipient of special privileges. Social interaction in the form of lunch outings, get-togethers, baby showers, and sporting events may give the appearance of exclusivity or partiality to one group over another. For interns, the

Table 6-2
Can You Work with Each of These Persons?
A teenager who is having unprotected sex with multiple partners
A middle school student who is using drugs
The parent who believes in corporal punishment
A mother who blames the teacher for all of her daughter's problems
The school principal who is away from work frequently but has a secretary to cover absences
A high school student who is considering gender transformation
An interracial couple seeking parenting advice
A woman who takes in foster children without being able to care for them adequately
A coworker who is having an affair with the supervisor
A child who is accompanying her mother who shoplifts

possibility of being hired during or after the internship may represent favoritism (or be perceived as such, even when it is not).

Work situations are not always fair. Favoritism in regards to promotions, raises, and recognition may well exist in your workplace. The professional must decide how to react, whether on the receiving end or the losing end. The choice of reaction may be as extreme as whistle-blowing (turning in a colleague for illegal or unethical conduct) or not burning bridges and ignoring the action.

Another workplace situation could be that the job requires you to work with persons whose background or values are different from your own, either as clients or as coworkers. Assess your ability to get along with others whose values may conflict with your own (see Table 6-2).

Personal conduct in the workplace returns us to the discussion of a personal code of ethics. If the polices are not explicit, the individual's values drive decisions about alcohol consumption, such as at a restaurant meeting or business meeting; dating colleagues or superiors; and other matters of personal conduct.

✳ IMPACT ON CLIENTS, CHILDREN, AND FAMILIES

As a student, you have known the power of a professor or instructor in interpreting and assessing your performance. You have experienced that perspective; now, you may be on the other side of the equation and find yourself setting standards for others' performance. In the classroom, you may be the judge of a child's potential; working with families, you may be the link to services they would never seek otherwise. Your credibility as an expert may be much greater than you think. Your words, even those spoken casually, can have long-lasting effect—positive or negative. Your verbal and nonverbal communication can heal, or hurt, or honor a child you are working with. Remarks that stereotype have the power to restrict a child's long-term career choices. For example, we know that some women can recall being told that girls are not proficient in math. These women, despite their abilities, avoided college majors that required advanced mathematics.

Although you may have a humble appreciation for your knowledge and experience, it is likely that you will be viewed by children, clients, and families as an authority. Having a conscious awareness of your clients' best interest is more demanding than simply wanting the best for them. Being attentive to clients' needs requires that you self-monitor at all times. Consciously selecting your words stimulates the attitude that will then be communicated in other ways besides language.

✳ ETHICS AND DECISION MAKING

Making ethical decisions is not always easy. It's also not always a straightforward, rational process. You can't always follow a 1-2-3 model of decision making; you may stop after one step or repeat steps or even change the order. Emotions and feelings often become involved in the interpretation of what is best for others or what plan of action is appropriate. Ethical decision making does not simply involve memorizing a set of rules or a formula. It does involve being sensitive to the situation at hand and aware of the different perspectives that are possible. You can develop tools to help you make ethical decisions.

One such tool is the C^4 model of ethical decision making in Table 6-3, which outlines a four-step process. First, the situation or issue must be clarified. Second, the decision maker collaborates or consults with other professionals. Third, risks, possibilities, and implications are considered. Fourth, a choice is made to proceed with a decision or not.

Clarifying the situation is the first step in ethical decision making. What is the problem? What issues are involved? Gather information about legal requirements, written policies, or unwritten guidelines that relate to the problem. Make sure you are aware of the most current laws or regulations; ask a coworker or mentor if you are unsure.

Collaborating with the client and coworkers may be the most important aspect of your ethical decision making. Sometimes it is also advisable to document your consultation—who you have asked for help and what their advice was. Look at the issue from different perspectives, taking another person's **POV** (point of view). Consider the voice of the client or the child involved. Identify who is involved and what different points of view might be. Are there ways that you can involve the family or the client in the decision? Involving the

POV

Point of view; perspective or choice of context for opinions or beliefs.

Table 6-3 C^4 **Model of Ethical Decision Making**

Clarify the situation and issues.

Collaborate and consult.

Consider risks, possibilities, implications.

Choose to decide or not to decide.

autonomy

Self-determination;
being able to make
decisions and life
choices without
relying on others.

ambiguity

More than one correct
interpretation or
multiple good choices.

family members may empower them so that they can resolve a similar issue on their own in the future. One of your objectives as a professional is to encourage **autonomy** in others.

Consider the issues and risks involved. How will your decision relate to any ethical principles guiding your behavior? Would you violate the principle of beneficence? Do the standards or codes of your professional organization offer any specific help or suggest a solution? The professional codes might include state or federal laws, licensing regulations, and resource materials on similar issues. Consider possible courses of action; solutions are not always possible. Brainstorm with your site supervisor or peers for possibilities and the implications or consequences of each alternative. Try to think through the implications for yourself, the persons involved, the agency or site, the community, and the profession.

Choose what appears to be the best course of action available at the time. Sometimes that involves no action on your part. How does your choice fit with your personal code of ethics or the code of your professional organization? Is further action needed at this time?

While you may wonder if you have made the best decision, try not to second-guess yourself. There is almost always more than one right choice. While you may be uncomfortable with the **ambiguity**, sometimes there are many gray areas rather than absolute answers. Often, ethical dilemmas are situations of "right versus right."

Ask yourself what you have learned from the process. What could you change or do differently the next time? How might others evaluate your decision? While being familiar with the professional code of ethics most relevant to your occupation does not necessarily guarantee ethical behavior, the guidelines are an appropriate focus. Ethics guidelines are not meant to be blueprints; you still need to apply a deliberative, thoughtful approach. Especially early in your professional life, you will frequently benefit from using a mentor or supervisor as a sounding board for discussing your ethical decisions. Establish a relationship early in your internship with someone whose professional experience and judgment you respect and whose values seem similar to your own.

Dealing with Questionable Behavior of Others

Sometimes during the course of the internship you might encounter what you consider to be unethical behavior in your coworkers or peers (see Table 6-4). Most professional organizations have clear guidelines about challenging unethical practices or behaviors. If you observe questionable behavior that seems to involve ethical violations, first consider an informal discussion with your supervisor or the colleague. If you still have concerns, ask about more formal procedures for reporting and exposing unethical behavior. Assess the seriousness of the violation in terms of harm to others or immediacy of the issue.

groupthink

Going along with
the consensus of the
group.

Sometimes groups of people, such as a close group of coworkers, convince each other that questionable behavior is acceptable. At the extreme, such thinking has led to acts such as mob rule or massacres. In the workplace, group consensus can override individual beliefs or ethics. As an intern, you may be vulnerable to such **groupthink**. In an attempt to fit in, you shouldn't silence your own ethical opinions or views. Often, one of the advantages to an organization of having an intern is the fresh ideas or questioning attitude you might bring to a discussion. Your perspective is valuable.

Table 6-4

What If . . .

. . . you are encouraged by your supervisor to engage in unethical practices?

. . . your supervisor exhibits strong attraction for you?

. . . a coworker demonstrates strong negative feelings toward a certain type of client on a regular basis?

. . . your supervisor hesitates to refer clients because the agency needs the income?

. . . you overhear a coworker discussing a client's case while in a restaurant at lunch?

. . . your site supervisor recommends discipline methods not consistent with your cultural beliefs?

. . . your work as an intern is not being adequately supervised?

✳ RESEARCH ETHICS

As a student, you may have been involved with research, perhaps assisting a faculty member with collection of data or as a participant answering a survey, or conducting an experiment in class or reading others' research and writing reports. Your colleagues at the internship site might also be involved in ongoing research. Research is valued as a way to generate new knowledge, products, or processes. Research is also a way for professionals to give something back to their profession by sharing their results and benefiting society.

When conducting research or program evaluations, professionals are aware of their responsibilities to the participants. All aspects of the research are planned and conducted with respect and consideration for the safety and dignity of participants. All school districts, social service agencies, hospitals, or other worksites that receive any federal funding have their own institutional review boards (IRB) to review proposed research involving human subjects prior to its beginning and to monitor ongoing research projects. The panel of reviewers are especially thorough in considering research on vulnerable populations; topics of a sensitive nature, such as sexual behavior, sexual orientation, or illegal practices, or research that exposes participants to high risks.

The student or professional in a research role is obligated to obtain **informed consent** from all participants. Participants must willingly agree to be involved and be allowed to discontinue their involvement at any time, with no penalties. The principle of voluntary informed consent would be violated if participants were forced to participate or if someone in position of authority coerced or threatened participants. While children cannot give legal consent, researchers seek children's **assent**, meaning that they willingly participate. Consent for their participation must be obtained from their legal guardian.

The researcher discloses up front to the participants details about the purposes of the research, any potential risks from participating, possible benefits, and how their confidentiality will be protected. Risks of involvement could range from loss of time to health risks. Benefits might include monetary incentives, free food, or increased knowledge from results of the study. Researchers may also provide referrals to appropriate resources if questions or issues arise after the research is concluded.

✳ **informed consent**

Agreement by a participant to be involved in a research project after receiving full information about procedures and any risks or benefits.

✳ **assent**

Agreement by a child to participate in research.

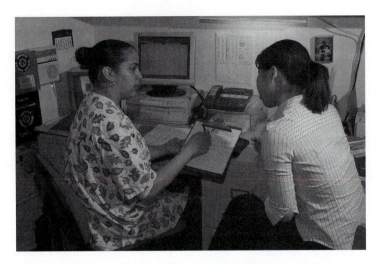

The student or professional in a research role is obligated to obtain informed consent from all participants.

The researcher strives to protect the confidentiality of the participants and the data. This means that only those who are authorized to access the data will be able to do so. The researcher promises not to provide names or addresses of participants or reveal details in the findings that can be traced back to individuals.

Another aspect of ethical research is presenting the results clearly and honestly. The results should not be skewed according to what the researcher hoped to find or what the funding agency wanted to hear. Ethical researchers do not manipulate the findings to support their own views or opinions.

✳ APPLICATION OF ETHICAL THINKING TO PUBLIC POLICY

advocacy

Actively supporting a cause or position, especially for the benefit of others.

personal agency

An individual's self-efficacy, or ability to care for self and advocate for one's own needs.

public policy

Laws and regulations by which the government allocates resources and sets priorities for action and funding.

Advocacy may be embedded in a code of ethics or may emerge from ethical practices. Advocacy refers to the use of professional position and knowledge to protect or promote the interest of others. Professionals often speak for segments of the population who have less **personal agency** or less "voice." People may be overlooked or simply less visible in society.

The professional may be most capable of helping such individuals through group action. For example, a professional organization's **public policy** initiatives may serve to advocate for special populations more effectively than a single professional could. Maximizing effort as group members (instead of as individual contributors), professionals may still make individual calls to government representatives or provide information to staff members of legislatures. The impact of many individual calls and efforts can be great.

Even if you cannot dedicate time to public policy initiatives, you can participate through your professional organization, knowing that the power of numbers (lobbying, advocating for a cause) and the strength of the organization are your contribution to the common good.

Public policy makers focus on what is good for society as a whole. Within a family, sometimes a choice is made for what is best for the entire family even if it requires individual sacrifice. The same principle is evident when choices are made for the good of society. Cultural values influence how people approach policy decisions, highlighting the culture's orientation toward individual rights versus collective rights. As Table 6-5 illustrates, individual or group perspective

Table 6-5 **Good of the Individual or the Group**

	Individual	Group
Gain	I win	We win
Loss	I lose	We lose

Table 6-6 **Case Study Exercises**

1. You notice a box of software that you have been wanting. You could easily bring your laptop to the office and install the program. Should you ask about restrictions of the site license for that software?

2. You notice that your agency-provided computer is loaded with software programs for which there are no site licenses. What is your responsibility?

3. You need a letter of recommendation and your mentor is out of the country but has always said that he or she would be happy to serve as a reference. Can you write the letter yourself and submit it, in your mentor's absence?

4. The agency prohibits use of the Internet for personal e-mail; however, you are able to access the Web site of your free e-mail account. If there is no tracking of your Web usage, would you use e-mail anyway? Would you use it during the workday or only after hours?

5. You have tickets for a concert on the same evening that you were scheduled to begin teaching a court-mandated parenting class. What do you do?

6. Your coworker has used up her vacation days but needs to run personal errands one afternoon. She asks you to cover her desk and not tell anyone she has left for the day. What would you do?

7. You learn that a coworker has taken a client and her baby into the coworker's home. This is clearly against agency policy. What would you do?

can be charted in terms of gain or loss. You can view a result of policy in terms of the trade-offs it asks of individual citizens. For example, a school tax is paid by every resident of a community in order to provide an educational system that benefits all ("We win"). Public policy reflects a shifting between the perspectives of self and others.

✳ ETHICAL DILEMMAS

Ethical dilemmas, by definition, have no single, correct answer. The professional considers the context, their personal standards, and experience in deciding on a course of action. For the intern, there is value in working through hypothetical situations, such as those posed in Table 6-6, in order to grasp the complexity of most decisions and the role of ethics.

◉ REVIEW OF CHAPTER CONTENTS

Introduction to Ethics: Ethics guide behavior, conduct, and decision making.

Themes of Professional Standards: Across professions, rules of conduct may be similar.

Elements of Ethical Codes: Similar elements are found in many codes of ethics.

Legal Requirements: Some codes cite conduct that is required by law.

Confidentiality: Protection of privacy and transfer of information is addressed through confidentiality clauses.

Conflict of Interest: Roles, inside information, and potential personal gain may present conflict in the ethical conduct of professional responsibilities.

Accountability: Accountability refers to taking responsibility for one's actions and being aware of consequences.

Conduct: Ethics influence behavior on the job and in personal life, as well as how you treat people.

Responsibility to the Profession: Even a new professional has the responsibility to contribute to the profession through shared standards of excellence and monitoring of ethical decision making.

Collegiality: Professionals demonstrate collegial relationships through mutual respect and shared activities.

Cultural Competence: Development of self-awareness and appreciation for other cultures reflect competence.

Assumptions: Professionals strive to avoid making assumptions and to accept people where they are.

Plagiarism: Unauthorized use of others' materials or words constitutes illegal use.

Articulating a Personal Code of Ethics: The internship presents an opportunity to consider and articulate a code of ethics.

General Points and Readiness: Self-assessment is the starting point for thinking about ethics.

Professional Conduct: The process includes examining your own behavior.

Application of Academic Learning: Questions focus on your training and readiness.

Working with Diverse Populations: A recommendation in developing your code of ethics is to acknowledge and self-monitor your biases.

Effectiveness of Practice: Knowing one's limits and knowing how to offer constructive criticism are aspects of effectiveness.

Self-Care: Ethics include taking care of self and modeling responsible limits for others.

Workplace Ethics: From the job or internship application to reporting a time sheet of hours worked, ethical behavior is crucial.

Impact on Clients, Children, and Families: Interns and professionals should be aware of potential long-term impact of their verbal and nonverbal communication.

Ethics and Decision Making: The C^4 model specifies four steps in decision making: clarify, collaborate, consider, and choose.

Dealing with Questionable Behavior of Others: Violations of ethics codes require response, which may be difficult without prior thought.

Research Ethics: In conducting research, professionals employ standards such as informed consent, confidentiality, and honest presentation of results.

Application of Ethical Thinking to Public Policy: Advocacy and personal agency are key elements of the involved, ethical professional.

Ethical Dilemmas: Professionals acknowledge that there is no single, correct answer for many situations encountered in working with people.

◉ DISCUSSION QUESTIONS

1. In the opening case study of this chapter, how many examples of ethical behavior can you identify? Are these examples represented in published codes of ethics?

2. Locate at least two codes of ethics for professional organizations. Develop a chart comparing their main elements.

3. Write a case study about confidentiality relevant to your internship site.

4. Identify a research project at your internship site or your college; how were ethical considerations addressed?

5. Describe your plan for contributing to your profession. How does the responsibility differ for interns and working professionals?

6. In Table 6-2, "Can you work with each of these persons?," this chapter identifies 10 situations to assess your ability to resolve value conflicts. Select at least two of these situations and outline your ethical approach to them.

7. Apply the C^4 model of ethical decision making to a current issue.

8. How might priorities for self-care differ among professionals in these settings: a K–3 classroom, a suicide hotline phone center, a juvenile detention center, an after-school program?

9. Write a role-play script or perform an extemporaneous skit for one of the scenarios under "Dealing with Questionable Behavior of Others" in this chapter.

10. Write your own code of ethics. Identify the sources for elements you selected.

◉ GUIDED PRACTICES

Guided Practices offer structured exercises in critical thinking, observation (including self-observation), synthesis, and self-expression. The title of Guided Practice sums up the purpose of providing a guide: an opportunity that permits practice and does not require a final, ultimate effort.

All of the guided practices can be used by one person or by a group of people. The practices are designed as self-report instruments, meaning that answers are reported by the respondent and not collected by an interviewer or by another person who may speak with or observe the respondent.

There is not a standard amount of time to spend on the exercises. One person may use a guided practice for making a quick check while the next person may choose to spend hours on the same practice. Individual interest in a topic makes a difference in use, as does current need for the topic.

The greatest value is derived when the guided practice is completed with honest answers and observations. Any instrument may generate socially desirable answers, the kind of responses that a person thinks will be acceptable or expected. Especially when related to academic study, an instrument that calls for self-disclosure or self-evaluation risks being answered this way.

Guided Practice:
Making a Great Referral

Help clients make the connection to professionals in the community.

Tool	Strategies	How I Can Do This
Community directory/network	Community help lines in your PDA Business card of help line, shelter, etc., to give to people	
Professional contacts	Contacts from other agencies or schools Rolodex Flyers from conferences	
Established relationships	School counselor Youth officer/security guard Staff psychologist	
Response	Role-play and practice phrases such as "Are you afraid you may hurt yourself?" "Are you afraid you may hurt your child?" "Is your home without electricity right now?" "Do you have food for today?" "May I walk you to the counselor's office right now?"	

**Guided Practice:
Vulnerable Populations**

Identify possible vulnerable populations at your site or in your community and explain why they are vulnerable.

Population	Why Vulnerable
Middle school students	Power differential
Homeless citizens	Few personal resources Lack of access to public resources

Guided Practice:
Equal Treatment?

Identify which behaviors or practices are appropriate and which are inappropriate.

Behavior or Practice	Appropriate	Not Appropriate
An employer refuses to hire a tattooed job applicant because some clients might be offended by the tattoo.		
A counseling agency has separate toilet facilities for staff members and clients.		
An adoption agency allows only heterosexuals to adopt children.		
A manager grants an extended deadline on a report for an employee whose child was sick.		
A school district disqualifies a pregnant teenager from recognition as class valedictorian.		
A supervisor awards a bonus to the caseworker with the most number of clients served each month.		
A teacher permits a student on crutches to go early to lunch.		
A parent educator has a program targeted to grandmothers raising grandchildren.		
A family resource center reserves parking spaces closest to the building for clients while staff must park in a distant lot.		

 Guided Practice forms are also included on the accompanying CD-ROM.

ADDITIONAL RESOURCES

Helpful Web Sites:

Codes of Ethical Conduct published on Web sites of professional organizations:

American Association of Family & Consumer Sciences (AAFCS), http://www.aafcs.org

American Psychological Association (APA), http://www.apa.org

American Sociological Association (ASA), http://www.asanet.org

National Association for the Education of Young Children (NAEYC), http://www.naeyc.org

National Association of Social Workers (NASW), http://www.socialworkers.org

National Council on Family Relations (NCFR), http://www.ncfr.org

Society for Research in Child Development (SRCD), http://www.srcd.org

REFERENCES

Code of Ethics of University of Southern California (n.d.) Available at: http://www.usc.edu/about/core_documents/usc_code_of_ethics.html

Gilligan, C. (1982). *In a different voice: Psychological theory and women's development.* Cambridge, MA: Harvard University Press.

Perry, W. G., Jr., (1981). Cognitive and ethical growth: The making of meaning. In A. Chickering (Ed.), *The modern American college: Responding to the new realities of diverse students and a changing society* (pp. 76–116). San Francisco: Jossey-Bass.

For additional material and resources to complement this chapter, the Online Companion Web site can be accessed at http://www.earlychilded.delmar.com.

CHAPTER 7

Assessment and Evaluation

CASE STUDY: After years of stressing out over tests, Yolanda was looking forward to a class with no tests—or so she thought before the internship began. She felt like teachers were always asking the wrong questions, rarely asking what she had studied or learned about a subject. Yolanda complained that most tests didn't measure what she knew or what was important. She could never understand why we had to have grades anyway. What did it matter what grade she had made in a course her first year of college? Finally, she would be graded on what she could do in a real-life situation, instead of just the answers she could memorize.

Yolanda was a little anxious about how her supervisor would know whether or not she was doing a good job. How would she compare Yolanda's job performance with any other intern or job applicant? Yolanda looked over the job description for her internship and decided that she could do all of those tasks, some easily and some with a little assistance.

When she looked on-line at the forms for her internship class, Yolanda was surprised to see rubrics and assessments and other things she was unsure about. There seemed to be measures of personal things—even how she dressed—and professional things—even her punctuality. This grade might not be so easy after all.

assessment

Measure or test that reports on ability or performance. Purposes can include screening, determining aptitude, and measuring skills.

evaluation

Measuring (often with multiple assessments) that supports analysis and conclusions about ability or performance.

gain score

The difference between a pretest score and a posttest score.

norm

Usual score or value, typically determined by national testing; also called a *standard score*.

standardized test

Assessment or measure that has been used in multiple settings with many test takers to produce a norm or standard score; also called *norm-referenced test*.

As you have learned through your own academic studies, learning and progress are measured through an assortment of tools. The general terms for such measurement are **assessment** and **evaluation**. They often are used interchangeably, but we will assign particular meanings to them in this chapter. To be brief, we will place assessments (measures of performance) under the larger umbrella of evaluation (measuring performance with intention of drawing a conclusion about the merit or worth of the performance). Assessment and evaluation are usually part of an analytic system or process that drives improvement in the future. In public education as well as funded social service programs, such analysis has become increasingly important. Historically, educators and professionals have always evaluated their curricula and programs; what has changed is the emphasis on documenting that evaluation and identifying what improvements are made.

As a student, you have been measured many times. In this chapter, we will discuss you, as the intern, needing to be evaluated, and then we will shift the discussion to the program level, which you are likely to observe during your internship. As in most professional endeavors, vocabulary changes according to the respective field of study. Thus, our language in this chapter will include a variety of terms that you may run across in your own formal and informal study of evaluation. Terms are defined with their most common meanings in the social sciences and education.

✳ WHY EVALUATE?

Humans make comparisons constantly, so our interest in assessment and evaluation comes naturally. Consider the teenager who weighs herself daily: she is making daily assessments and, probably, comparing them. If she draws a conclusion about the measurements, she is making an evaluation. We'll return to this example later to explain some basic vocabulary. For now, we'll assume that the teenager has a reason for making a daily assessment. What might be the reason? The most neutral language would be *to track change in weight*. An observer might be inclined to say, more conversationally, that the girl is looking for progress. But that word would then have to be defined. For one girl, a drop in weight might be progress; for another girl, an increase in weight might be progress; for still another, no change in weight might be progress. So, it helps to think about measurement in terms of change or difference, without making assumptions about progress or another evaluative conclusion.

In your education, no doubt you have been measured hundreds of times. Most of the time, your assessments have come in pairs or sets to measure change. The purpose was probably to look for differences in your command of a body of knowledge. In short, the measures have been made to see if you learned more knowledge since your last assessment. This would be called *knowledge gain*. **Gain scores** are easy to spot and track, but they are often assessment traps, as described later in this chapter.

Sometimes, in your schooling, you were measured only once because the comparison to be made was not against your own learning but against a **norm** or usual score established by a large group of people. An example is the PSAT, a **standardized test** that most high school students take only once. That measure allows comparison between the individual student and many other students across the nation. Tests typically taken later, the SAT and ACT, may serve two purposes: to allow comparison between the student and national norms

Students (and interns) are regularly
assessed to look for knowledge gain.

and, also, to allow comparison between the student's first effort on the test
and a later effort.

If your education included a **mastery approach**, then you also took
criterion-referenced tests. Criteria were identified as necessary elements of
knowledge or as necessary skills for you to learn, and then your performance
on the test reported on how many of the elements or skills you had mastered.
Your test performance was treated as an individual reflection of your learning,
and it was not compared to other students' performance.

Your educational assessments did not measure only your performance.
They also measured your schools' performance. When students' results are
combined (aggregated), they serve as indicators of the quality of the school.
Similarly, when family professionals conduct a program in community, they are
likely to make assessments that will help evaluate the program—some of those
assessments may produce **aggregated data** from program participants.

Selecting the right measures is important. You can imagine that some people associated with a high school would not be in favor of just three measures,
such as those shown in Figure 7-1, reflecting overall quality. The power of
evaluation comes from comparison; if all schools were to be compared on just
these three measures, and then receive their share of funding based on the
results, then the choice of measures could work for your school or against it.

If a high school promotes students taking the PSAT and offers free tutoring beforehand along with free MP3 players to listen to test prep lectures,
would it have an advantage in a comparison with high schools across the
state? Not necessarily! The promotion (and popularization of any activity with
free MP3 players) might attract all the students in the school, ranging from
high to low testing ability. The mean score for the school, then, may be lower

mastery approach

Educational
consideration of a
student's learning
based on what the
student knows or
what the student can
do. This approach
does not compare the
student's performance
to other students'
performance.

criterion-referenced

Test or measure of a
student's skill level or
knowledge against
one criterion (or
several criteria) that
would reflect mastery.

aggregated data

Data that are
systematically
collected and
combined, reflecting
assessments over time
and/or assessments
from multiple
locations or sources.

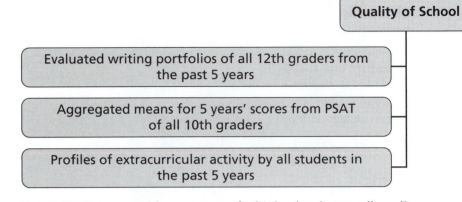

Figure 7-1 Three possible measures of a high school's overall quality.

than a neighboring school that counts on only the Honor Society students getting up at 7 a.m. on a Saturday to take a college-oriented standardized test.

What about the measure of extracurricular activity? If the high school's population is like most today, it includes a sizable proportion of students with after-school jobs. They may have limited time and little inclination to sign on for more activities in their afternoons and evenings. So, a measure of extracurricular activity may be lower for one school than another whose students do not have jobs (either because they don't need jobs, or because they are in a high unemployment area and cannot find jobs).

Some stakeholders in a school community might insist that laboratory science should be reflected in a quality check, another type of assessment.

A stakeholder in a school community might insist that laboratory science be reflected in a quality assessment.

Other stakeholders might be more interested in oral communication skills. Or athletic opportunities. Or athletic competition championships. The debate over how to measure schools is an ongoing one. The great variety of possibilities actually ends up promoting the option of standardized tests as the primary measure simply to avoid the debates surrounding the choice of other measures.

The question of what measures to select becomes more complex when we begin to check the **reliability** and **validity** of each measure. We can return to our daily weigh-in example for quick definitions of these terms. When the teenage girl weighs herself daily, a set of scores develops: 128, 130, 127, 129, 129, 131, 130, and so forth. The variation, or variability, of the weights over a week's time makes us think about reliability. How reliable is this measure of the girl's weight? Two thoughts emerge: (a) maybe the variability means that the bathroom scale is not reliable, not capable of consistently reporting true weight; and (b) maybe the variability means that daily weight fluctuations (which are normal and expected) make the daily scores not the best choice for tracking weight. Assuming the bathroom scale itself can be checked and declared reliable, the daily scores could be replaced with a weekly score, either an average of the daily scores or a sample score taken regularly on the same day of the week. With a little reorganization, we can assure the reliability of the weight scores that will be tracked.

We can consider whether the teenage girl's measure is valid by asking what her purpose is. If the purpose is to track weight in pounds, then the bathroom scale (after its reliability is confirmed) can produce valid results for her. If the purpose is to track body fat, then the scale does not produce a valid result (no matter how reliable it may be). Similarly, if the purpose is to track health, the bathroom scale is not the best measure. The girl would be better served to consult with a health professional about multiple measures of health to produce a valid evaluation.

In our bathroom scale example, we brushed past a major rule about reliability and validity: a measure can be reliable without being valid, but a measure is valid only if it is also reliable. Consider an experience from education: if a student took the PSAT in 10th grade, she took a test that is considered both reliable and valid in measuring math achievement. It is a reliable test because students score (about) the same if they take it more than once; it is a valid test because it accurately determines the level of students' math achievement. (It measures what is intended.) If a student sitting for the PSAT found instead a 2nd-grade test of arithmetic, we'd be likely to call it a measure that was reliable (assuming the student would consistently score 100% if taking it multiple times) but not valid. A test of elementary arithmetic would not be a valid test of math achievement for a student at the PSAT level.

To repeat the question we began with: why evaluate? We measure and evaluate in order to know how we are doing. By assuring reliability and validity of our measures, we can count on our evaluations being meaningful.

reliability

A check on the consistency of a measure, meaning that the measure will produce the same score, time after time.

validity

A check on whether an assessment is measuring what it is intended to measure.

✳ MEASURING THE INTERN

How might an intern be evaluated? Are multiple measures likely to be used? Are multiple evaluators likely to be involved? Answers will vary from one internship to the next and from one university to the next. For some internships, formal assessment is not recorded; rather, the internship is completed satisfactorily through submission of a report, project, or portfolio. A research based internship may have as its goal the publication of a scholarly paper or an article in a student research journal. A project or paper may thus represent an entire semester's work. Such a completion project requires discipline on the part of the intern because there may be few supports along the way to begin or complete the documentation of the project. Supports that the intern can take advantage of or initiate are conferences with the academic advisor or site supervisor, checkpoints at regular intervals to record progress, and goal dates for first and final drafts of the report.

From a higher education perspective, field experience brings new challenge to assessment—both in earning grades and in assigning grades. Your semester of field experience may include some traditional school functions, such as writing papers and attending seminars. But the heart of your experience is in the doing, and that is harder to assess for grading purposes. Common assessments of the field experience are the student's journals or logs and the site supervisor's evaluation of the student. Together, these assessments may comprise as much as 80% of the student's grade.

This discussion of evaluation of the intern begins with the site supervisor's evaluation. The variety of internships means there are many styles of supervisors' oversight of interns and eventual assessment of them. Examples here draw on common themes of assessment: competencies, performance, and evidence items. At the end of this chapter, you will find a Guided Practice called "Sample Rubric for Evaluation of Intern by a Site Supervisor."

Competencies of the Intern

The most general **competency** types are personal and professional. Personal represents the intern's traits, characteristics, and abilities that would presumably be in place no matter what the setting. Professional represents the expression of abilities in the workplace. While professional competency may rely heavily on personal traits, it can also be learned and expressed in spite of a person's natural temperament.

Personal competency may relate to **personality** traits, typically defined by Goldberg's **big five** (Goldberg, 1990), a scheme further developed as the **five factor model (FFM)** (Costa & McCrae, 1997; McCrae & Costa, 2003). Personality traits have been found to be stable across adulthood by many research studies. Most researchers point to young adulthood, the 20s, as the beginning point for stability of traits. This implies that personality develops all through childhood and adolescence; life span theorists tell us that development continues across the life course, although presumably a stable trait does not change greatly. The terminology surrounding personality development is important: some theorists take care to refer to change agents as *influences* on development, so as not to overstate the amount of change that personality undergoes.

The big five and FFM personality traits are the factors that tend to reappear in study after study. They do not stand for theories of personality; they simply are the labels for the most commonly reported results of personality testing. As descriptors, the labels represent words and meanings that most people can relate to. Scientists who study personality also consider the source of traits, looking for ways to test the question of **nature versus nurture**. Most scholars acknowledge that the OCEAN traits identified by the FFM relate to the temperament that a person is born with; however, personality develops over a lifetime, and therefore, the traits may change. Thus, the FFM is a biosocial model—it assumes that both biology and social environment influence the development of personality.

---

competency

Proficiency or ability to perform at a high level.

personality

The collective qualities, traits, and behaviors that are unique to an individual person.

big five

A noncausal explanation of personality traits that appear to be defined across many languages: intellect, conscientiousness, surgency (extroversion), agreeableness, and emotional stability. Tests of the big five indicate overlap among the domains.

five factor model (FFM)

A biosocial explanation of personality as consisting of domains of openness to new ideas, conscientiousness, extroversion, agreeableness, and neuroticism. The model's domains are also known by the acronym OCEAN. Tests of the FFM identify people's traits in all the domains and do not sort people into personality types.

Personality develops all through childhood and adolescence.

nature versus nurture
The scholarly debate of the relative influence of nature (genetics) and nurture (social environment) on human development, including personality development. Most scholars today maintain that the debate is not *versus*, meaning nature *or* nurture, but a combination approach that incorporates nature *and* nurture; however, the proportion of those elements and, potentially, other elements continues to be debated.

The FFM connects openness, conscientiousness, extroversion, agreeableness, and neuroticism. These five descriptions of personality have appeared in research and theory, with emphasis on different elements by different researchers in different cultures. Openness, in some Western countries like the U.S., is usually interpreted as being open to new ideas and being curious; it is sometimes measured as intelligence. In other countries, there is less emphasis on the intelligence aspect and, instead, an added interpretation of rebelliousness. Conscientiousness appears to be nearly universally recognized; it is commonly labeled as "dependability" or "work-focus." Extroversion is another

Conscientiousness and agreeableness are two personal competencies often evaluated during an internship.

widely recognized trait in all cultures, but its measure may be as power, or self-confidence, or self-expression, or assertiveness. (It is also sometimes spelled *extraversion*.) Agreeableness is known variously as social adaptability, compliance, friendliness. Neuroticism, which sounds very negative, simply takes its name from one end of its spectrum; at the other end, a person may be described as emotionally stable.

In the workplace, including the internship workplace, the evaluation of personal competency is considered a **pragmatic** necessity. This fact may startle the newcomer, who may counter, "But a person cannot help being stubborn. If that's an inborn personality trait, then it isn't fair to be judged on that." Let's make a pragmatic examination of stubbornness in the workplace. We will not be as detailed or clinical as an **industrial psychologist** would be, but we can locate it in the domain of agreeableness and think of it in practical terms.

Accepting that agreeableness is a function of personality, we can explore all the meanings it has. The first meaning is a neutral one: agreeableness is simply the degree to which a person agrees with others. (Without knowing what the person is agreeing to, that could be either wise or foolish, of course.) In a social context, agreeableness means that the person can adapt to social conditions and work (or play) with others. In a social hierarchy, agreeableness means that the person knows when and how to comply with the group priority or to the group's authority. When would agreeableness be a problem? Being *too* compliant would reflect high agreeableness (and possibly low judgment). And being zero compliant (lack of agreeableness) could reflect what is often called stubbornness, or unwillingness to agree. The agreeableness domain also includes the disagreeable, the argumentative, and the combative. For these, conflict may be a consequence. Is that necessarily a problem? In some contexts, it could be a solution. For example, in war, being combative and not complying are expected. In a courtroom, being argumentative may be a sign of success (although even the most argumentative trial attorney would also know when to comply with a judge's rule).

Context must be considered to know if expression of a personality trait is problematic. (In extreme cases, context plus diagnosis will establish whether a trait is a **personality disorder**. For most people, such a diagnosis is rare and would follow a history of interference with daily life.) For our example of stubbornness, the workplace context is pertinent: consider a scenario in which an adult who is stubborn in goal achievement is met with a group of fearful children who refuse to follow the adult's instructions. In a youth swimming program, the stubborn adult can cause much damage to fearful children if priority is placed on reaching the adult goal of getting all the children into the water. But in firefighting, the stubborn adult will save children's lives by putting the goal of emptying a burning building ahead of the children's fear or disobedience.

For a less dramatic example, consider the stubborn individual's *other* personality traits that also have an effect on behavior. The stubbornness may reflect a dislike for change. For some people, acting stubborn is more about adjusting to change than putting an individual goal ahead of everyone else's needs. Thus, the stubborn behavior is not a daily trait but an occasional response to certain stimuli. For this person, selection of job (or internship) should take into account the likelihood of frequent change.

Thus, when an intern is evaluated on personal competency, the evaluation may reflect how well the intern's personality matches the context of the workplace. (It may also reflect how well the intern self-monitors and adjusts, if the match is not a good one!) When an intern is evaluated on professional competency, the assessment reflects how the intern assumed professional responsibilities. In most internships, professional competency is not weighted

pragmatic

Concerned with practical matters; approaching a problem or situation with practical experience or observation, rather than with theory or ideology.

industrial psychologist

Professional trained in the branch of applied psychology that addresses workplace behaviors, management of a labor force, and other issues of the workplace.

personality disorder

Expression of one or more personality traits that interferes with a person's long-term functioning in addition to daily functioning. Diagnosis of a disorder is made by a trained counselor, therapist, or doctor.

heavily; the intern is recognized as a novice or beginner in most areas. However, when an intern does perform at a professional level, that is typically highly rated by the site supervisor.

When an intern is evaluated on personal competency, the evaluation may reflect how well the intern's personality matches the context of the workplace.

Performance Areas

Job performance is almost always assessed across multiple areas (see Table 7-1). Interns are not expected to score high across the board. Rather, a typical evaluation will report some high performance levels and some low. The more concrete terminology of assessment enters at this level of assessing

job performance

Workplace behaviors related to the process or accomplishment of a job function or role.

Table 7-1

Personal Competency Performance Areas	Professional Competency Performance Areas
Dependability	Attitude
Cooperation	Resourcefulness
Consideration	Leadership
Adaptability	Language/Writing
Enthusiasm	
Judgment	
Alertness	
Emotional Maturity	
Initiative	
Appearance	

performance on the job, making the personal and professional competencies easier to describe. Well-known terms, such as *dependable* and *cooperative*, describe personal competency in a way that does not require explanation. Similarly, *resourceful* is immediately understood as it relates to professional competency. Most words used to describe job performance have **consensual meanings** in the workplace.

Scale Items for Evaluation

A performance area such as dependability could be measured and reported in a number of ways. Two measures are punctuality and efficiency. Other measures of dependability might be "completes work" and "reports to work regularly." Such measures may be called *indicators, evidences,* or *scale items*. Indicators or evidences are behaviors that a site supervisor could reasonably expect to observe over the course of an internship. While the performance areas are largely consensual across many settings, the indicators may have to be defined for the individual internship.

For example, in the performance area of cooperation, a general indicator is how well the intern works with people. That statement may need to be more

Table 7-2 **Typical Indicators in General Performance Areas**		
Competency Type	**Performance Area**	**Indicator, Evidence, or Scale Item**
Personal	Dependability	Is punctual and efficient
Personal	Dependability	Completes work/projects
Personal	Cooperation	Works well with people
Personal	Consideration	Courteous, friendly, and thoughtful
Personal	Adaptability	Meets new situations calmly
Personal	Adaptability	Accepts suggestions and criticism
Personal	Enthusiasm	Eagerly attacks jobs
Personal	Judgment	Knows when to ask for help
Personal	Alertness	Is sensitive to others' needs/feelings
Personal	Emotional maturity	Is poised and self-controlled
Personal	Initiative	Starts tasks without prodding
Personal	Appearance	Is neat and well groomed; dresses appropriately
Professional	Attitude	Evaluates own work
Professional	Resourcefulness	Is imaginative and creative
Professional	Resourcefulness	Seeks resources when needed
Professional	Leadership	Brings out the best in people
Professional	Leadership	Can coordinate group work
Professional	Language/Writing	Writes effectively and correctly

For the intern assigned to a preschool, cooperation might be measured as the intern's participation in rotating duties, such as cleaning up after snack time.

specific to a workplace in order to fairly evaluate the intern's performance. For the intern assigned to a high school, cooperation might be measured as the intern's willingness to join (or take turns with) staff members in supervising students, grading papers, recording test scores, writing reports, and attending meetings. For the intern assigned to a preschool, cooperation might be measured as the intern's participation in rotating duties of preparing centers, supervising snack time, cleaning snack trays, leading story time, greeting parents, and so forth. Each of these tasks further defines the indicator or evidence of a performance area. See Table 7-2 for typical indicators in general performance areas.

Performance areas of professional competencies are similarly defined by specific indicators or evidences (see Table 7-3). Having an appropriate knowledge base for the internship is likely to be an influence on how well the intern performs—in how highly the intern is rated in that area. In a school setting, a professional competency is knowledge of child development. The measure of performance could be how well the intern communicates with children using appropriate vocabulary. For an intern working for a suicide helpline, a professional competency might be knowledge of crisis management. In that setting, the indicator for evaluation might be the following of instructions or how well the intern understood and recalled the protocol for handling a crisis.

Indicators can be measured and reported many ways. The simplest form would be a checklist on which a site supervisor could simply place a check mark if the intern exhibited the evidence of the desired behavior. Some evidences can be described as **dichotomous**, having only two possible answers, such as "Yes" or "No." The following are dichotomous measures of common performance areas.

Yes/No   The intern arrives at the site on time.

Yes/No   The intern returns from breaks on time.

Yes/No   The intern keeps the work area in neat order.

Yes/No   The intern answers e-mails within 24 hours.

A checklist can quickly establish whether minimum standards or, perhaps, common expectations of the job are being met. But most interns and university supervisors want feedback on performance beyond the basics. In most cases, a scale is used to distinguish different levels of performance as **quantitative data**;

dichotomous

Divided into two parts or two classifications. Common examples are on/off, yes/no, included/excluded.

quantitative data

Information in the form of numbers, such as test scores and responses to close-ended questions on surveys.

Table 7-3 **Sample Indicators in Specific Settings**

Competency Type	Performance Area	Indicator, Evidence, or Scale Item
Professional competency in a school setting	Knowledge of child development	Communicates with children using an appropriate vocabulary
Professional competency in a medical facility	Knowledge of legal requirements	Handles information appropriately, following HIPAA and other guidelines
Professional competency in a detention facility	Knowledge of intake procedures	Maintains calm in stressful situations, such as intake interviews
Professional competency in a nursing home	Knowledge of older persons' needs	Adjusts pace and volume of speech to accommodate needs of residents
Professional competency in a police internship	Knowledge of crisis management	Follows appropriate procedures and instructions in a crisis situation
Professional competency in a child care setting	Knowledge of safety standards	Examines environment in terms of hazards, risks to young children
Professional competency in various settings	Self-knowledge	Self-monitors for choice of words, tone and volume of voice, appropriate silence

qualitative data

Information in the form of words, such as written answers to open-ended questions on surveys or oral answers to interview questions.

scale item

Statement that can be responded to with a value; typically several items are listed to permit response about a concept; the values of the responses can then be summed and averaged.

additionally, **qualitative data** in the way of comments are usually included in evaluations. If an evidence or indicator is rated on a scale, it may be called a **scale item**. Frequently, the measurement scale is presented to a site supervisor in survey format, with the indicators listed as items in the survey. A **unidimensional scale** is typically used so that the response merely indicates "more" or "less" performance; a famous one is the **Likert scale**. You have probably taken many surveys that asked for a rating of 1 to 5, with 5 meaning "Strongly agree," for example.

When a scale is used in evaluation, an important decision is whether to make it an even-numbered scale or an odd-numbered scale. Four choices (four being an even number) might read, "Strongly disagree," "Disagree," "Agree," "Strongly agree." Having exactly four answer choices requires that the respondent identify his or her position as either agreeing or disagreeing. There is no middle ground! The respondent cannot sit on the fence and be neutral. By contrast, a five-choice scale (five being an odd number) might read, "Strongly disagree," "Somewhat disagree," "Neither agree nor disagree," "Somewhat agree," "Strongly agree." On this scale, the respondent has the option of being neutral, of neither agreeing nor disagreeing. In research, the odd-numbered scale is sometimes accused of not providing any data. But in some situations, the researcher may want to give the respondent the choice of being neutral, or not having a vote. The same may be the case in evaluation of an employee or an intern. Should the evaluator always be forced to indicate a positive versus negative rating? Or might the intern's performance be rated "neutral" in some cases? Some evaluation forms solve the issue by including a place for the supervisor to identify an item as "Not applicable," meaning the internship did not provide opportunity for that measure. Of course, a site supervisor may indicate the same thing (or unwillingness to rate an item) by simply skipping it on the evaluation form.

Four labels for a scale measuring intern performance might be: "Accomplished," "Developing", "Novice," and "Unacceptable." The labels themselves may not be defined because the terms are common words, and their placement indicates relative value, with the best at one end and the worst at the other end. If those terms are entered into a **rubric**, extra text may be added to suggest what the label can mean (see Table 7-4). In such a rubric, the text serves as an **operational definition** for the performance standard. When site supervisors have a rubric or other evaluation form with definitions, the intern and the university can feel more confident in their understanding of how the supervisor rated the intern. The rubric is still based on the same principle as the Likert scale: performance is rated along one dimension, with either an even number of rating choices or an odd number of rating choices.

✳ **unidimensional scale**

Measurement in terms of just one aspect, such as "ranging from heavy to light," without assessing any other characteristic.

✳ **Likert scale**

Specific type of scale or instrument that has a set of at least several items and a horizontal row of labeled response levels. The originator, Rensis Lickert, intended the items to produce an average response to represent an attitude. (Pronounced "Lick-ert.")

Table 7-4 Rubric for Personal & Professional Competencies

Performance Areas	Accomplished	Developing	Novice	Unacceptable
Personal competency: judgment **Knows when to ask for help**	Recognizes own lack of experience or knowledge and promptly contacts a mentor	Sometimes recognizes own lack of experience or knowledge and contacts a mentor, but not consistently	Recognizes own lack of experience or knowledge but does not follow through by contacting a mentor	Does not recognize own lack of experience or knowledge; acts without a mentor's guidance
Personal competency: initiative **Starts tasks without prodding**	Takes initiative to start tasks on his or her own	Sometimes takes initiative to start tasks on his or her own, but not consistently	Rarely takes initiative to start tasks on his or her own, but responds quickly when prodded to begin	Does not take initiative to start tasks on his or her own, and is not responsive when prodded to begin
Professional competency: attitude **Evaluates own work**	Evaluates own work and either makes corrections or articulates related needs	Sometimes evaluates own work and sometimes makes corrections or articulates related needs	Rarely evaluates own work, but is responsive when a mentor outlines corrections	Does not evaluate own work and is unresponsive when a mentor outlines corrections

Table 7-5 **Sample Labels for Evaluation Rubrics**

Scale of . . .	Highest	Next to High	Next to Low	Lowest
Accomplishment	Accomplished	Developing	Novice	Unacceptable
Learning	Mastery	Learning	Beginning	Not learning
Ability	High ability	Moderate ability	Low ability	Unable
Performance level	Proficient	Able	Minimal	Below minimal
Level compared to average	Above average	Average	Below average	Failing
Mentoring	Little need for guidance	Moderate need for guidance	Great need for guidance	Need for guidance is too great; intern is not in an appropriate placement
Numerical	4	3	2	1
Numerical	3	2	1	0
School grades	A	B, C+	C−, D	F
Percentages	90%–100%	75%–89%	60%–74%	59% and below

rubric

Guideline for assessing performance or learning. Sometimes created as a template for reuse in future assessments, a common style is a table with outcomes listed in the left-hand column and values for rating listed on the top row.

operational definition

Explanation or definition of how a word is used in the current context. For example, in a rubric for scoring a preservice teacher's performance, "unable to articulate rationale for choice of literacy materials" may be the explanatory text for the rating label of "Novice."

Whether creating a scale for use in a survey or a set of labels for a rubric, the choice of labels to represent the ratings can help set the tone for the meaning of the evaluation (see Table 7-5). Some labels suggest an educational approach, and encouraging terms appear at even a low rating: "beginning" and "novice" are examples. Comparable labels in other scales are "low ability" and "below average." The implications are very different for the people on the receiving end of the ratings! In school studies, you may have noticed the impact of the + (plus) or − (minus) on a letter grade. Was B+ considerably more flattering than B−? The power of rating labels cannot be denied, and sometimes, it cannot be avoided. When receiving a rating of "below average," a person must seek information about the context of the rating. If the evaluation form for your internship was created by your university, you have the university instructor as a resource to learn about the rating system. If the evaluation form was created by the internship site, you will have to learn about the site's purpose and style of evaluation.

Data collection methods used for evaluation may include in-person interviews with the site supervisor and university instructor, on-line surveys, and print surveys placed in sealed envelopes and mailed to your instructor. Evaluations are most efficiently collected through on-line survey forms. In some programs, the intern never sees the full evaluation form after it has been completed by the supervisor. In other programs, the intern is invited to discuss the results, either with the site supervisor or with the university instructor. These variations are almost always the standard procedures of the site and the school and not subject to change.

When you begin the internship, you can ask about how you will be evaluated. Orientation packets or training often include information about the process, but interns may not attend to the information. This is a typical occurrence when people must take in a lot of new information; only the most relevant data can be absorbed. Of course, information about evaluation will be relevant at some point, but in an orientation session, the intern understandably places higher importance on the details of starting the job. University instructors can provide insight into the how and why—and when—of evaluation. Specifically, you should ask your instructor about checkpoints that may be scheduled during the internship. A checkpoint allows feedback or even a full evaluation during the internship that helps the intern know how work is being perceived (either by the instructor or by the site supervisor).

Because an internship is often a blend of academic studies and the workplace, the evaluation may also be a blend. It may be more pragmatic than a school grade and, simultaneously, more generous than an employee evaluation. Some site supervisors have a strong opinion about intern evaluations. For example, some supervisors firmly believe that no intern or employee can (or should) receive a perfect score. Thus, they begin their top scale at what you might call a grade of B. Other supervisors almost always award top ratings to their interns. If you work with a site supervisor who is a "hard grader," you should talk to your university instructor about the impact on your semester grade. Most internship classes use multiple measurements to protect against the variability of ratings from the sites. You are likely to also create a self-assessment of your internship accomplishments, and your instructor may have even more assessments to add to the grading of your internship course.

What about the site supervisor who gives all high ratings? While that may feel good on the receiving end, it has a downside: you will not receive the thorough feedback you need (and want) about your performance. If this is the case, you may ask the site supervisor for an appointment to discuss how you performed on the job. Because you will already know that this mentor does not like to rate people, you should prepare a different approach to learning about your performance. You can plan a set of questions that relate to the rating categories. Here are three different ways to ask about how you worked with coworkers. You can draw from these examples that follow to design questions that suit you and the site supervisor.

1. Did you notice how I got along with other people at the site?

2. I liked joining a team, but I didn't always feel as though I fit in. How did you see it?

3. Your agency puts a lot of importance on teamwork. This was new to me and so it took me a while to understand how the professionals work together. How might I have done this better?

Securing feedback after a negative evaluation, from either the site supervisor or the university instructor, can be a daunting task. But the rewards will be high, not only in gaining an understanding of the negative evaluation, but in overcoming the natural reluctance to have such an interview. A first consequence of a negative evaluation or low rating is that one's feelings are hurt. Other possible reactions are defensiveness, anger, and depression. Rarely is an evaluation negative across the board, but seeing the high ratings and positive comments can be a challenge in light of the defensiveness to the negative rating. In the U.S., much emphasis is placed on measurement, and we adopt language

---

Table 7-6 Strategy for Finding Perspective on a Negative Evaluation

1. On the first reading, try to focus on all parts, not just negative parts.

2. Set the evaluation aside for a few hours.

3. Reread the evaluation and break it into small parts.

4. Highlight all the positive ratings or list them on a piece of paper.

5. Read negative ratings carefully, making sure you understand all the words.

6. Notice the language used to describe abilities and performance.

7. Consult the instructor about the balance of evaluation items, positive and negative.

8. Set the evaluation aside for a week or more.

9. Revisit the evaluation after you have written your own self-assessment.

10. Consider whether the negative rating is a feature of your work that you would change in a future work assignment. Sometimes a negative rating becomes the source for change; other times, it may be set aside as not pertinent to future settings. "Putting it into perspective" means either putting it to work or putting it to rest.

---

that supports that emphasis. For example, we are told to accept and appreciate constructive criticism, but we are rarely warned about the emotional toll of being on the receiving end of criticism. The supportive nature of an internship is a rare opportunity to be evaluated, and even criticized, with the chance to analyze and integrate the information—not just react to it emotionally.

A good strategy for the review of a negative evaluation is to make an appointment with the university instructor. The instructor can help the intern to interpret the evaluation, putting negative aspects into perspective. The instructor is also a good sounding board for the question of whether or not to discuss the evaluation with the site supervisor. In an employment setting, an employee would be likely to discuss a rating with the supervisor, but even then, an outside interpreter might be of help and that would typically be a representative from human resources or a similar office. Other strategies for finding perspective on a negative evaluation can be found in Table 7-6.

Sometimes, the intern may be surprised when an evaluation by a site supervisor is *not* negative. In some settings, the intern may focus on errors while the supervisor takes them in stride. Even if the supervisor is aware of mistakes or poor performance, that professional may choose not to emphasize them in an evaluation. A common reason would be that the supervisor considers making mistakes an expected part of the internship. Thus, errors are not held against the intern. The supervisor may instead emphasize what the student did well.

Another reason for an unexpected positive evaluation is that the intern has been more critical of herself or himself than any supervisor was. If you are highly critical of your performance (and that may be a personality trait that you have already been aware of), accepting a positive evaluation may be just as difficult for you as it is for another intern to accept a negative evaluation. Highly self-critical people often discount positive evaluations (including high grades in school) as not being accurate. Putting the positive evaluation into perspective is just as important as putting the negative evaluation into perspective. To gain the maximum advantage from the evaluation, consult your instructor to help you interpret and then apply the knowledge gained.

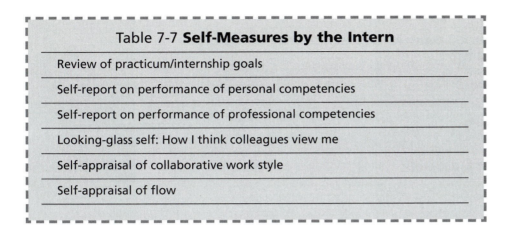

Table 7-7 **Self-Measures by the Intern**
Review of practicum/internship goals
Self-report on performance of personal competencies
Self-report on performance of professional competencies
Looking-glass self: How I think colleagues view me
Self-appraisal of collaborative work style
Self-appraisal of flow

Self-Measuring by the Intern

Very likely, self-measures will include a review of goals, a self-report on personal and professional competencies (mirroring the evaluation items rated by the site supervisor), and additional assessments of what was learned during the internship (see Table 7-7). Because of the subjective nature of an internship, the intern's own self-appraisal may be the most valuable of the evaluations that emerge. This does not mean that the site supervisor's and university instructor's assessments are less important, only that they may not hold the personal value that will influence career and life decisions.

Review of Practicum/Internship Goals. As the 3-A model in Chapter 3 proposes, goals of the internship should be measurable. Ideally, all your goals were measurable with clear evidence of success. As valid and reliable indicators, those measures can be analyzed to produce an evaluation of your experience. Realistically, you will review the evidence of success and find that some goals were not fully achieved. If you revised goals along the way, you may already have recognized what objectives were not suitable. Making a good measure does not rely on success or achievement of the goal, however. An internship may be considered very successful even if fewer than half the original goals were achieved. A review of goals, such as the one shown in Table 7-8, is the opportunity to both record levels of success and reflect on how the experience of the internship matched initial expectations. Some questions to ask in a review of goals include:

Did my prior knowledge/impression of the agency match actual activities?

Were my goals congruent with the goals or mission of the agency?

If my goals changed, what were the factors?

What other variables (internal and external) influenced success?

When student goals are not met over the course of the internship, the leading cause is insufficient knowledge of the site. The goals may not have matched what was available in terms of assignments, or the agency focus may have overridden student preferences. Typically, students find there is little they can do to change such circumstances after the internship is underway. Thus, restructuring of goals is likely. Formative (ongoing) evaluation of the internship helps to regain the maximum benefit possible, and university instructors are often the support for such evaluation.

Self-Report on Performance of Personal Competencies. Whether a requirement or not for academic credit, the wise intern will take time to

Table 7-8 **Sample Review of Internship Goals**

Goal or Objective	Accomplished	Were Resources Available?	Could You Stick to Your Timeline?	Level of Success
Learn about the professional credentials for the field of _____				Exceeded my expectations; didn't just learn about credentials but also acquired some
Evidence #1: Attend professional conference	✓	Yes—Mentor provided information and conference fee	Yes—Conference date was during my internship semester	
Evidence #2: Interview my mentor	✓			
Evidence #3: Complete CPR and First Aid training	✓	Agency paid training fees and made it part of my internship hours		
Learn to work with diverse populations				Partial success— Introduced to two populations but really worked with only one; expected more opportunities
Evidence #1: Make in-home visit to grandparent-headed household	✓	Yes—Shadowed professionals before participating in program functions		
Evidence #2: Conduct parent education program for incarcerated parents			Unable to schedule visit during my work hours at the site	

Table 7-8 **Continued**				
Goal or Objective	**Accomplished**	**Were Resources Available?**	**Could You Stick to Your Timeline?**	**Level of Success**
Make a professional presentation				Limited— Although presentation was prepared, it was not presented
Evidence: Present mini-lesson at in-service staff development		Created lesson from agency library and added a new Webliography as an appendix	Yes—Worked on this throughout the semester (my time filler)	No—The in-service was cancelled due to bad weather
Identifying county resources for homeless families				
Evidence: Research and create a directory for agency Web site publication	✓	Updated previous directories; located additional information at other agencies	Yes—I scheduled 2 hours a week; at the end, I increased the hours for the proofreading and uploading	Highly successful—I met my learning goal and provided a service for this agency and the entire county

self-assess on the same personal competencies that the site supervisor used in the intern evaluation. Typically, personal competency covers performance on dependability, adaptability, enthusiasm, emotional maturity, and similar areas. A self-evaluation is a good exercise (even before the internship ends), but its real value may be when you compare your own ratings with the site supervisor's. Is there a gap in perception? Perhaps you rated your promptness as outstanding, but the supervisor rated it as acceptable. Your perception might have been that a few late arrivals to the workplace were tolerated, and *overall* you still deserved an outstanding rating. But a site supervisor may reserve "outstanding" for the worker who arrives on time every day, without exception. Frequency of events may matter, and *overall* tendencies may not!

Self-Report on Performance of Professional Competencies. Similarly, you can rate yourself on the professional competencies: professional attitude or demeanor, resourcefulness, and leadership. Sometimes the internship permits skill building in professionalism, with opportunities for public speaking or networking. Because performance in these areas can almost always be compared with professionals' performance (for example, your first public speech at a conference might have followed a speech by a middle school principal or an agency director who has made dozens of such

Table 7-9 **Looking-Glass Self: How Colleagues View My Conduct with Clients**	
First step— **How colleagues see me**	Colleagues see me being cautious and a little quiet with the intake interviews.
Second step— **How colleagues judge my performance**	Colleagues probably judge my caution as understandable but needing to change.
Third step— **How I feel about that judgment**	I have to agree: I have been so cautious that I haven't tried to emulate the professionals' interview techniques. This makes me want to step up my interviewing performance. The professionals' presence is my safety net, so I can responsibly step away from my caution.

addresses), it is too easy to downgrade your performance. You may want to rate it as "unacceptable" or "low ability." But a rating on a professional competency deserves a qualifier: what is the rating *considering it is the intern's first speech in front of 350 people?* Even the most self-critical intern is likely to rate the effort at a higher mark with that kind of qualification, and appropriately so.

Looking-Glass Self: How I Think Colleagues View Me. A challenging, but potentially fun, self-assessment is to borrow the language of Cooley (1902) and consider how you appear in the looking glass. Cooley said that humans' self-image develops largely as a function of how others see us. That is, we react to how others see us and incorporate that information in our own perception of self. You can make a self-assessment along these lines to examine your *professional* self-image or possibly to assist you as you adopt a professional persona. As shown in Table 7-9, the first step would be to list on paper (or just imagine) how colleagues at the internship site see your performance. Second, consider what judgment colleagues make about your performance. Third, and finally, consider what your own reaction is to that judgment. The theory of the looking glass self predicts that your reaction will influence how you view yourself.

Self-Appraisal of Collaborative Work Style. Most internships permit an appraisal of your collaborative work style, at least regarding in-person collaboration. On-line collaboration is also important for workplace success. It is facilitated by on-line services, groupware programs, including intranets of computers and Web collaboration software. More important than the technology or even the individual's skill in using the technology is the individual's attitude toward such work. The importance of attitude toward virtual collaboration highlights the commitment required for effective collaboration. That commitment, whether on-line or in-person, comes from the professional's willingness to set aside convenience and put the collaborative effort ahead of all else. This sense of priority, essentially an attitude, is what produces a collaborative work group.

Personal work style preference is highly related to your attitude toward collaboration. Self-knowledge about your attitude is key to understanding what type of workplace is best for you. While it is easy to simply say, "Yes, I value collaboration," the more important information is how well you work in that mode. If you are an individual contributor, your highest value to an organization is in maximizing that role. If you are highly competitive, you may be drawn to the role of individual contributor rather than to teamwork. You may still need to build skills in collaboration, but you should have an accurate view of yourself in terms of natural preference. To gain that view, you can rely on diagnostic instruments to identify personality traits, work style preferences, and workplace strengths. You can take assessments on-line or at a career counseling center on campus even if they are not included as part of your internship or class.

So-called 360 (or **360-degree feedback**) assessments offer an all-around view of an employee from the perspective of coworkers, supervisors, and workers who report to the employee. This type of diagnostic tool is expensive because of the multiple measures that it employs. Thus, a traditional 360 assessment may be reserved for managers only. However, the concept of 360 degrees, or full circle view, has become popular, and less extensive tools have been developed in order to approximate the all-around evaluation. While interns' evaluation is not designed in this model, it is interesting to note that the multiple views typically employed in an internship resemble the 360 perspective.

Self-Appraisal of Flow. Another key element of self-knowledge that the internship may provide is awareness of when, where, and how you are most satisfied. For some people, satisfaction is equated with feeling creative; for others, it is the feeling of being immersed in the work. Some people report they are happiest at work when they lose track of time or become oblivious to their surroundings. The creativity scholar Mihaly Csikszentmihalyi (1990) referred to the state as **flow**, which he defined as the total involvement in activity that one performs for its own sake. All abilities and skills are used to their utmost, and the person typically is completely engaged so that time does not matter.

360-degree feedback

Multiple reports on one's performance from other employees in the workplace. Typically collected anonymously, the reports are treated as feedback information for the focus employee and are not necessarily a part of the official evaluation process that leads to raises, promotions, and job assignments.

flow

Mental state characterized by intense focus or concentration on a task and virtually no awareness of time passing or of local events or setting.

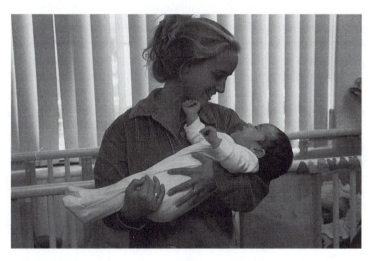

A key element of self-knowledge is awareness of when, where, and how one is most satisfied, such as when providing direct care to infants.

Knowing about your own flow state does not mean identifying a career path or a single pursuit for the rest of your life. You may have many flow states ahead of you! And you may *not* have experienced such a mental state yet. For our purposes in making a self-evaluation of the internship experience, we can draw on the principles of flow noted in Table 7-10 and help to establish some

Table 7-10 **Principles of Flow: You and the Task**
Your personal skill level matches the task's challenge.
You already have an understanding of the task's requirements.
Your mind may go blank or in a trance or become perfectly relaxed preflow.
Your focus on the task involves complete concentration and commitment.
Your creative thinking puts the task above the day's mundane matters.
You experience immediate feedback (which keeps you in the flow).
Your focus on the task removes any focus on yourself.
Your satisfaction is high and your enjoyment is high.
You are immersed in the task and "in the zone."
You seek more tasks that generate flow.

of your preferences and tendencies. Some questions to help identify the preferences can come from the daily intern experience; these include:

What part of the day flies by and what part drags on?

Which offices or rooms do I gravitate toward?

Am I more efficient or less efficient when working alone?

Does working with a partner stimulate me or slow me down?

Does being in a group charge my batteries or drain me?

✳ MEASURING THE PROGRAM

At some internship sites, program evaluation is an obvious activity, but at others, it may be an administrative function that is visible only during reporting times. As an intern, therefore, you might have high participation in activity such as surveying program clients—or never see a single assessment being made. As a working professional, you will surely be involved in evaluation, so whatever opportunity you have now to observe or help facilitate evaluation at the site should be taken. The previous discussion about evaluation of the intern is not unrelated to the larger picture of program evaluation. With some overlapping vocabulary, new terms form a **lexicon** that is general enough to apply to most evaluation processes.

Reasons for Program Evaluation

Virtually all organizations today include **accountability** in their processes and publications and, sometimes, even embed the word in their mission statements. Accountability refers to the organization's ability to demonstrate that its work is sound and that activity is appropriate to the purpose of the organization. For example, a school district is accountable for the direction of educational activities for children in the community, for the responsible expending of funds, and ultimately for the academic performance of the students. A system of reports,

lexicon

Specialized vocabulary, or stock of terms, that is applicable in a particular profession, field of study, or style of work.

accountability

Responsibility of an agency or institution to do the job it is charged with.

audits, and evaluations must be developed whereby the school district can demonstrate that it is responsibly carrying out its charge.

Another common word in organizations' mission statements is **effectiveness**. This concept is a usual indicator to report on accountability, but there is great variation in how institutions define effectiveness. Some may put it in economic terms, meaning that programs or processes are efficient and cost-effective. Another use is to identify outcomes as being effective: the preservice teachers' training will be evaluated in terms of teaching performance in the K−12 classroom after graduation. In program evaluation, the usual meaning of program effectiveness is that the participants were well served or that their needs were met. A simple shorthand definition is also appropriate: *effectiveness* means it works, whether *it* is a program, a training, or the delivery of a service.

Often a program's effectiveness is so well known to the professionals that evaluation is not conducted (or is partially conducted but not in a systematic manner). This seeming contradiction is understandable in terms of program pressures: professionals and programs may be underfunded and, therefore, unable to get everything done. Not willing to cut short time and services for clients, they let evaluations and reports go untended. Thus, documentation of program effectiveness has frequently been lacking in community programs, and yet, this documentation is key to maintaining funding because of accountability requirements.

The heart of documentation is a report on the program's objectives as to whether they were met or unmet (Muraskin, 1993). What happens to that documentation is just as important as creating it: documentation will have value only if it is shared. Professionals may have several purposes for sharing, and those may change over time. For example, an initial report may serve to set benchmarks for a program. With repeated offerings, a program is likely to be improved, and the documentation about effectiveness can drive the necessary changes. This is typically called **formative evaluation**. By the end of a program's life, accountability standards call for a **summative evaluation** that will summarize, analyze, and report a judgment about the value of the program. Such an evaluation cycle may lead to the renewal of a program or the creation of new programs based on the experience gained by the program. Figure 7-2 offers a flowchart of this evaluation and assessment process.

The Processes, People, and Products of Program Evaluation

The process of program evaluation starts in the program's planning stage rather than as an ending to the program. A first evaluation, called **needs assessment** or *needs analysis,* establishes the basic design of a program and may even determine whether a program is required. Whether the program is intended for community or classroom, there are basic considerations to survey for: who will benefit from the program; what are their needs; how are program supports best delivered; how will the processes of the program be evaluated; and how will everyone know if the program succeeds? Results of the needs assessment may not provide the full information required for program design, but it can provide the starting point for design work.

You can think of evaluation as a means for providing constant feedback all along the life cycle of a program. Feedback puts the emphasis on the process of the program, implying that we don't have to wait for a product. This is exactly correct: formative evaluation that is ongoing not only allows examination

---

effectiveness

How well a program or initiative accomplishes its goals or aims.

formative evaluation

Ongoing assessment of a program's effectiveness and other measures of performance.

summative evaluation

Final assessment of a program's effectiveness and other measures of performance, typically conducted at the end of a program's total life cycle and typically shared with interested parties.

needs assessment

Analysis of initial conditions to determine the need, scope, and feasibility of a program.

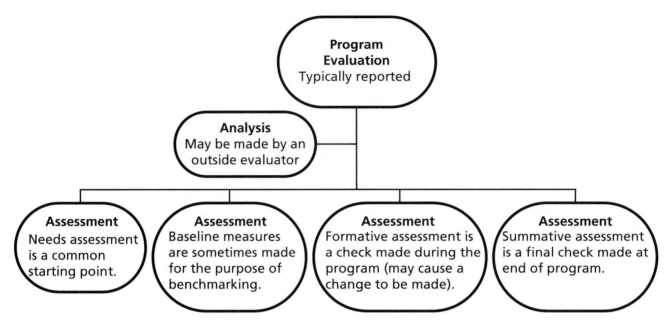

Figure 7-2 A program evaluation and assessment process flow chart.

continuous improvement

Program goal of ongoing improvement in terms of more efficient processes or more effective outcomes.

stakeholders

The people who care about the accountability and effectiveness of a program.

of the process as it occurs (as the program is delivered), but also allows adjustments to be made to the process. Some programs specify **continuous improvement** as a goal of evaluation, and that may refer to improvement along the way (through formative evaluation) or improvement between program cycles (through summative evaluation).

Evaluation is made of the outcomes (intended and unintended) of programs. They may be identified concretely as deliverables. In most human service areas, the evaluation model is participant-centered, meaning that the program is measured in terms of the outcomes for clients. But even when defined as outcomes-based, aims frequently extend to the outcomes expected by more **stakeholders** than only the clients. Among the people who have a stake in the program and, therefore, care about its accountability and effectiveness are the following:

- Funders, donors
- Sponsors, referrers
- Customers, clients, consumers
- Elected representatives
- Policy makers
- Program staff
- Agency staff
- Taxpayers
- Community citizens

Program evaluators can include any of the stakeholders, but in the main, evaluators are specialists who bring an objective (and trained) eye to the process. Most grant-funded programs today designate a portion of the budget for evaluation, and this makes the use of professional evaluators likely. A choice that varies from program to program is the use of internal evaluators, external evaluators, or both. As the words suggest, internal evaluators are employees of the agency or institution, while external evaluators are consultants who work for another entity. Some funders express preference for external evaluators because they will presumably have no self-interest to protect in making a full and authentic assessment of the program. But institutions may prefer to have their own in-house professionals make evaluations. To protect against biased evaluations, the internal evaluators may not be active players in the program. For example, school districts frequently maintain a staff for evaluation and testing. As district employees, evaluators may know the system very well, but still have an objective approach to individual programs because the evaluation office is in a different division or branch of the organization. An evaluation staff may include researchers, statisticians, analysts, and technical writers.

Typical Programmatic Evaluation Measures

What are typical programmatic evaluation measures? In a specific field, there may be existing standards and accreditations. For example, the NAEYC accreditation for child care facilities is so well known that its standards are widely published and taught. It may serve as a guide to evaluation measures even for centers that do not seek NAEYC's official accreditation. At the community level, the United Way agency may be a leading source for guidance on outcome assessments. Programs supported by tax dollars are likely to have measures outlined for them by government offices (at both federal and state levels). All of the following indicators can be found in the thousands of annual reports published every year to address program accountability.

- Attendance at programs
- Cost (often in terms of dollars per client)
- Standardized tests of effectiveness (testing learning gains, for example)
- Validated instruments to measure client's attitude or personality trait
- Evaluation of facilitators in terms of qualifications and effectiveness
- Client/customer satisfaction (often documented through surveys)
- Grass-roots involvement in selection of programs
- Empowerment of local clients to help shape their own programs
- Visibility in the community (how aware of the program are individuals, from the county judge to the person on the street)

Standards and Safeguards of Effective Evaluation

Programs can draw from many different evaluation models, but the common theme should be improvement. In other words, evaluation is a process whereby program weaknesses can be seen and changes can be made. Setting goals that are 100% achievable may not produce the evaluation that drives self-improvement. Sometimes we have an urge to set the bar low so that we are assured of scoring 100%. But that sort of evaluation does not give us new information about the program. Thus, it does not drive improvement.

There is another place to look for 100% scores: what outcomes are so important to the program that we must check for and strive for 100% compliance or learning? Think of this example: flight training for pilots requires 100% learning because everyone must know how to land a plane. At the agency or program, what must everyone know or be accomplished at? What skills must a teacher have at the 100% level?

With authentic goal setting comes the responsibility to select appropriate evaluation methodology. A program aimed to improve skills (in parenting, for example) should measure the skill level, probably at the start of the program and again at the end of the program. This type of pretest/posttest design presents a potential assessment trap: the gain score that may not reflect a program-induced difference. A higher score on the posttest might result from familiarity with the test because it was also used as the pretest. A gain in points could also be due to chance, a particular problem of programs that have a small sample size. Finally, a gain score may be the result of the social desirability effect, whereby participants perform on the test to please the facilitator while the performance does not reflect the real skill or commitment to put the skill to work. Although gain scores can be misleading, a sound evaluation plan can, nevertheless, safeguard against measurement error and report on whether skills were built. A follow-up test, perhaps six months after the program's end, can check on long-term retention of skills, which may be the preferred aim of the program. Many programs are not able to include follow-up evaluations due to attrition: the sample will be smaller as time passes due to people moving or simply deciding not to participate in the program any longer. Such challenges to program evaluation mean that facilitators must be prepared to make multiple measurements of program effectiveness. Additional assessments could include baseline measures, attitude scales, diagnostic tests, and observations.

Many programs collect data on program satisfaction, which is easier to demonstrate than skill building but doesn't necessarily speak to the effectiveness of the program. Typically assessed with a **self-report instrument**, satisfaction is, thus, a subjective measure. In some programs, satisfaction may have high value. For example, a job training program for adults may appropriately be judged by how satisfied the attendees are. Presumably, satisfaction would be reflected by high scores in "adequate preparation for the job" or "satisfactory training in order to be a competitive job applicant." In effect, the satisfaction measure is trustworthy because the adult making the report has concluded that either the training did or did not help the adult in getting a job. By contrast, a satisfaction measure by children might not be appropriate if the young attendees are not mature enough to judge the effectiveness of training.

At certain points of a program, a satisfaction measure is the most appropriate evaluation to make: to ensure that logistics are suitable for the audience. A short survey can help facilitators review times, locations, and similar practical concerns. Thus, a check on satisfaction can sustain a program, especially if participants have not spoken up about their preferences. An old joke from parenting education describes the risk, that dissatisfied parents will "vote with their feet," meaning that rather than speak up about their complaints, they will use their feet and walk out (and not return).

In addition to the variety of assessments, there is a variety of data collection methods possible. Surveys and questionnaires can be distributed in paper-and-pencil format (through the mail or in-person) or on-line. Facilitators or evaluators can also gather information through interviewing program participants. Interviews are, by their nature, a costlier means of data collection than surveys. But the qualitative data collected through interviews may be richer than the quantitative data of questionnaires and can provide needed information about the program and the participants. Group interviews, conducted in focus groups of six to 12 participants who are similar in some way, create another dynamic that generates valuable information.

self-report instrument

Measurement tool that the person fills out or answers without assistance. Common self-report instruments are print and on-line surveys.

Surveys and questionnaires can be distributed to participants in person, via e-mail, or via regular mail.

The following list summarizes standards and safeguards of evaluation that are likely to be found in most programs.

Systematic plan providing for both formative and summative evaluation. While the overall plan may call for ongoing or continuous evaluation, there will be certain points at which results will be analyzed and reports will be written. These points will mark the cycle of evaluation and serve as deadlines or goal dates. A cycle may be described as a five-year plan or 10-year plan, for example, if it is tied to overall strategic planning of the organization.

Needs assessment or needs analysis. An early evaluation to establish the need for and scope of a program may be run as a formal measurement sampling multiple stakeholders. But it is often an analysis created by staff members using published statistics or making a review of the published literature on the subject.

Benchmarks. Starting points, or known levels of performance, serve as comparisons for measurements taken at the end of a program. Benchmarks are sometimes set through pretesting before the program begins.

Pilot program or pilot test. A pilot is a small-scale effort that serves as a trial and, therefore, allows changes before being conducted for a larger population. A pilot program is run with a small group of people for a limited time; similarly, a pilot test or pilot instrument is administered to a small group of people so that results can be checked for reliability and validity. In both types of pilots, the participants may be invited to comment on processes so that the pilot is evaluated for ease of use, for example, as well as for its reliability and validity.

Model of evaluation. Use of widely accepted models assures that evaluation reports will be understood and respected by all stakeholders. For example, a model that focuses on outcomes will have greater meaning than a simple report of attendance numbers.

Choice of evaluators. Identifying evaluators who are a good fit for a program may mean going outside the staff to employ external evaluators. When interval evaluators are used, the report should acknowledge that and explain why they were the best fit.

Permission to collect data. Responsible evaluators assure that they will conduct their work ethically, with the consent of the participants (even when participants submit responses anonymously). If children are the participants, their assent is sought, along with consent by their legal guardians. The entire plan for data collection may need to be reviewed by a governing board or an institutional review board. These supervising bodies may require extensive documentation of evaluation processes; typically, permission of a board is required before any data collection commences.

Multiple measures and methods. Over time, a long-term evaluation plan uses multiple measures and also multiple methodologies. Through triangulation, results are confirmed, and evaluators can draw sound conclusions. When a long-term plan is in place, evaluators can schedule both quantitative and qualitative measures, assuring that data are varied and complementary. Also, multiple sources of data can be utilized.

Adequate sample size. A common problem in program evaluation is sample size. If a program is conducted many times and its content is standard, results from consecutive evaluations can be aggregated or combined. For example, a survey from only six participants has limited meaning (beyond the scope of that small group). But if six participants are surveyed in each of 10 programs using the same curriculum and the same survey, the aggregated sample would be 60 participants. The aggregated results would be more likely to allow conclusions about the program's effectiveness than any one of the ten surveys.

Appropriate analyses. Recognized methods of qualitative and quantitative analysis should be used in program evaluation. For example, descriptive statistics may be appropriate for certain quantitative data that cannot be used in inferential statistical tests. Making the appropriate analysis of the data not only allows sound conclusions but also lends credibility to the report when shared with others.

Publication of results. A report of evaluation findings may draw conclusions about program effectiveness and also outline implications for the future (see Table 7-11). Shared results benefit the program and its participants, as well as the community. Colleagues learn from the findings of one program as they plan their own programs.

Profiling the Program

Another measure of a program or agency can be compiled as a profile, a lengthy description that does not necessarily rely on evaluations conducted with participants. As an intern, you can benefit by creating a profile of your organization, and your perspective as a newcomer may produce a superior picture of all the aspects of the organization. The following outline for a profile can be amended to fit most organizations.

> Historical background
>> Date founded, by whom
>> Rationale for creation, mission
> Programs
>> Purposes
>> Audiences, clients
> Stakeholders
>> Funders, community, professionals, clients, families of clients
> Reputation
>> Ranking among like organizations
>> In community
>> Among professionals
>> Visibility within the profession

Table 7-11 **Example of an Evaluation Plan for an Agency**

This evaluation was designed for The Parenting Center (Fort Worth, Texas), for one of its long-standing and successful educational programs.

PEPS (Parenting Education Program in the Schools) is a multiday curriculum on child abuse, family strengths, and resilience. It is known by its nickname, PEPS. Published by the Parenting Center (TPC), PEPS is delivered by TPC staff in metropolitan school districts. Students are in high school Health classes; all classes in the area are visited by the PEPS educators.

PEPS was first introduced in high schools in 1980. More than two decades later, the program underwent an in-depth evaluation. The procedures are described below; they combined new assessments with the historic assessments of the program.

Step 1: Review by the PEPS Program Coordinator

Historically, PEPS has collected evaluative data from students, the classroom Health teachers, and the PEPS educators. These data have been used for program and agency evaluations. For the reevaluation project, the program coordinator **examined several years' data.** She found **trends** that pointed to one conclusion: both students and classroom teachers considered the PEPS curriculum out-of-date.

Step 2: Review by the Agency's Administrative Leadership

The trends in the data were shared with the TPC executive director and the director of programs. These top administrators consulted TPC staff and board members for additional reactions. The administrators decided that the program coordinator had correctly identified a need for action: a consultant was hired as an **outside evaluator** to investigate further and make **program recommendations,** with expectation that the review would include a revised curriculum.

Step 3: Review by the Consultant

The consultant reviewed the curriculum in light of **current research,** comparing PEPS to curricula on similar topics delivered to secondary school students in other parts of the country.

The consultant recommended a **needs assessment** to guide program changes. TPC administrators agreed that a needs assessment would be valuable. Thus, any resulting changes to PEPS would come from **multiple perspectives,** rather than from only the program coordinator. In this case, the needs assessment was geared to the adult **stakeholders,** not the high school students.

Step 4: Needs Assessment

The consultant worked with the program coordinator to outline a **multimethod needs assessment plan** that would be feasible in the summer months when school was not in session. The coordinator withdrew from the project at that point so that respondents would be free to speak frankly about the program. (The stakeholders who were to be included in the needs assessment all knew the coordinator as the primary program administrator.)

The consultant first made a **literature review** of research-based programs and studies related to the same topics (abuse and resilience) and the same population (adolescents). Scholarly literature and curricula were sampled to identify elements of contemporary programs that were comparable to PEPS and its objectives.

A **paper-and-pencil survey** was designed to collect qualitative data from classroom Health teachers. In a four-week period, three dozen teachers were contacted by mail and offered the survey, to be completed **anonymously.** The response rate exceeded 30% but the sample was small. The nature of the data (qualitative), nevertheless, made the results valuable for analysis.

The same survey was revised slightly and administered to PEPS educators. In addition, PEPS educators were invited to participate in **focus group interviews** with the consultant. Two focus groups met and discussed their views about needed program changes.

(Continued)

Table 7-11 *Continued*

Through qualitative **data analysis,** the consultant identified major themes from the two types of stakeholders. She shared the themes and summaries of the data with the program coordinator, who served as an **outside reader** to review the data and provide another interpretation of their meaning. Results of the data analysis guided the consultant in writing curriculum changes.

Step 5: Revision and Review of the PEPS Curriculum

Revisions and additions were made to the PEPS curriculum, with many **checkpoints** along the way to include TPC personnel in the process. New curriculum modules were posted to a Web site available to the administrators at TPC as well as TPC staff members who expressed an interest in the process.

Step 6: Pilot Test of Major Curriculum Modules

The newly created curriculum modules were **pilot tested** in the next semester in selected high school classrooms in one of the school districts already using PEPS. Both the consultant and the program coordinator made classroom presentations of the new material.

Student and classroom teacher evaluations were conducted in the pilot tests; improved reactions by students were noted. The pilot test continued for several weeks in different classrooms to confirm that the improved evaluations by students were the result of the new curriculum and not a particular PEPS educator's delivery of the curriculum.

Additional observations during the pilot testing were made by the agency's program director as well as an experienced PEPS educator. Following those observations, the experienced PEPS educator then tested the new elements in a high school outside of the usual school districts in which PEPS is delivered. Thus, program elements were reviewed by **multiple observers** and tested in **multiple settings.**

Step 7: Refinements to Curriculum Modules

Results of the evaluations and observations made during the pilot testing served as **feedback** to the consultant and program coordinator. The curriculum modules were then refined before being shared with PEPS educators.

Step 8: Training for PEPS Educators

Training in the new curriculum was prepared for both in-service workshops and videotape. All PEPS Educators learned of the study results and the pilot testing in addition to learning the new curriculum modules. A training Web site as well as print notebooks displayed sample scripts to be used in the classroom, visuals and manipulatives to serve as teaching aids, summaries of the research base for all elements of the curriculum, and information about adolescents.

Step 9: Sharing of Results

Besides being shared with the PEPS educators, all **study results** were shared with the agency's administrators and board of directors. Changes in the curriculum were **summarized and published** to a larger audience through articles in the agency newsletter mailed to a wide variety of **stakeholders,** both in TPC and the community.

Step 10: Continued Evaluation

Historically, the PEPS program has used student evaluations of the curriculum, pre- and posttests in first period classes in the high schools, survey evaluations by the Health teachers, and survey evaluations by the PEPS educators. The program continues to use these methods, but with updated pre- and posttests to reflect the new curriculum and with a new design for the student evaluation. The other evaluation tools have withstood the test of time and remain unchanged. With continued evaluation, the program will be able to check both content and processes to continually move from **evaluation to analysis to improvement.**

Growth or expansion/Decline

    Numbers of programs, clients, staff members

    Turning points in growth/decline

        Funding, grants

        Change in director, executive staff

        Change in board of directors, advisory board

        Economic shift in near environment

Physical plant

    Location (chosen or by default on basis of affordability), square footage

    How acquired (or received as gift of space)

    Visibility in neighborhood, in larger community

Infrastructure

    Staffing (size, turnover, composition, male/female ratio, absenteeism)

    Consulting sources

    Investment in physical components

    Investment in technology, including Internet services

Budget

    Size, sources (including fees if paid by clients)

    Grants or funding

    Major expense categories

    Percentage spent on overhead, percentage reaching clients

Processes

    Accountability standards and methods

    Methods of conducting programs

    Style of conducting evaluations, including employee evaluations

    Standards for achieving success

    Safeguards (audits, review board, professional evaluation staff)

    Management method, philosophy

Communication

    Public communications, including public relations

    Marketing communications

    Advertising means (Yellow Pages, ads, Web sites, billboards)

    Publications (print, broadcast, Internet)

⊙ SUMMARY OF CHAPTER CONTENTS

Why Evaluate? Reasons to evaluate include tracking changes or differences, determining mastery of skills or concepts, and comparing with other programs, techniques, or attempts.

Measuring the Intern: An intern can be measured using multiple measures or multiple evaluators, both formally and informally.

    Competencies of the Intern: Competency types are both personal and professional.

Performance Areas: Workplace behavior is assessed across multiple areas with interns rarely expected to score high in all areas.

Scale Items for Evaluation: While indicators or evidences are often consensual across many settings, the indicators may be defined for the individual internship with unique ratings or responses.

Self-Measuring by the Intern: Self-evaluation includes a review of goals, a self-report on competencies, and subjective assessments of what was learned during the internship.

Measuring the Program: Some interns have the opportunity to assist with program evaluation.

Reasons for Program Evaluation: Many organizations evaluate in order to demonstrate that their work is effective and that activity is appropriate to the purpose of the organization.

The Processes, People, and Products of Program Evaluation: The continuous process of program evaluation examines the outcomes (intended and unintended) of programs.

Typical Programmatic Evaluation Measures: NAEYC accreditation standards are an example of measures used to assess quality.

Standards and Safeguards of Effective Evaluation: Safeguards include a systematic plan, needs assessment, benchmarks, a pilot test, appropriate model of evaluation, choice of evaluators, permission to collect data, multiple measures and methods, adequate sample size, appropriate analyses, and publication of the results.

Profiling the Program: At some locations, a profile of the program consisting of a detailed description could be prepared to assess effectiveness.

⊙ DISCUSSION QUESTIONS

1. Reread the opening case study of this chapter, then prepare a three-minute presentation for Yolanda on the benefits of evaluation at her worksite.

2. Describe at least one norm-referenced test you have taken. Describe the limitations of such tests. What standardized tests are used or could be used at your worksite?

3. Compare the process of evaluating interns with evaluation of employees at your site. How are the processes similar?

4. Describe an ideal approach to evaluating an intern. What measures do you think are valid and reliable?

5. What elements of personal competency do you think are most appropriate for evaluation at your worksite? What elements of professional competency are most appropriate?

6. Develop a rubric for evaluating job performance at a worksite other than your own.

7. Give an example of how both nature and nurture have influenced your development as an intern this semester.

8. Compare your self-assessment with your supervisor's assessment of your performance. Why would there be differences?

9. Apply Cooley's concept of the looking-glass self to make a self-assessment. First describe how you think colleagues at the internship site see your performance. Second, describe what judgment colleagues make about your performance. Third, describe your own reaction to that judgment.

10. How do you react to the phrase, "constructive criticism"? Why?

GUIDED PRACTICES

Guided Practices offer structured exercises in critical thinking, observation (including self-observation), synthesis, and self-expression. The title of Guided Practice sums up the purpose of providing a guide: an opportunity that permits practice and does not require a final, ultimate effort.

All of the guided practices can be used by one person or by a group of people. The practices are designed as self-report instruments, meaning that answers are reported by the respondent and not collected by an interviewer or by another person who may speak with or observe the respondent.

There is not a standard amount of time to spend on the exercises. One person may use a guided practice for making a quick check while the next person may choose to spend hours on the same practice. Individual interest in a topic makes a difference in use, as does current need for the topic.

The greatest value is derived when the guided practice is completed with honest answers and observations. Any instrument may generate socially desirable answers, the kind of responses that a person thinks will be acceptable or expected. Especially when related to academic study, an instrument that calls for self-disclosure or self-evaluation risks being answered this way.

Guided Practice:
Sample Rubric for Evaluation of Intern by a Site Supervisor

Performance Areas	Accomplished	Developing	Novice	Unacceptable
1. Personal: Dependability **Is punctual and efficient**				
2. Personal: Dependability **Completes work/projects**				
3. Personal: Cooperation **Works well with people**				
4. Personal: Consideration **Courteous, friendly, and thoughtful**				
5. Personal: Adaptability **Meets new situations calmly**				
6. Personal: Adaptability **Accepts suggestions and criticism**				
7. Personal: Enthusiasm **Eagerly attacks jobs**				
8. Personal: Judgment **Knows when to ask for help**				
9. Personal: Alertness **Is sensitive to others' needs/feelings**				
10. Personal: Emotional Maturity **Is poised and self-controlled**				
11. Personal: Initiative **Starts tasks without prodding**				
12. Personal: Appearance **Is neat and well groomed**				
13. Personal: Appearance **Dresses appropriately**				
14. Professional: Attitude **Evaluates own work**				
15. Professional: Resourcefulness **Is imaginative and creative**				
16. Professional: Resourcefulness **Seeks resources when needed**				
17. Professional: Leadership **Brings out the best in people**				
18. Professional: Leadership **Can coordinate group work**				
19. Professional: Language and Writing **Writes effectively and correctly**				
20. **Overall Performance**				
Comments:				

Guided Practice:
Performance Indicators

Talk with your worksite supervisor about the indicators, evidences, or scale items used to measure each performance area. Include other performance areas appropriate for your worksite.

Competency Type	Performance Area	Indicator, Evidence, or Scale Item
Personal	Dependability	
Personal	Cooperation	
Personal	Judgment	
Personal	Initiative	
Personal		
Personal		
Professional	Resourcefulness	
Professional	Leadership	
Professional	Writing skills	
Professional	Attitude	
Professional		
Professional		

Guided Practice:
Review of Goals

Review your individual, specific goals that you hoped to accomplish at your site. Note some variables that influenced your success on specific goals. Then address the overall questions to help evaluate your experience.

Goal:	Accomplished	Some Progress	Not Accomplished
1.			
2.			
3.			
4.			
5.			

Overall Questions:

How well did my prior knowledge of the agency/site match my activities?

_____

How congruent were my goals with the mission of the agency?

_____

If my goals changed, what were the factors or reasons for change?

_____

What variables influenced my success?

_____

Guided Practice:
Looking-Glass Self

Consider how you appear in the imaginary looking glass at your field experience site. Then, consider how you think others see your conduct at work. The last step is to think about your reaction to how others see you.

How does your reaction influence your performance? Are there things or tasks you do differently because of that perception? How are you influenced by how you view yourself? How is your professional persona developed?

Looking-Glass Self: How Colleagues View My Conduct
First Step— How colleagues see me
Second Step— How colleagues judge my performance
Third Step— How I feel about that judgment

Guided Practice forms are also included on the accompanying CD-ROM.

REFERENCES

Cooley, C. H. (1902). *Human nature and social order.* New York: Scribner's.

Costa, P. T., & McCrae, R. R. (1997). Personality trait structure as a human universal. *American Psychologist, 52,* 509–516.

Csikszentmihalyi, M. (1990). *Flow: The psychology of optimal experience.* New York: Harper & Row.

Goldberg, L. R. (1990). An alternative "description of personality": The Big Five factor structure. *Journal of Personality and Social Psychology, 59,* 1216–1229.

McCrae, R. R., & Costa, P. T. (2003). *Personality in adulthood: A five-factor theory perspective.* New York: Guilford.

Muraskin, L. D. (1993). *Understanding evaluation: The way to better prevention programs.* Washington, DC: U.S. Department of Education.

For additional material and resources to complement this chapter, the Online Companion Web site can be accessed at http://www.earlychilded.delmar.com.

CHAPTER 8

After the Internship

CASE STUDY: As her internship at Early Childhood Intervention (ECI) drew to a close, Christy felt sad—and worried. She enjoyed having a professional identity and being treated like a real ECI worker. Making home visits with the team of specialists made her feel so worthwhile. She loved the warm way a family greeted the workers when they arrived to work with a child. Whenever anyone asked how the internship was going, she truthfully answered with enthusiasm. However, she hadn't told the whole story. While she enjoyed being a team member, she knew she didn't have enough skills to meet the job description on her own. Also, she wasn't sure if she really wanted to work with very young children. She had always pictured herself working with adolescents.

The problem was that graduation was looming. She knew what would make her family happy: for her to stay in the area and to have a job waiting after graduation. But without knowing what type of job to apply for, Christy's indecision and frustration grew to include even uncertainty about where she wanted to live.

The week before graduation, Christy decided to drop by the office of her internship instructor. She asked, "Is it too late to begin career counseling?" The instructor was sympathetic to Christy's situation but did not have a magical three-step solution to reduce Christy's anxiety.

The instructor did offer confirmation that many college graduates go through a transition from school to employment—and the transition varies from individual to individual.

✳ SELF-ASSESSMENT AND REFLECTION

While some students may think of the internship as the culminating experience of college, you can also think of it as a beginning point. The internship may launch your career—or may launch your career search. After the internship comes self-assessment and reflection of how to put the field experience to best use. This time of reflection can help you in the decision making process revolving around a myriad of questions, such as what to do and where to live. It's not unusual to begin the job search process feeling overwhelmed by all the choices. How can you find the perfect job? How will you know if it's the right job for you? One important thing to remember is that you don't have to find the *perfect* job—or at least not right away. Most people today expect to change jobs several times in their work career. You don't have to know the answer to all those hard questions immediately. Sometimes it helps if you look for *a right job* rather than *the right job.* Think about what will meet your needs now or where you can make a difference now.

Career-Matching Criteria

One approach to narrowing down the search for a job is to use a strategy of matching. You can deliberately implement such a strategy on your own or locate professional help. For example, career consultants might try to match your

One approach to narrowing down the search for a job is to use a strategy of matching one's interests, such as a love of crafts, with a particular job choice.

interests and personality type with job choice. The tools used to make these matches are called *interest inventories, personality profiles, skill identifiers, type matching instruments,* and so forth. There is not a single best instrument that answers all needs. Thus, if you decide to pursue this type of testing, you will probably use several instruments. Some tests are *forced choice* questionnaires, meaning that you must choose between optional answers. An example might be answering whether you prefer to work inside an office with windows or to work outside without a desk. Other personality matching tests are written more like multiple-choice tests that you have taken in school. Results may come in the form of scores or categories, and some even sort you into a color coding. You might be told what clusters or groups of jobs best match your personality type or your color coding.

Critics of these instruments warn that a person can skew his or her own scores by intentionally playing a role while answering. Instrument designers acknowledge that the tests' validity rests with the person's willingness to answer questions honestly. No single instrument should be the authority on your suitability for an occupation. Avoid overreliance on the test; you will not have a definitive answer after taking a test or even after taking several tests. It's also possible for your scores or results to change at different points in your life. The value of such testing is in the exploration and the thinking time that results. Going through the process of reflecting and answering the questions helps you to know more about yourself.

Career testing and career inventories are also available on the Internet, many of them for free. The reports are typically produced instantly and provide explanations of how you may fit employment categories or workplace environments. Just as a career counselor advises that a test result should not be considered absolute, these Web-based instruments couch their results in terms of possibilities and ideas for you to think about. Don't expect highly valid results from free on-line quizzes. You can use them as an exploratory tool.

It's a good idea to use multiple sources of data in determining your job profile. Researchers call this process triangulation. In this case, triangulation could be consulting with a college advisor, consulting with family members, taking standardized matching instruments, visiting with a career counselor or life coach, and even interviewing with an employment agency. Your own view of self is one piece of data that is well supplemented by other perspectives and data from other sources. Sometimes others can identify your strengths and gifts more clearly than you can.

Assessing Likes and Dislikes

Reflection on the best and worst of the internship and your other work experiences can guide your career planning. During the internship, did you find yourself absorbed in certain projects or activities to the point that you lost track of time? Were there certain days that you stayed beyond the required workday? Did you look forward to returning each day? Look back over your journals or logs for your most positive statements. These signs indicate that the worksite was a good match and may point you in the direction of a career choice. By the same token, if you cannot answer positively to those questions, you have an indication of the need to search further.

Even though you may not have positive feelings about the particular site, probe deeper before eliminating the type of work or career field. You might not have enjoyed the student teaching experience in that specific classroom, with that group of students or with that supervising teacher—but you might still want to be a teacher. Try to ask yourself what has contributed to your feelings of liking

Reflection on the best and worst of the internship can guide the intern's career planning.

the site or disliking the site. If possible, separate your feelings about the site (including specific clients or supervisors) from your feelings about the work itself.

After going through much reflection and analysis of your feelings during the internship, you could eliminate some settings or types of work. An unhappy internship experience could be a turning point for the individual who realizes that the intended career was chosen to please someone else. Or perhaps you always thought you wanted to work with adolescents but learned that you have a unique talent for working with toddlers. Gaining this self-knowledge can help you make deliberate choices about your career path. If the internship has not been a good match, think about other jobs or hobbies that do provide satisfaction. What do you choose to do when you have free time, when you have a choice about your activity? Can that activity be found in a job? The activity probably isn't simply fun and easy—it is likely to hold challenge for you, and this becomes a good measure of something you would enjoy doing over time.

Workplace setting is an important part of your choice of employer, and your experience in the internship will inform this choice. Did you work in an open office with many people in view? Was that stimulating or distracting? Your preferred amount of contact with other people can drive a job choice.

Another key factor is the match between your personal mission in life and the purpose of the workplace. You might have chosen an organization for a field experience because of its unique mission statement or purpose. After working there, perhaps you found that the intended clients were not well served and that the beneficiaries were really the managers or supervisors rather than the people needing services. That experience might have made you realize that you want to work directly with the clients rather than with the middle man. Reflecting on your internship experience in this light can inform your job search and yield better results.

A different approach to career choice after college is to travel or participate in service learning. Programs, such as Americorps*VISTA, Teach for America, and Peace Corps, offer a wide variety of experiences and some include training. These programs may not pay much, but they provide opportunity to learn more about yourself and the world. They offer sponsorship and support, which may be important to people who would hesitate to travel on their own or move to a new part of the country. You could also acquire or strengthen language skills, which are highly valued in most job settings. Longer-term commitments include military service. Civilian employment through the military is also a possibility; child care directors, classroom teachers, family advocates, and family service professionals all are found on military bases throughout the world. Children's activity directors and child care teachers are also needed on cruise ships and at resorts. For some child and family professionals, these are short-term jobs featuring travel before making decisions about where to live permanently.

Some students see the post-college years as an opportunity to explore interests and hobbies to combine with their careers. Your talent in working with children might lead to a career as a photographer specializing in children's portraits. A love of the outdoors could result in being a camp director or even establishing your own camp. In making your career decisions, don't overlook your hobbies or activities that you might have long pursued in your spare time. Those activities are clues to what is most important to you.

One additional way to find out about yourself is through volunteering. If you think you would like to be a child life specialist but aren't sure if you are suited to work in a hospital and be around sick people, volunteer in a local hospital or hospice. If you are unsure of your patience with children, volunteer in an after-school tutoring program. If you are interested in being an advocate for children but aren't sure about your commitment, volunteer as a Big Brother or Big Sister for one-on-one time with children of different ages. Most local agencies, and even some local newspapers, have volunteer matching services that could help you find a place for your service, on a long-term basis or short-term assignment. You might want to serve meals in a homeless shelter during the holidays, an example of a short-term volunteer role. In addition to providing needed help, you would learn about future career options and could meet new mentors. Sometimes volunteering your services for free can help you find a paying job within the same agency; you can demonstrate how valuable your skills are and what a contribution you can make.

If an intern is unsure of his patience with children, he could volunteer in an after-school tutoring program.

Quality of Life Indicators

The community you will join is just as important as the employer you choose. While you might think you can be happy anywhere ("I'll go wherever the job is!"), that may not be the case. Following the job may still be necessary, but a working knowledge of the location can narrow the gap between expectations and reality. Think about the type of community that is needed for your quality of life. Experts use a variety of indicators to rate or compare living conditions in different areas. Depending on your stage of life or main interests, some of the variables will not matter to you while others will be of primary concern. The cost of living in a certain community and the climate are usually considered critical to most people. The cost of living will impact the availability of affordable housing. Related to that might be the median income in the area (the midpoint with half the people having income above that amount and half the people having income below that amount). The cost of living might be a more important factor than the actual amount of salary you are quoted in a job offer.

Understanding the long-term effects of environment and climate might include awareness of number of days of rain, length of seasons, amount of sunshine, and altitude. A health condition may require that you seek a dry climate. Some areas are more prone to extreme weather such as hurricanes and tornadoes; some states regularly experience earthquakes. Ask yourself what your own preferences are. You might not know how much you would miss the sun until you move to an area with daily rain. Knowing your own tolerance for these extreme conditions will help you prioritize geographic areas.

Other considerations might include the zoning or distance of residential areas from work areas. Are you a born commuter? Can you deal with traffic or long-distance drives on a daily basis? The cost of gasoline and car maintenance is only one part of the equation; if you measure a commute in terms of time out of your day, that will be an extra cost. By contrast, if you love to drive, you might see the commute as enjoyable transition time between your home and workplace. If you plan to bike to work, you would likely look for an area that is bike-friendly with trails and designated paths on the streets.

Other transportation considerations include public transportation (bus line, light rail) as well as access to airports. Even the airline routes may be important if your job will involve travel. Maintaining family ties may be a consideration of transportation. Airport proximity can affect travel to family events or the frequency of family members' visits. Are there direct flights available? How easy are the connections?

What kind of a physical environment is important to you? Do you need to see green spaces or mountains? Do you envision yourself hiking on weekends or relaxing on the beach? Landscape and scenery are important to some people but not to others.

For others, weather or climate is not important, but the recreation opportunities are crucial for leisure in nonworking hours. This could include anything from being able to attend sporting events to support your favorite team to your access to cross-country skiing or other recreational facilities. Some students know they want to stay near their college or duplicate the atmosphere of a college town. Low cost concerts are often a feature of college towns, as are cultural events such as art shows, plays, and speaker series.

Size of the community may dictate the number of opportunities for recreation and social events. Size may also be an indicator of density of housing. Seclusion or isolation may not be a disadvantage for you; for others interested in a more active social scene or peers of their own age, research into the age or marital status of residents will be important. Size and location of community may even impact the availability of Internet and cable services. Malls, movie theatres, and restaurants may seem unimportant until you don't have them.

Other services of the community include health care, special schools, and resources such as libraries. Parks, tennis courts, and public swimming pools are some other examples of city services. Less obvious community concerns are crime rate statistics, level of safety and security, and emergency services (police, fire, ambulance). For some people, the overall quality of the school system might be the number one factor in deciding where to live. How are the schools rated? How many people have college degrees? What is the level of support for public education? Are community education courses available?

The most important consideration for you might be ethnic diversity of the community. What does the population look like? Do you see people like you? Do you see a mix of people living and playing together comfortably? If possible, visit some public spaces and watch the people interact. You can also check county and city statistics on government Web sites or even chamber of commerce sites. If you can't visit the community in person, investigate the location as thoroughly as possible before moving or accepting a job there. Your assessment of the quality of life there will have much influence on your overall feeling about the job. Use the Guided Practice "Importance of Community Aspects of a Job" at the end of this chapter to begin your own exploration of job location preference.

The most important quality of life indicator for an intern seeking a position might be ethnic diversity of the community.

✳ THE JOB SEARCH

When you are ready to begin a job search, you will find a specialized vocabulary describing the people and processes. In the employment world, a *headhunter* is a recruiter who specializes in a certain type of professional. Headhunters are typically paid by employers to search and screen job applicants. *Recruiter* is the typical term for a human resources or employment office employee of a company who visits campuses to recruit applicants for only one company.

Employment agencies are businesses that hope to be the connector between job seekers and employers. Some charge fees to the employer and some charge fees to the applicants. If you are approached by an agency and offered help in making applications, you should clarify the cost involved. If a fee is charged, you will want to evaluate the services provided to decide how worthwhile the help is. Don't send money before you have checked out exactly what services you will receive. Be cautious about any agency that offers guaranteed employment. You might not want the jobs they suggest.

Campus Resources

Support for making career choices and learning about yourself is available on most college campuses. Whether called the career services office or employment placement center, specialists offer guidance about applications as well as interest testing, job listings, resume and interview practice, and some even help with clothing choices. Cost for such services is typically free on campuses while a student is enrolled. Like most campus services, the best experience comes from making appointments ahead of time and asking lots of questions. You may find it necessary to make multiple visits and talk to multiple people. Initial results could be limited but follow-up can produce more success.

On-campus interviewing may be scheduled in campuswide job fairs or as networking in your academic department. Teacher Career Day states its purpose clearly. Area school districts send recruiters or human resources staff members to meet with college students. One advantage of going to such fairs is that you will learn about whole categories of employment even if you do not find a fit among the jobs at that fair. Other advantages are listed in Table 8-1.

Strategies for success at job fairs require preplanning on your part. You can usually find the list of participating companies and organizations in advance. Check the university Web site or the career placement office. Do some preliminary research about the companies you are most interested in. Tailor your resume to highlight your skills or interests for jobs at those companies; print at least a dozen copies of your resume to carry with you. Print business cards that give your contact information. The day of the career fair, dress appropriately: business or casual business attire. This may mean a dressier look than your usual classroom attire. Business suits are always appropriate but not necessarily required. Casual business attire refers to slacks and dress shirts. Carry a folder or file to keep your resumes crisp and clean; you will also use the folder to collect business cards and recruiting material from the companies.

At the career fair, set a personal goal of approaching at least two companies or organizations that were previously unknown to you. This will give you the opportunity to describe your skills and practice searching for a fit. What can you

Table 8-1 **Benefits of Campus Employment Fairs**
Exposure to new fields of employment
Practice in introducing yourself
Practice interviews with recruiters
Networking with contacts for follow-up
Learning about trends in employment
Learning about benefits before even applying
Comfortable, low-anxiety setting
Practice describing your personal strengths
Practice in explaining your major or interest
Opportunity to share your resume and get a reaction to it

do for that company? What do they have to offer you? You might be pleasantly surprised that your skills are marketable in a variety of companies or industries.

After the fair, take time to reflect on what you learned and how you presented yourself. An important step is to record the names of recruiters you spoke with. If you decide to follow-up with a company, you will probably want to refer to having spoken with the recruiter at that event.

Off-Campus Networking

Job searches revolve around the completion of application forms and the writing of resumes, but the great majority of job offers come as a result of networking. Of course, the paperwork of searches must still be tended to, but with understanding that they are not the central activity that produces job offers. Tapping into networks is the productive activity. Often students accept a myth of networking that they must join a network in the industry where they seek employment to make direct contact with the person in charge or the decision maker. Or students think they are dependent upon who they already know (friends and family already employed) and, therefore, will never make contact with the right network. These perceptions are not accurate: networks operate by connecting systems. The power lies in the links between one person or system and another. It's not who you know—it's who *they* know.

The great majority of job offers come as a result of networking.

Granovetter (1973) described the source of most job offers as *The Strength of Weak Ties.* Parents and parents' friends may represent strong ties, but the more productive networking emerges from the weak ties—those people who are casual acquaintances or business colleagues two or three levels away from the applicant or the applicant's immediate circle. This circumstance is counterintuitive to most people. We assume that our immediate friends and relatives would be the most supportive and therefore the most helpful. The reason this inner circle cannot be the most productive source is that the people are all too much alike. They are involved in the same activities, they know the same people, and they may even have the same preferences in leisure. In short, the amount of new information is limited.

By contrast, the network that extends through weak ties (occasional visits or contacts, for example) represents much more new information and many more avenues for activity and employment. Different perspectives are more likely, even of the job applicant. Within the inner circle, your current reputation may lock you into one role or at least not allow people to envision you in a new role. In the outer circle of acquaintances, you can be seen as eligible for a new role or recognized as an expert. Some college alumni associations offer sponsored networking for employment, and their services may be available on-line. The Internet version is referred to as social networking and offers the advantage of being able to update your information instantly and also to surf the network to see what connections exist among people you know.

Even though networking produces most job offers, you may need to include making "cold calls" as part of your job search strategy. A *cold call* is a phone call, e-mail, or visit to an employer that is uninvited. You might select two dozen companies to approach with cold calls because of their reputation or because you like their products and use them yourself. Whether the company is large and has an employment office or small and operates from a manager's office, certain business protocol is expected. For some job seekers, making cold calls is very difficult—you may feel awkward talking to strangers and talking about yourself. You may worry that making a cold call is asking for help, but another way to view the call is that you have something to offer the company: your enthusiasm for their products or an interest in their services. Table 8-2 provides a protocol for making effective cold calls.

Phone etiquette, such as speaking and listening carefully, is part of the protocol but should be extended with tips more pertinent to job searching. Be prepared to leave a short and clear message if you reach voice mail; consider what you will do if offered an on-the-spot interview. Dress as if the person you are calling can see you. Some people find it helpful to look into a mirror while

---

Table 8-2 **Protocol for Cold Calls**

Identify a gatekeeper or a manager's name.

Know what you're asking for: internship, entry-level job, or information.

Research the basics to indicate genuine interest on your part.

Practice your self-introduction.

Arrange your own best time and location to make the call.

Ask if your timing is convenient or ask for an appointment.

Take notes and do not trust your memory for addresses, times, etc.

Ask if you may follow up with your resume.

Ask if you may call again in a month.

Thank the individual for taking time to speak with you.

Repeat your name and contact information, spelling it if necessary.

Offer to send a follow-up e-mail with resume as text as well as attachment.

speaking on the phone, aware that facial expression can be communicated through the voice. (Smile!) Even though you may not need it, have your resume within reach, along with a list of your strengths and skills that you could rattle off, if invited to describe yourself. If you have a computer on your desk, that can be a resource for quick information, but it can also be a distraction that could make you sound uninterested. Turn down all competing sound makers, including cell phones and e-mail alerts. Arrange for privacy so that you are not likely to be interrupted by visitors, call waiting, or other distractions.

A detailed search of a single institution or company can make a cold call less intimidating. This search can be conducted efficiently on the Internet. If a specific company or organization does not have a Web site, a search may still yield information. For example, an agency may be profiled on a United Way Web site or other umbrella organization. A school may have its own Web site, or it may be described on a school district Web site.

Internet Research and Resources

The Internet can be used for formal research into employment as well as informal searching. The same strategies recommended for internship searches in Chapter 2, "Placement," can be employed in the job search. Commercial sites dedicated to posting and circulating resumes as well as posting job openings include the well-known Monster.com. Maximizing your exposure on these large sites should include moving beyond the resume. In fact, the value of the Internet is much greater for your own researching rather than for posting your resume. Only a tiny fraction of jobs hired result from an on-line resume; thus, your submission of a resume is just a small part of your job search. (But not one to be skipped!) If you do post your resume, keep in mind the following precautions.

- Make a list of all submissions so that you can return regularly to update or remove the resume.
- Recall that you are intentionally disclosing personal contact information on a public space.
- Keep in mind that your job search intentions potentially become known to everyone (including your current employer).

Job searches at Web sites such as Monster.com, jobsonline.com, and jobbankusa.com can produce jobs lists in the thousands and tens of thousands. Those overwhelming numbers can also bring a search to a screeching halt. The best search is conducted with filters or keywords, so that you do not have to narrow the search repeatedly. For example, a search for "K–12 education jobs" + "New Mexico" + "metropolitan" areas will immediately focus the search. Even more specific keywords may be in order: "Head Start teacher" + "Albuquerque." This very focused search produced seven listings on a popular search engine and also provided related job titles for broadening the search. Related jobs can lead you to other entry-level experiences you might not have tried otherwise. For example, a similar search at Monster .com produced these alternative suggestions: substitute teacher positions and family advocacy program assistant.

Psychologically, the broadening option in an Internet search is less daunting than the narrowing option. When broadening, the searcher is adding slowly to the pool of possibilities; when narrowing, the searcher may despair at ever reaching a manageable number of links to explore. Librarians are experts at making Internet searches, and you can consult them for help, either at a campus library or a community public library. Especially on campuses, we tend

Using specific key words, such as "preschool teacher" + "New York City", will help the intern narrow an Internet job search.

to think of librarians as sources only for academic work, but their training can be applied to any search for information.

One of the most helpful features of employment Web sites is the identification of the length of time the job has been listed. Finding a job listing that is less than a day old (or just 28 minutes old) can boost your interest in following through. Listings usually include the closing dates. These are the deadlines for submitting applications; however, you might still be able to apply if the job has not been filled.

Job fairs, also called career fairs, are frequently listed on the Internet and are worth your time to attend, if only to practice introduction and interview skills. Your university Web site will be one source of information on local fairs.

Virtual interview services with career counselors or career coaches are also available on-line. Either through chat or e-mail, you can submit questions and receive customized advice. Clarify whether there is a charge for such services. A free service used for your own practice is worth your time. Do not expect to receive extensive personal feedback; that sort of support is more likely to be found at your campus career placement center.

Another useful feature of the Internet could be access to the information listed in Table 8-3, such as a personnel directory. A preservice teacher investigating school districts will be more confident calling a principal whose name is confirmed in an on-line directory rather than calling a school office as listed in the telephone book. That teacher is also able to say to the principal, "I have read about your school's exemplary program, and I would like to be a part of such a program." Finding the names and titles of employees will help you to discover commonalities and connections prior to calling for information.

Other criteria to search for include institutional accreditations (such as NAEYC for preschools) and professionals' credentials (such as Certified Family Life Educator, advanced degrees, licensure). Your course work in your major can guide you on quality assurance measures.

Internet searches could be focused on geographic area, occupation title, or industry sector. For example, a graduate in human development who seeks a child life specialist career will begin with a search of the country's pediatric hospitals and the largest metropolitan and research hospitals that serve

Table 8-3 **Internet Search of a School District**
Community demographic profile
Student demographic profile
Individual school Web sites
Qualifications of current teaching staff
Directory of names and contact information
Pay range for beginning teachers
Job descriptions for district personnel
Benefits, such as graduate tuition reimbursement
School calendars for a building as well as the district
On-line homework information/chats
Ratings of the school, test scores
Minutes and agendas of school board meetings
Disciplinary policies and procedures
Student code of conduct, dress codes
Extracurricular opportunities for students
In-service and other training for teachers and staff
Description of physical facilities
Enrollment history and current size of campuses

children. The resulting list of hospitals would then lead to a search of the cities of their locations. Comparisons of Seattle and Boston, even just on basics such as climate and cost of housing, can be made through city Web sites, on-line newspapers, and chamber of commerce Web sites.

Your Support Team during the Search

Both during the job search and through your first few months on the new job, you will benefit often from the involvement of mentors, family, and supportive friends. You will need proofreaders for your resume, fashion advisors to critique interview outfits, sounding boards to listen as you describe pros and cons of job choices, financial advisors (but not negotiators), or financial supporters until that first paycheck comes in. The first few days on a new job feature many decisions about benefits. Sometimes it's hard to focus on decisions, such as long-term life insurance needs or to compare retirement plans, when you are still trying to find out where to park your car. It's often helpful to have a support team to provide advice or to listen.

New employees are sometimes dismayed at how long it is between the first day of work and receipt of the first paycheck. There might be deposits required for a new apartment or other move-related expenses, creating unexpected shortfalls in cash. Before asking the new boss for a loan, think through other options. Maybe a family member or close friend can help. What are the disadvantages of using a debit or credit card? What are your first and last resorts for help? How long can you wait before student loans are due? If you have to travel and rent a car for work, what is the legal age requirement for car rentals? Be prepared with a plan for emergencies, financial and otherwise.

A new job is often overwhelming at the beginning, with potential to create much self-doubt. It's not unusual to question why you took the job or wonder how you'll ever learn as much as the other people who work there. Your support team can help talk you through some of these doubts. You must have some strengths and skills, or you wouldn't have been hired!

Sometimes, the job really is not a good match for you. Maybe the job description did not accurately portray the daily tasks. Or maybe the supervisor who hired you has already moved on before you even start—leaving you with a boss that you aren't well suited to work with. Before quitting, talk to someone in the human resource office or a mentor from your campus. Talk through the problem and see if strategies can be found to create a better situation. Think through how long you should stay before looking elsewhere.

✳ THE RESUME

You are an expert on you. You know what you are good at, but you may not have practice in expressing that. In fact, you almost assuredly have not done a lot of talking about your strengths and your abilities. The resume is the place to put that information.

Articulating your strengths is a process that precedes the writing of the resume. Identify your skills, without discounting something that you might think of as minor or commonplace. You may find yourself stumped at listing your strengths. Try talking to a friend or peer, especially someone who has worked alongside you in the internship, in volunteer work, or in class. Such a friend can help you think through success stories that depict your abilities. You may also find that you trust a mentor or teacher in this role. For most people, an outsider is more acceptable than a family member as a partner in making this assessment with you. While a parent or sibling may know you very well and be able to articulate your strengths, you may find yourself resistant to the family member's comments. You may wonder if a family bias is producing the assessment; even when this is not the case, your perception may work against you and make you discount what is said.

Personal Success Stories

Identifying your success stories may start with a review of the facts on your resume. If the resume lists your part-time job of two or three years with the same company, what success does that indicate? It speaks to your stability in a part-time entry-level job and demonstrates your dependability. It takes maturity to fit into a workplace for so long. Just knowing that you showed up on time can be a big plus to the prospective employer.

A friend may know about a hobby or activity unique to you and be able to elaborate on how that relates to your job search. For example, your mention of bicycle riding as a hobby may be only that—a mention. But your friend knows that you rode from Austin to Anchorage as a fund-raising effort for a charity. The perseverance demonstrated by this activity represents a success story that would impress a recruiter or interviewer. Such a story becomes a way for the recruiter to remember you; you will stand out from all the other applicants with similar qualifications.

Success stories represent transferable characteristics to the workplace. You may not be able to share the stories until you are in an interview, but the basics of the stories should appear in the resume. For example, by listing bike riding and charity fund-raising as interests on the resume, you have provided the key words for later telling a success story. Success stories are the events that were milestones for you, the turning points of your life. They are worthy of sharing and being documented in the resume.

Finding Words to Describe Yourself

Descriptions such as *enthusiastic* and *cooperative* need additional information. What is it that you are enthusiastic about? When are you cooperative? When you extend your descriptions with the actual context or setting you mean, you communicate more useful information (see Table 8-4).

When potential employers read your descriptor in the resume, will they also find evidence of it? For example, if you ended the resume with the descriptor, "dedicated to child wellness initiatives," is that dedication reflected in another part of the resume? Is there a volunteer task force or summer job that clearly relates to child wellness?

For child and family professionals, it can be difficult to communicate an outstanding aptitude for interpersonal relationships. Frankly, everyone in this field could say, "relates well to people." You will have to describe specific characteristics that indicate your unique strengths to anyone who reads your resume. The Guided Practice at the end of the chapter, "Specifying Context for Resume Self-Descriptors," will help you identify descriptors that need contextual description.

Style of Resume

The resume is a biographical representation of your work and education. In education, it may be referred to as a *curriculum vita;* in public relations, it may be referred to simply as a *bio.* The different names suggest that this representation is used differently in the settings. This is certainly true. The academic-oriented curriculum vita is a detailed document that may run a dozen pages by the time a person has completed graduate school. The employment-oriented resume is

Table 8-4 **Context for Descriptors**	
Cooperative	Cooperative in large and small groups
Dedicated	Dedicated to child wellness initiatives
Enthusiastic	Enthusiastic about working with families
Optimistic	Optimistic about positive outcomes for abuse victims
Patient	Patient with parents as they learn appropriate guidance techniques

typically recommended to run just one or two pages. The publicity-oriented bio is usually somewhere in between.

In the job search, your resume can be customized several times so that it is targeted to specific employers. You will highlight different skills or experiences for each opportunity. The basic information should be the same, of course, and that begins with a professional-looking heading that includes your most reliable points of contact. An e-mail address can help establish your image with the employer: if possible, use your university or college e-mail address.

Styles of resume are chronological and categorical. Variations on these two styles can be seen in an Internet search of the many resume help sites that now exist. If you have an extensive work background already, the chronological resume may make sense for you. The usual order is most recent job on top, working backward in time so that your earliest work experience will be at the bottom. There is no firm rule about what to leave out of the resume, but it should match the same work history you would provide on a job application. For education history, list your current degree even if you have not graduated: "Bachelor of Science, Expected Graduation August 2009." If you had a high GPA or if you were named on the dean's list, that information can be listed alongside the degree.

The categorical resume (sometimes called *functional resume*) presents your strengths and interests. This style is appropriate for the person who has no or little paid work history. Section headings can highlight what makes you a good choice for a particular job. For example, an application to a private school might include the resume with these headings: "Education," "Volunteer Work in Head Start," "Campus Leadership Roles."

Content of Resume

A common first element for the resume is a short statement of your career goal. You can try writing it as a complete sentence or as a phrase. You can also think of the goal as being near future, not far future. Compare these statements and consider which works for your situation.

Near future: Entry-level position as Head Start assistant teacher

Far future: Professional career in early childhood education

The words in the career goal should be congruent with elements in the resume.

The goal should be realistic and appropriate for someone at your skill or experience level. A widely shared resume may skip such an opening statement. The goal statement may be added when the resume is being sent to a targeted audience. This keeps the goal statement fresh and relevant for carefully selected recipients.

For prospective teachers, the resume or job application may need to include a philosophy of teaching. A one-sentence statement may suffice in a resume. Do not include a full statement of philosophy unless that has been specifically requested. If submitting a teaching philosophy, use only your own words. Quotes from books or well-known persons are not appropriate, either in a philosophy or on a resume. (Similarly, such quotes should not appear in e-mail stationery.)

The length of your resume should be based on your purpose and your audience. A common error is to write a five-page resume in an effort to be as complete as possible. But if your audience is company recruiters who throw away anything that comes with a staple, your resume will not even be read. A common advice is to write the resume on one 8.5 × 11 sheet of paper.

A common first element on the resume is a short statement of the intern's career goal, such as "professional career in early childhood education."

Exclude personal information in the resume. A potential employer wants to focus on your qualifications and not be distracted by details such as marital status, age, weight, family composition, or religious preference. Photographs are usually not recommended.

Just as important as the content is the accuracy of the information. Be sure that you do not exaggerate or misrepresent any details about your experience or training. Double-check your dates of employment, grade point average, degrees received, and job titles. Lying and misleading potential employers can cause many problems when detected.

Selecting and Recruiting References

Selecting references (and then securing them) involves thinking through who can address your suitability for a position. All of these people are potential references: former or current employer (can include part-time jobs or occasional work such as babysitting), college advisor, internship supervisor, professor, sponsor of honor society or other campus organization, supervisor of volunteer work, former or current coach. Relatives are not usual choices, but friends of the family may provide a credential or connection that makes their appearance as reference appropriate.

You may or may not use the same three references for every job application. When time allows, you can ask particular people who match the field. For example, in an application for youth director in a faith-based organization, you could request references from your church or temple. This example could also call for a reference from your Scouting experience in your adolescence. In a different setting, more recent references might be the better choice. Consciously evaluating all potential references puts you in the position to make the best choice for each application.

Secure permission before listing the person's name on a reference form, application, or resume. You should know your reference well enough to know if permission should be sought in person, through telephone, or through e-mail. If your request includes a letter of recommendation, some references will want to be asked for each use of the letter; others will provide you with a general letter that you can use multiple times. When you ask someone to serve as a reference or write a letter, allow time for a response. This may mean that you need to begin contacting references even before you decide on where to send your applications. If you are asking for a reference from professors, consider the best time to capture their attention. Avoid obvious busy weeks such as start and end of semesters; avoid holidays and semester breaks. A query could be phrased, "if you feel you can make a positive recommendation of me." If a professor hesitates, that should be your cue that another selection is in order.

Supply your reference person with a copy of your resume and a brief description of the specific job or type of job you are seeking. Remind the person of how he or she knows you. For example, what classes did you have with that person, or what years were you an employee, or what office did you hold in the campus organization? Having this context will permit the reference person to provide more details about your skills and abilities. If you have reminded the person of a specific project or achievement, the recommendation can describe your suitability for a particular position.

In arranging for a letter of recommendation, specify when and where you need the letter. Electronic? Print? Letterhead? Some employers require that letters of recommendation be mailed directly from the reference or be delivered in a sealed envelope (typically with a signature across the seal). By contrast, some employers accept reference letters in electronic formats.

Presentation of Resume

Imagine an employer receiving your presentation, whether that is an electronic or print copy of your resume or an entire portfolio. What tone is communicated by the e-mail address, as an example? Is it professional sounding? Is it easy to reproduce if the employer must type it into e-mail? The ideal e-mail address identifies your name accurately. Your goal is for the employer to remember your name and be able to contact you easily, without frustration at decoding an e-mail address.

If your cell phone or landline number is listed and the employer called it, what message would this person hear on your voice mail? Is it even your voice? Perhaps you use a default message that came with your phone system, or perhaps you had a friend record a welcoming message. Listen to that recording as if you were a potential employer and consider what the message communicates. A humorous message or music may not be appropriate during the job search.

Your college may provide personal Webspace where your resume can be displayed, or you may have your own Web page. If you link to a personal Web site, be sure that all of the contents are such that you would wish a potential employer to view. If you have a profile in Facebook or MySpace, consider temporarily removing or altering personal information. Ask a mentor to preview the pictures posted in order to have a second opinion on acceptability for professionals. Conduct a vanity search of yourself on-line to learn what others will find if they google your name. Make the search through several search engines.

The opening of your resume or portfolio is likely to be a cover letter, designed to introduce you to the potential employer. This letter should clearly identify the position you are applying for and state why you are seeking that position or why you would be a good fit for that position. The cover letter should be just that: to cover. Think of it as a title page or a very short table of contents: refer to the attached resume or other materials in the packet. Whenever possible, address the cover letter to a specific person (instead of "To Whom It May Concern"). If you met that person at a job fair or conference, refer to the meeting briefly, "As we discussed last month in Atlanta at NAEYC, I am submitting an application…" The cover letter is ideally just two or three paragraphs. It should be concise and focused.

Print or electronic? You need both. Sometimes you need to be able to put a print copy of your resume in someone's hand. Job fairs and in-person interviews are the obvious settings, but you may also need to have a print resume to mail to the employer. Some agencies cannot receive attachments to e-mail and, therefore, rely on your having a print version; some people prefer hard copy to an electronic version. By designing your materials from the start in both print and electronic formats, you will be able to provide the preferred version at any time. Of course, a priority for all versions is careful proofreading so that your presentation reflects your professionalism.

Specs for the Printed Resume. Some standard **specs** for resumes are provided below. The Internet provides numerous guides and samples of resumes; comparing your own first effort with published examples will help you critique your resume before you submit it anywhere. Recall that your campus may provide free resume-writing consultation or service.

> ✳ **specs**
> Shorthand for specifications, the details such as size, color, weight of paper.

Size: 8.5 × 11 paper is the only acceptable size in the U.S. Using a different size to stand out on a recruiter's desk means that your resume will be the first to be tossed in the trash can. Odd-sized paper doesn't fit file folders well and requires extra handling; do not expect anyone to accommodate an unusual size or shape.

Color of Paper: White or ivory is acceptable. Avoid high brightness, which is indicated with a numeral on package labels. For example, "Brightness 110" is a very bright paper that might be used for an announcement flyer. For business and resume purposes, it is glaringly white and may irritate the reader.

Weight of Paper: 24 lb. weight is appropriate. Photocopy paper is 20 lb. weight and sometimes 16 lb. These are too light for the purpose of a resume.

Content of Paper: Smooth bond or linen are typically good choices. Avoid papers that are textured or include decorative fibers.

Typeface and font: The traditional typeface choices are Times Roman and Arial. The font, or size of type, should be no smaller than 11 point and no larger than 13 point. Most default settings of word processing software are 10 point and 12 point; be aware of this and change 10 point text to 11 or 12. The worst choice is to set the type in a script typeface or one of the standard typefaces in italic. The resulting text is hard to read and may make the resume unacceptable. Similarly, do not use ALL CAPS in the text and do not boldface more than a few words.

Electronic typesetting: Because most resumes must also be sent electronically, it is important to format them so that they will be received unchanged. For this reason, use one of the standard typefaces (Times Roman or Arial) and do not use underscoring, italics, or tables. Do not use justified margins; instead, select Flush Left typesetting. Use centered text very sparingly; at most, use it for category headings. Send the file to yourself and open it on several different computers to test the formatting.

Color of Ink: Black ink on white paper is the preferred choice. Other ink colors may not photocopy clearly or, in electronic versions, may not appear in the shade you intended.

Margins: Leave a minimum of 1 inch on all sides.

Length: One page is typically expected.

Photograph or other image: Do not use in the resume.

Additional Specs for the Electronic Resume. *File type:* Some employers specify Word documents (.doc file extension) but, most of the time, you will not see a file type requested. The safest submissions are rich text format (.rtf file extension) and portable document format (.pdf file extension). Rich text can be produced by any leading word processing software; select it through a "type of file" option when saving the file. Always check a rich text file to see if it carries the formatting you intended. From virtually any type of document, a PDF file, readable with Adobe Acrobat, can be created. If your computer cannot generate a PDF file, you can submit a Word document or other file to free Web services that convert it to the Adobe format. Search for "PDF converter" on the Internet. PDF documents embed the formatting and fonts so that the resume appears just as you created it. The resume can be read on virtually any computer in the world. Avoid file formats that are not common, because they generally require special software on the recipient's computer. Opening and reading files created in WordPerfect and Microsoft Works is not always possible, for example.

Delivery mode: As you distribute the resume, keep in mind that an electronic copy is almost always received as an attachment to e-mail and, therefore, needs a filename that is immediately recognizable and easily retrieved. Your surname and the word resume is a safe label: "Jones_Mary_resume.rtf" would communicate what you need a recruiter to know. This filename would signal the recipient that applicant Mary Jones has submitted her resume in rich text format. Having your name on the file will help keep recipients from losing your resume among all the others submitted—or having to take the time to rename it. Appreciate the value of a file that identifies you in the filename rather than one labeled "resume.doc" or, even worse, "resume-final-version .doc"! A one-page resume should be of small file size and easily e-mailed; send the resume to yourself first to confirm that it arrives and that it is the final version that you intended to send. This trial e-mailing is a good time to include your proofreader for a final check on text and format. Someone else can spot errors that you cannot see because of your familiarity with the page.

✳ THE PORTFOLIO

What is a portfolio? While the resume is a one-page snapshot of your qualifications and work history, the portfolio is a collection of examples of your work and evidence of your performance or potential. The portfolio is usually a selected collection intended to highlight your best work (see Table 8-5). While art students have traditionally prepared portfolios to display their work, the student portfolio is now seen in wider use across disciplines. If you completed a portfolio during your schooling, you may be able to use that as the basis for a job search portfolio. Format can be print or electronic; the electronic portfolio has the advantage of being available over the Internet or on a CD or DVD. It can be easily duplicated and, therefore, left with the potential employer. A print portfolio, commonly bound in a notebook, might be able to be duplicated, but few employers would be interested in storing it.

Table 8-5 **Possible Contents of the Portfolio**

Basic documents	Resume
	Statement of philosophy
	Educational history, course list, or transcript
Samples of course work	Lesson plans submitted to demonstrate understanding of DAP
	Webliography of parenting support Web sites
	Policy brief on grandparents' legal rights
	Interview with K–3 curriculum specialist
	Report on observations at a NAEYC-accredited preschool
	Audio clip or podcast describing community services for seniors
	Research paper on American applications of Reggio Emilia
	Paper comparing state standards for infant care
	Images of self-created learning materials
	Photographs from study or travel abroad
Samples from the workplace	Video clip of leading story time with young children
	Video clip of leading recreational activity with school-aged children
	Video clip of working with a child with developmental disabilities
	Report or reflection on internship
	Internship supervisor's evaluation
	Log of hours from internship
	Photograph of internship site, brochure about site
Samples of professional development	Certificate of in-service training
	Membership certificate for local NAEYC chapter, student NCFR chapter
	Honor society activities and membership
	Evidence of community education course on conversational Spanish
Evidences of qualifications	Audio clip of dialogue in Spanish or other languages
	Evidence of computer technology training or skill
	Certificate of CPR training, First Aid Training
	Photographs of products demonstrating unique skills

The portfolio has the potential to make you a memorable job candidate. Evidence of your abilities can be visual, such as photographs of products demonstrating unique skills. For example, if you are applying for a teaching job in family and consumer sciences, a photograph or video depicting your cake decorating ability would be appropriate. Other examples of your skills might include the actual learning materials that you created for a "Make-and-Take" workshop for parents of toddlers, such as a recipe with a photograph of the matching healthy snack, or a lesson plan on healthy snacks for toddlers illustrated with a photograph of your sample served to the participants.

Share your portfolio with multiple reviewers—peers and instructors—for their reactions to your selection of evidences. You will want to be certain that your meaning is clear as well as your files easy to load. These evidences should showcase your best work and make an employer want to see more. This same portfolio could be used after you get the job to introduce yourself to the parents of the children you will be serving or presented in a staff meeting with new colleagues.

Specs for the Print Portfolio

A print portfolio is probably not your first choice for delivery method. A potential employer might not want to receive a bulky notebook—accompanied by problems of storage or returning it to the applicant. The print version is also more difficult to circulate among hiring decision makers. However, if a print copy is requested, you will want to be able to provide it, being selective about the contents. Try to avoid the appearance of a scrapbook stuffed with photos and memorabilia. Provide a table of contents with clear organization. Use photographs only related to your work, with appropriate professional captions. Stickers and cute artwork should be reserved for your personal albums, rather than the professional portfolio. Stick with the standard 8.5 by 11 inch size for ease of sharing. Do not use plastic sleeves for every page in the notebook. Include easy-to-read and easy-to-handle tabs to divide the materials into logical sections. Identify your name on the outside spine and front cover of the notebook; include your name and mailing address on the inside cover, along with other contact information.

Specs for the Electronic Portfolio

An electronic portfolio can be distributed or shared by providing the URL to potential employers. E-mail yourself with the link before e-mailing it to others so you can make sure it links to the site you desire and is not a broken link. If you have other links within the portfolio, such as links to your own Web site or to a Web site for an organization where you completed your internship, also check those links.

Use restraint in the use of graphics, animations, animated gifs, videos, and sound effects. Just because you are technically able to animate something doesn't mean it is necessary or advisable to do so. Also, the recipient of your portfolio may not have the same equipment as you; the colors could change or the animation could falter. Video clips should be no longer than one minute in length. If children are shown in any photographs or videos, be sure you have obtained parental consent.

File types should be the most common ones used on the Internet and opening/downloading times for files should be measured in seconds, not minutes. Design the portfolio so that it is equally effective if viewed from a CD or DVD. If you distribute such media to employers, test every CD beforehand to check that it opens properly, is easy to access on any type of computer, and is clearly labeled.

Make a conscious decision about including personal information on a portfolio housed on the Internet. Although you may have already distributed your address and phone number through a Web posting of your resume, the portfolio is a more substantial representation of your life. You may choose to display only an e-mail address on screen. To minimize the chance of search engines picking up that e-mail address (for sale to marketing lists, for example), you can display an image of the address rather than a typed address.

If your Web-based portfolio includes academic course work, review each item for appropriateness. A project cowritten by other students is not a good inclusion, even if your coauthors do not object. A class paper recounting an interview or observation may not be a good choice because your interviewee probably did not consider Web publication when giving permission for the interview. A project from your internship similarly may not be appropriate because your site may have approved the project for sharing in your campus class but not imagined wider public display. If such items from an academic portfolio are removed before posting to the Internet, you will then need to make a detailed technical review of the portfolio. Check to see whether the menu for the portfolio needs to be edited so that removed items are not indicated. Check to see that actual files were removed, instead of just deleting hyperlinks to them. Add copyright notices and explanation of authorship as needed.

✳ THE INTERVIEW

When the job search produces an invitation to interview, you may become highly anxious. Remember that the employer has invited you because a manager or recruiter recognizes the potential of a good match. You can assume that you have a chance of securing the position because the employer does not waste time on unqualified candidates.

Arrangements for the interview may include travel. Some costs may be paid directly by the employer (such as air travel and car rental). Other costs may be reimbursed after the interview. Read guidelines closely so that you understand the procedures and know what records you should keep. If you will need a rental car, be aware of age and insurance restrictions.

The first step in the process might be a phone interview, especially if you live at a distance. Phone interviews help screen for the best candidates and allow the employers to clarify questions about your resume or experience. You also have the benefit of asking direct questions to insure that you want to pursue the opportunity further.

Use the list of frequently asked questions in Table 8-6 to role-play or rehearse your answers. While you want your responses to sound natural and unmemorized, it helps to anticipate difficult questions.

On-site interviews may be scheduled in individual or group formats. You might meet several representatives of the company at once in the group interview. This format can be intimidating as the questions multiply. This structured setting may be more strenuous than a one-on-one interview, which is more likely to feel conversational. To your benefit, the group interview allows you to see different players within the group or understand how the job interfaces with different parts of the company.

Table 8-6 **Frequently Asked Questions in Interviews**

1. What is your ideal job?
2. What should we know about you?
3. What are your strengths and weaknesses?
4. What do you know about this organization?
5. What motivates you?
6. What would a former boss or former colleagues say about you?
7. Why are you interested in this position?
8. What are your long-term career goals?

Testing could a part of the interview day, including anything from personality testing to drug testing. These are likely to take place in a human resources or employment office. Testing in the interview might include asking you how you would handle certain situations or scenarios. An example might be, "How would you answer a frustrated parent who asks, 'Why isn't my three-year-old learning to read in your class?'" In a Child Protective Services office, an interview question might be, "What makes a good parent? Are you prepared to recommend that someone's parental rights be terminated?"

An all-day interview might include a shared meal with several employees. If this is the case, be conscious of your table etiquette and brush up on rules of manner if you need to. Know how much is appropriate to tip. Order a menu item that you can eat neatly and that will allow you to take part in conversation. If you have special dietary preferences, quietly discuss that with your server or order an item that requires no special preparation. Do not order an alcoholic drink, even if everyone else at the table does. Be prepared to pay for your own meal; the policies of reimbursement vary among companies, and you may also need to secure a receipt.

Be alert throughout all the activities and assume that you are being observed at all times. Your behavior in the waiting room may be reported by a gatekeeper, such as a receptionist. Some companies consider this person's report a key part of the interview record. Your polite demeanor should extend to all people in the environment. Be courteous to everyone, making no special demands. Keep any complaints, comments, or frustrations to yourself. Wait until you have left the site before updating friends or family.

By the end of the interview, you may be anxious to know how you did. In most cases, you will not be given an answer or offered a job on the spot. Thank the interviewer for the opportunity of applying and ask if there is any other information you can provide. Follow up with personal notes to the people who participated in your interview. A simple thank you is appreciated; you may comment that you hope to see them in the future. The note can be sent as e-mail or handwritten.

Logistically, you may have other follow-up if you are to be reimbursed for travel expenses. Act promptly to submit receipts as directed. Note limits to the reimbursement and do not ask for amounts over those limits.

✳ ETHICS OF THE JOB SEARCH

Nearing the end of your undergraduate career and entering the exciting phase of job searching, you may like the change of pace and focus in your life. In addition to talking to recruiters locally, you may be offered interviews that involve traveling to other cities. While a free trip is attractive to most students, think about the ethics involved in accepting such a trip. Are you seriously interested in the position? Would you really move to that location if offered the job? Is it fair to the company involved for you to take the trip at their expense if you have no intention of considering that job?

Some job applicants also push the boundary of what is ethical by collecting job offers to use as bargaining chips with a company they really want to work for. In other words, applicants might think it's possible to increase their worth to a company if they have multiple offers from other employers. The idea is that it might be possible to negotiate a better salary. Again, such a strategy isn't ethical or aboveboard if you are not serious about the offers. Misleading recruiters or employers could cause problems later if you decide to apply at a company you have previously turned down.

Ethics also come into the job search when you are competing for a job with other applicants. Some employers might ask you to comment on why you are superior to other applicants. It's a good idea to role-play such a situation; think through how you can highlight your own strengths without criticizing another applicant. You might even know the other applicant. There may be a temptation to bad-mouth a peer who you know is applying; such a strategy almost always backfires, because company recruiters consider the applicant's comments a personal reflection and not an accurate assessment of the other job candidate.

Another question to ask yourself during the job search is how long you are willing to commit to a position. The expectation from the employer is often for a commitment of at least a year. If you terminate before a year's anniversary, you could be asked to reimburse the company for any moving expenses or travel funds. Even if the company has not paid for your moving, they have invested in training and orienting you to the position. It's unlikely that they will realize a return on their investment if you are with the company for less than a year.

One of the most perplexing job search ethics concerns, for both female and male applicants, is the question of how home responsibilities may impact starting a new job. The question often arises for women about whether or not to disclose a current or anticipated pregnancy. While there is no legal responsibility to inform a potential employer, applicants may struggle with the ethical question of whether withholding information is misleading. Private information decisions extend to medications, former illnesses, and even family medical histories.

Privacy concerns are addressed in law, and modern regulations such as the Family Educational Rights and Privacy Act (**FERPA**) guide institutions in terms of handling and sharing personal data. These foundations serve to make employment fair, but they do not solve everyone's concern about disclosing or not disclosing all conditions.

Some questions are off limits in all employment settings, including the interview: personal background, marital status, lifestyle choices, sexual orientation, and history of pregnancies. Candidates may decide which topics they *want* to share with recruiters or interviewers. For example, an applicant may want the recruiter to know of an upcoming wedding because the applicant

FERPA

Family Educational Rights and Privacy Act, the federal legislation that protects privacy of student records, through control of access.

prefers to begin a job only after that event. Vacation plans present a similar dilemma for some people, as might family pressures about participating in traditional holidays.

✳ THE JOB OFFER

The excitement of receiving a job offer is quickly replaced with worry about what to do next. The answer may be directed by the method through which the job offer is made. If you receive a telephone or e-mail offer, your next step is to ask what the timeline is for your response. If you receive an offer letter (in-person or through the mail), you are more likely to have that timeline spelled out in print already. Employers usually do not expect applicants to accept an offer on the spot; you will probably have at least several days to consider how you want to respond. Pragmatically, your response will be influenced by how many other offers you expect to receive.

From the employer's perspective, what's the supply of graduates with your degree? If you are in a large pool of applicants, the salary may not be negotiable. On the other hand, if you have a highly valued, unique skill that is in demand (the pool of applicants not being likely to duplicate your skill), the salary and other aspects of the job may be negotiable.

Even if you don't consider salary negotiation an appropriate activity for an entry-level job and your instinct is to take whatever salary is offered, you need to be aware of the long-term impact of initial salary. Often future raises are percentage increases, based on your starting salary. Starting low might mean you stay low for your tenure with that organization. It may be worth stating this to the hiring personnel to see if the salary has any room for negotiation.

Salary, of course, isn't the only reason to accept or reject a job. You might value the experience of the type of employment or working with a certain colleague or even the chance to live in that location. The job might be considered a "starter job," or one that provides entry into your chosen profession. It could be important to start at the bottom to gain the necessary experience to be promoted later.

If a job offer is received, ask how negotiable the start date is. You might need to take a break after graduation rather than start work immediately. Or, you might need to start as soon as possible in order to get that first paycheck sooner! Sometimes the start date is planned to overlap with an employee who is leaving so that you can receive training from that person. If this is the case, but you need time to relocate to the community, ask the employer about any support you can have to make a smooth transition. The employer may be able to help with temporary housing or pay for a house-hunting trip (also appropriate for apartment hunting) so that you can report to the job at the most advantageous time.

✳ ON-THE-JOB CHALLENGES

Having an appropriate wardrobe is sometimes a challenge for a new job holder. Observe the clothing of others in similar positions; sometimes you can learn tips from observing what works for others. Many large department stores offer seminars or the services of personal shoppers who can help with putting together basic wardrobes. Focus on classic looks rather than the newest fads. If you are working with different groups or teaching different classes each day, you might need fewer outfits. Remember that your clothing is not the focus. You don't

When selecting a starting wardrobe, an intern should observe the clothing of others and focus on classic looks rather than the newest fads.

want to be remembered on the job for what you wear—good or bad. Let your performance be the focus rather than inappropriate clothing or accessories.

Another challenge once you are on the job could be the lack of praise or encouragement from mentors, teachers, or family members. You might wonder how well you are performing. How does your work compare with other employees? For a student accustomed to receiving regular feedback on assignments or tasks, the lack of comments may be a big change. A new employee could have a probationary period with a review scheduled at a certain time interval. However, other new employees may have to wait for a once-a-year review, sometimes on the anniversary of their hire date.

New employees are often faced with many decisions at the start of a job, including those about insurance and benefits. It is often wise to seek counsel from those with special expertise or knowledge in these areas. Be cautious about signing away any rights to insurance benefits or waiving insurance access. Be honest about preexisting conditions that might be relevant to eligibility.

A frequent challenge is making it through the first month before a paycheck arrives. If you relocate or move to new housing, there may be unexpected deposits to pay. Be aware of dates for repayment of school loans or other bills that may now be due. Try to establish a safety net of your own savings or support from family members or close friends. While you want to avoid having to ask your new boss for a loan to support you until payday, you also want to avoid accumulating debt that cannot be repaid. Plan in advance how you will handle expenses, including some that you cannot anticipate.

What if you accept a new job and then discover that it's a bad match? Maybe you are assigned to a supervisor who is impossible to get along with. Or maybe the job description changed because of a grant that didn't come through for the agency or because a school principal reassigned you to a different classroom. Maybe you received your dream job offer soon after you began a job at another workplace. Sometimes, the job just doesn't turn out to be what you expected. Be cautious about burning bridges at any location. Usually, honesty is the best approach. Talk to a mentor before proceeding impulsively. Consider your long-term reputation in the field. How will you be viewed by others? Will that matter? If you received a signing bonus, will you have to re-pay the money if you decided to leave the job? If you received special training, will you be charged those fees? Will you be asked to return travel reimbursements? Be sure you know all implications before resigning from a job that no longer appeals to you.

✳ PROFESSIONAL AFFILIATIONS AND PROFESSIONAL DEVELOPMENT

As a new employee, you will want to utilize various strategies to maintain your level of expertise and to develop new skills. Active membership in professional organizations is one such strategy. Membership dues usually include subscription to a journal with research findings relevant to your field, as well as a newsletter with current happenings within the organization or job listings. Organizations such as Society for Research in Child Development (SRCD), National Council on Family Relations (NCFR), and National Association for the Education of Young Children (NAEYC) have state or area affiliates; you may be able to participate in meetings and develop leadership skills through these groups.

Setting your own goals for expertise you would like to develop or for areas of growth is also an appropriate strategy. For example, you might set a goal of observing a master teacher in another classroom or volunteering in an after-school tutoring program in order to work with a different age group. Reading and travel can improve your cultural competence and language skills. If you find you need additional technical skills, most local school districts offer

Professional development is important. One strategy for gaining new expertise might be to volunteer in an after-school program in order to work with children of different ages.

community education classes; area universities may also offer short courses to supplement your skills.

Such organizations also offer opportunities for formal professional development or continuing education courses. In many occupations, there is a requirement for a certain number of hours of training beyond graduation or a minimum number of hours each year of continuing education units (CEUs). Check your professional requirements carefully to know many hours are required and what documentation is needed to verify participation. Some occupations require additional certification or licensure such as becoming a Certified Family Life Educator (CFLE) through the National Council on Family Relations. Being certified might give you an extra edge when you apply for a job or even when you seek a promotion. Such certifications are a recognized sign of your ongoing professionalism and desire to stay current in your field. Some employers might require that you begin formal course work toward a graduate degree, such as the MAT (master of arts in teaching), MSW (master in social work), or a master's degree credential in your selected field. Talk with your supervisor or mentor about the career ladder or expectations of professional development.

SUMMARY CASE STUDY

Marisha waved to Tiffany and Jennifer, eager to reconnect at the NAEYC conference. The three friends had last seen each other at their college graduation, having shared classes and their internship at Head Start. In the 10 years since, the three women had moved to different areas of the country. Their connection at NAEYC would provide a chance to renew their friendship and catch up on each other's news.

As Marisha listened to her friends' account of their travel to the conference, she wondered if their career paths were similar to hers. After graduation with her BS in Early Childhood Education, Marisha had accepted a job with Head Start, with responsibilities building on her college internship. She continued to enjoy working directly with children and their parents. With only one change in location during her tenure with the agency, Marisha already thought of herself as a lifelong teacher.

Tiffany was happy to share her experiences since college. While she had enjoyed her internship with Head Start, she knew it wasn't what she wanted to do beyond college. What she enjoyed most from the internship was working with the parents, and that led her to a decision to work in community education. Within two years of joining the staff of a family and parenting center, Tiffany began a part-time and on-line graduate program to earn her master's degree. Now, as a Certified Family Life Educator, she writes curricula as well as teaches about parenting. In her 10 years since college, she has worked for three employers. Relating her job history to Marisha and Jennifer, she laughed that her father thinks she changes jobs too often. But she knows her experience reflects a growing trend for her generation.

Jennifer interrupted with her own story—recounting her parents' frustration and worry mixed with pride about her choices after college. She used her Head Start experience to obtain a position at a franchise child care center. She advanced from preschool teacher to assistant director and finally to director, all within four years. At that point, she made the scary decision to borrow money to open her own center. While she works long hours, without days of vacation, she enjoys being her own boss. Profitable from the first quarter, Jennifer's business grew from a small setting to a chain of four centers. Her next goal is to seek NAEYC accreditation for all the facilities.

As the friends' conversation turned to personal lives, they realized the impact of their career choices on their home lives. Jennifer described herself as a workaholic, with little time for anything other than the business of the centers. Tiffany has been able to work from home some, while caring for her young children. As a single mother, Marisha envied Tiffany's home-based employment, having continued to teach every year even while having children. Marisha could never imagine missing the beginning of each school year and, therefore, had accepted that she would have less time in her own home.

As the three women reviewed their career choices and made comparisons with their friends' experiences, they each found something to admire about the others' paths. Having had a common start in an internship, they had nevertheless made very different choices about career and family.

⊙ SUMMARY OF CHAPTER CONTENTS

Self-Assessment and Reflection: Following the internship, taking time to reflect on the experience can ease the pressure of job search decisions.

> *Career-Matching Criteria:* Interest inventories and similar tests can help identify good matches in employment.

> *Assessing Likes and Dislikes:* Your internship may help you realize your preferences for employment, as may your hobbies and volunteer work.

> *Quality of Life Indicators:* While selection of a job may be a first consideration, selection of a community is also important and may encompass decisions about climate, cost of living, commuting distance, access to public transportation, landscape and scenery, and so forth.

The Job Search: Headhunters and company recruiters are among the specialists who aim to screen job applicants to make hiring efficient.

> *Campus Resources:* Offices of career services and employment placement offer guidance, testing, resume consultation, interview practice, and similar supports for graduating seniors. Career fairs are especially valuable for practicing conversation with recruiters.

> *Off-Campus Networking:* The strength of weak ties refers to the highly productive networking between systems of family, friends, and acquaintances.

Internet Research and Resources: The Internet is your best tool for researching employers and geographic locations.

Your Support Team during the Search: Mentors, family, and friends can serve as proofreaders, sounding boards, and informal advisors during the job search as in the early weeks of a new job.

The Resume: Articulating your strengths and abilities may be new to you. Find a friend to help you identify all your strong points for sharing in the resume.

Personal Success Stories: Identify the stories that not only illustrate your positive characteristics but also make you memorable to a recruiter.

Finding Words to Describe Yourself: Describe the context for words, such as cooperative, by detailing that you are cooperative in large and small work groups.

Style of Resume: Length of personal employment history may guide the choice between a chronological or categorical resume.

Content of Resume: Selective information, checked for accuracy, should be held to one page of text unless an employer specifies a different or longer format.

Selecting and Recruiting References: Seek references even before you make job applications so that you have permission to list a name on an application form. To request a letter of recommendation, explain the purpose of the letter and provide a copy of your resume to assist in the writing of the letter.

Presentation of Resume: Look at your resume and imagine how it will be received—either electronically or in print—by a potential employer. Consider the impact of your cover letter, too.

The Portfolio: Selective works compiled in a portfolio can illustrate qualifications and skills for employment.

Specs for the Print Portfolio: A notebook version of a portfolio should be reader-friendly, with clear organization and relevant samples.

Specs for the Electronic Portfolio: A Web-based portfolio requires technical proofreading and consideration of appropriateness of every file.

The Interview: Think through possible questions and answers in an on-site interview and be mindful that every minute of the day may be part of the interview record.

Ethics of the Job Search: Ethical considerations include accepting travel for interviews, commenting on other applicants, and committing to a period of employment.

The Job Offer: Initial salary and start date may be negotiable and worth discussing before accepting the first offer.

On-the-Job Challenges: Transitions to the workplace may include new clothing costs, unexpected bills, and a period of adjustment to the new environment.

Professional Affiliations and Professional Development: Through membership organizations and personal study, professionals maintain their expertise and gain new skills.

DISCUSSION QUESTIONS

1. In the opening case study of this chapter, Christy is unsure about what she wants to do—even after completing a successful internship. Develop a script for what her academic advisor or mentor might say to her based on specific advice found in this chapter.

2. Locate Web sites for two professional organizations. Develop a chart comparing their costs and benefits for persons at your stage of professional development.

3. After taking an on-line career interest inventory, compare the results with your own ideas about your potential career. How were the results similar to what you expected? How were the results surprising?

4. Describe what you enjoyed the most about your internship. How does Csikszentmihalyi's concept of flow (defined in Chapter 7, "Assessment and Evaluation") relate to your feelings about the job?

5. What areas did you determine are growth areas for you? Which of the on-the-job challenges described seem most problematic for you?

6. Compare and contrast characteristics of a resume with those of a portfolio, including both print and electronic versions of each. Describe situations or worksites where each form would be the most appropriate choice.

7. Describe personal information that you think could ethically be withheld in an interview. How would your perspective change if you were the potential coworker or employer?

8. Role-play a situation in which you have been offered a job that matches your interests but does not offer the salary you desire. Create alternative endings of the role-play; how do you feel about each ending?

9. Using the guidelines suggested in this chapter, practice making at least two cold calls to inquire about jobs. How can you improve the script suggested? Describe your results and feelings about the process.

10. Using the summary case study, compare yourself with Tiffany, Marisha, and Jennifer. Which person can you most identify with? Why? How does your own internship experience differ from theirs?

GUIDED PRACTICES

Guided Practices offer structured exercises in critical thinking, observation (including self-observation), synthesis, and self-expression. The title of Guided Practice sums up the purpose of providing a guide: an opportunity that permits practice and does not require a final, ultimate effort.

All of the guided practices can be used by one person or by a group of people. The practices are designed as self-report instruments, meaning that answers are reported by the respondent and not collected by an interviewer or by another person who may speak with or observe the respondent.

There is not a standard amount of time to spend on the exercises. One person may use a guided practice for making a quick check while the next person may choose to spend hours on the same practice. Individual interest in a topic makes a difference in use, as does current need for the topic.

The greatest value is derived when the guided practice is completed with honest answers and observations. Any instrument may generate socially desirable answers, the kind of responses that a person thinks will be acceptable or expected. Especially when related to academic study, an instrument that calls for self-disclosure or self-evaluation risks being answered this way.

Guided Practice:
Importance of Community Aspects of a Job

On a scale of 1 to 5, with 5 being "Very important" and 1 being "Not at all important," rate each aspect of community life that might influence your acceptance of a job. You may add other aspects to the list.

	Very Important 5	Important 4	No Opinion 3	Somewhat Important 2	Not at all Important 1
Commute of under 20 minutes					
Landscape, scenery of my preference					
Access to a college					
Recreation opportunities					
Climate of my preference					
Proximity to family					
Access to public transportation					
Physical facility (cubicle, private office)					

Guided Practice:
Specifying Context for Resume Self-Descriptors

What phrases would you write to explain the context (experience on the job, in a hobby, or in school) that allows you to claim at least three descriptors? You may add your own descriptors to the chart.

Cooperative			
Dedicated			
Enthusiastic			
Patient			
Reliable			

Guided Practice:
Networking

Expand your network of job contacts. Think about *who you know,* your friends and relatives that comprise your inner circle. Next, think about *who they know,* your outer circle of contacts. Talk with at least five friends or relatives in your inner circle to obtain names and contact information for persons. You could practice making cold calls to several of these persons to introduce yourself and state your job objective.

Name of Friend or Relative	Names of Persons They Know
1.	a. b. c.
2.	a. b. c.
3.	a. b. c.
4.	a. b. c.
5.	a. b. c.

Guided Practice:
Success

The purpose of this Guided Practice is to compare and contrast different definitions of success, then to derive your own personal definition, unique to you at this point in your life. For each person described or named, draw a symbol of what you think *success* means to that person. For example, for one person, success could be financial security; for another, success could mean fame.

1. A young child

2. A high school senior

3. A mother of a newborn

4. Your mentor at work

5. You, today, at this point in your life

Guided Practice:
Future Goals

This guided practice is to help you focus beyond the field experience, toward what you will do next in life. Think about your ideal lifestyle and how you will accomplish those goals during the next few years.

In five years, I will live in…

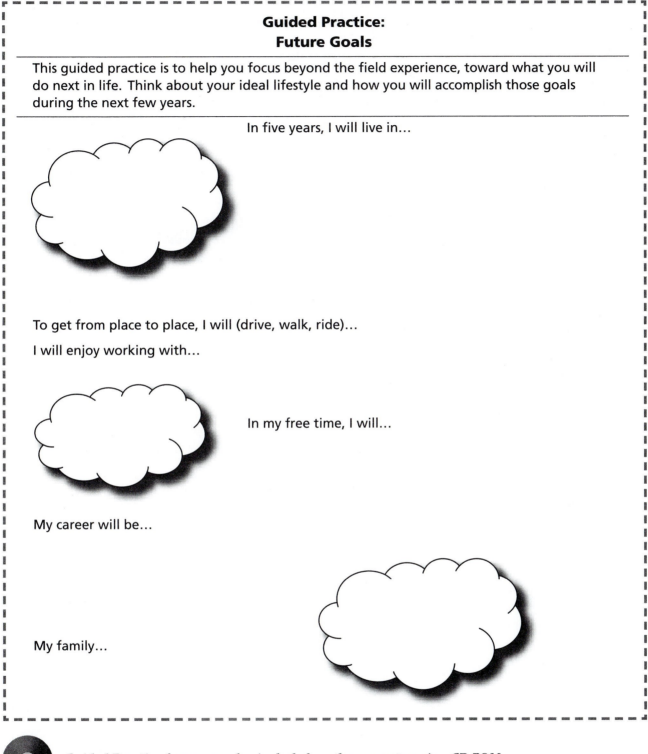

To get from place to place, I will (drive, walk, ride)…

I will enjoy working with…

In my free time, I will…

My career will be…

My family…

Guided Practice forms are also included on the accompanying CD-ROM.

ADDITIONAL RESOURCES

Helpful Web Sites: Rich Internet resources of data are available from organizations and agencies such as these.

Annie E. Casey Foundation, http://www.aecf.org

Council for Professional Recognition, http://www.cdacouncil.org

National Center for Education Statistics (NCES), http://nces.ed.gov

National Council for Accreditation of Teacher Education (NCATE), http://www.ncate.org

ZERO TO THREE: National Center for Infants, Toddlers and Families, http://www.zerotothree.org

REFERENCE

Granovetter, M. S. (1973). The strength of weak ties. *American Journal of Sociology, 78*(6), 1360–1380.

For additional material and resources to complement this chapter, the Online Companion Web site can be accessed at http://www.earlychilded.delmar.com.

Glossary

360-degree feedback—multiple reports on one's performance from other employees in the workplace. Typically collected anonymously, the reports are treated as feedback information for the focus employee and are not necessarily a part of the official evaluation process that leads to raises, promotions, and job assignments.

A

abstract thinking—cognition that uses concepts to form generalizations; typically contrasted with concrete thinking, which focuses on actual objects or things at hand.

accountability—responsibility of an agency or institution to do the job it is charged with.

acculturation—process of adapting to a different set of rules and behaviors.

ADHD—attention deficit hyperactivity disorder

advocacy—actively supporting a cause or position, especially for the benefit of others.

aggregated data—data that are systematically collected and combined, reflecting assessments over time and/or assessments from multiple locations or sources.

ambiguity—more than one correct interpretation or multiple good choices.

andragogy—study of learning by adults.

assent—agreement by a child to participate in research.

assessment—measure or test that reports on ability or performance. Purposes can include screening, determining aptitude, and measuring skills.

assimilation—process of adopting the characteristics and norms of the organization.

autonomy—self-determination; being able to make decisions and life choices without relying on others.

B

beneficence—helping others achieve their goals, as they understand them.

big five—a noncausal explanation of personality traits that appear to be defined across many languages: intellect, conscientiousness, surgency (extroversion), agreeableness, and emotional stability. Tests of the big five indicate overlap among the domains.

blog—shortened form of *Weblog,* which is an online journal or diary, typically posted in reverse chronological order.

boundaries—borders or limits; in a family system, borders may indicate membership or activity in (or out of) the family unit.

broken window thesis—idea that the condition of specific environmental elements (such as broken windows in a deserted building) reflects overall health of a community or residents' commitment to it; idea that untended elements in a community influence the processes of the community.

C

capstone—culminating event or decisive moment; the internship or practicum is often described as a capstone course, typically meaning it is a concluding course or represents the final stage of undergraduate education.

career credentials—certifications or documented training that enhance employability. Examples: First Aid, CPR, hotline response training, ROPES training, conflict resolution training.

change model—unique set of processes that describe how an individual or institution adapts to a changing environment.

clientele—target audience (such as a school population), clients, patients, program

participants, customers, service recipients.
(Terms are program-specific.)

collaborative work—professional activity conducted in small groups or teams, in concert with colleagues or coworkers toward common program goals.

community education—informal education or instruction, typically taking place outside of schools.

competency—proficiency or ability to perform at a high level.

concomitant learning—a gain in knowledge that is ancillary to the primary and intended learning. For example, in learning to drive, an adolescent gains knowledge about the main task (driving) and concomitantly learns about car maintenance (adding fuel, checking oil, checking air pressure).

confidentiality—protection of personal information and identity, sometimes utilizing anonymous or pseudonymous references.

conflict management—the use of skills, techniques, and attitudes to control the effects of conflict, even if the conflict is not resolved or ended.

conflict mediation—the use of procedures, especially those based in communication, to resolve conflicts through intervention by a specially trained facilitator.

conflict resolution—broad description of the study and practice of using skills for problem solving and ending conflict.

consensual meanings—shared meanings or definitions that most people agree to.

continuous improvement—program goal of ongoing improvement in terms of more efficient processes or more effective outcomes.

copyright—legal right granted to an author, composer, or publisher to exclusive publication, sale, or distribution of an artistic work or program.

cortisol level—measured level of steroid hormone produced in the body when a person is under stress.

court-ordered or **court-mandated**—required participation by a judge or court. Common examples: required educational program for hot check writers; parenting education for divorcing parents; parenting education for parents at risk of losing custody of their children.

criterion-referenced—test or measure of a student's skill level or knowledge against one criterion (or several criteria) that would reflect mastery.

crystallized intelligence—learned abilities or stores of knowledge gained through exposure to a culture; often associated with facts and experiences.

cultural competence—acceptance of and appreciation for other cultures.

culture—shared knowledge and practices in a defined setting.

D

deficit model—approach by the family professional that assumes problems or client's lack of ability to resolve problems; reflects opinion that something is lacking in the person or family, especially when compared to the professional.

delayed sleep phase syndrome—chronic disorder in which a person delays the start of sleep, but is able to then sleep soundly into daytime hours. Probably related to circadian rhythm and also associated with adolescence, the syndrome may change over the life course.

dichotomous—divided into two parts or two classifications. Common examples are on/off, yes/no, included/excluded.

diffusion theory—description of how a new technology, idea, or approach is adopted, typically over time and across an entire population.

divorce education—instruction on effects of divorce (especially on effects on children) directed to parents who are divorcing or divorced. Typically, sessions are short (half day or less) and number just a few.

dual relationship—overlapping personal and professional relationships, or overlapping multiple professional roles.

E

early adopters—first people in a group to adopt a new technology or idea.

eclectic method—making decisions or selections in terms of what is best for that situation (drawing from multiple sources, theories, or styles) rather than following one doctrine (or theory, or style) when a decision or selection is needed.

ecological—relating to the relationships and interdependence of humans and their environments (both physical and social).

ecumenical—nondenominational; representing many different faiths.

effectiveness—how well a program or initiative accomplishes its goals or aims.

elevator speech—concise and practiced speech that can be delivered in a short time span of 30 seconds to three minutes; typically delivered as a self-introduction, the speech can be used in any setting but was named *elevator* to draw attention to the requirement for a short presentation (as if in an elevator traveling between floors in a building).

empowerment—supply access or ability for a person to act on one's own.

ethics—personal principles leading to critical reasoning and reflection on conduct.

evaluation—measuring (often with multiple assessments) that supports analysis and conclusions about ability or performance.

experiential—hands-on learning activity involving participants.

F

facilitator—discussion or activity group leader (rather than teacher or lecturer).

family strengths—characteristics of a family that enable them to meet challenges and function on a daily basis. Examples of strengths: resilient attitude, sense of humor, resources such as employment or emergency savings, shared sense of purpose or goals.

fair use—allows limited use of copyrighted work for educational purposes without the written permission of the author.

faith-based setting—agency or program affiliated with or sponsored by a religious organization.

family life education—instruction in or facilitation of knowledge, practice, and skills that individuals and families can use to enrich their lives.

family life educators—professionals whose knowledge base includes human development and family processes.

feasibility—ability to be accomplished.

feedback—information that is returned to the system; as a process, a loop of information that returns and changes the system, which produces more output, to be returned to the system. In a family system, feedback is information that influences change and relationship dynamics.

FERPA—Family Educational Rights and Privacy Act, the federal legislation that protects privacy of student records, through control of access.

filter—software that blocks a computer's access of certain Web sites or certain content, according to settings that are amendable by the computer owner.

firewall—hardware or software that protects gateways (entry points) between the Internet and a network or computer system and prevents an unauthorized outsider from accessing the files and computers.

five factor model (FFM)—a biosocial explanation of personality as consisting of domains of openness to new ideas, conscientiousness, extroversion, agreeableness, and neuroticism. The model's domains are also known by the acronym OCEAN. Tests of the FFM identify people's traits in all the domains and do not sort people into personality types.

flow—mental state characterized by intense focus or concentration on a task and virtually no awareness of time passing or of local events or setting.

fluid intelligence—reasoning ability that does not depend on what has been learned in a culture; often associated with the nonverbal mental processing in solving puzzles or adapting to a new condition.

formative evaluation—ongoing assessment of a program's effectiveness and other measures of performance.

fraud syndrome—common response to stress or a new situation due to inability to internalize success, making the individual doubt his or her ability to perform at a task; aka imposter syndrome.

G

gain score—the difference between a pretest score and a posttest score.

gentrification—restoration of deteriorated neighborhoods, replacing old buildings through renovation or new construction. Typically, property values increase, necessitating a change in residence for some of the original owners.

GLBT—gay, lesbian, bisexual, and transgender people, referring to parents of a family; sometimes reordered as LGBT.

groupthink—going along with the consensus of the group.

H

HIPAA—Health Information Portability and Accountability Act, passed by Congress in 1996 to regulate patient access and control over their health records; designed to safeguard security and confidentiality of records.

I

IM—instant messaging through services such as Google and Yahoo!

industrial psychologist—professional trained in the branch of applied psychology that addresses workplace behaviors, management of a labor force, and other issues of the workplace.

informed consent—agreement by a participant to be involved in a research project after receiving full information about procedures and any risks or benefits.

innovators—inventors or creators of new technology or ideas.

internal organs—communication publications created by businesses and agencies for targeted internal and external audiences.

internship—structured and hands-on student activities across weeks or months, synthesizing content knowledge, observation, and field experience; also known as practicum or field experience.

intervention program—crisis- or problem-focused program incorporating clinical techniques through which professionals treat groups, families, or individuals.

interventionist—professional whose work is primarily in making interventions when individuals' crises interfere with daily functioning and require external help. Example careers include Child Protective Services caseworker, CASA family advocate in the courts, victims services coordinator for the police department, disaster response team member for Red Cross or FEMA, substance abuse counselor, and adolescent suicide prevention counselor.

J

job performance—workplace behaviors related to the process or accomplishment of a job function or role.

journal—record of events, typically written daily or weekly.

K

knowledge base—understanding of essential elements of a phenomenon or setting that lead to further learning and expansion.

L

laggards—people who resist change and delay adoption.

late adopters—those members of a group who are slow to adopt changes.

lexicon—specialized vocabulary, or stock of terms, that is applicable in a particular profession, field of study, or style of work.

liability insurance—protection against damage caused unintentionally in the conduct of your duty. In some fields, this is called malpractice insurance.

Likert scale—specific type of scale or instrument that has a set of at least several items and a horizontal row of labeled response levels. The originator, Rensis Lickert, intended the items to produce an average response to represent an attitude. (Pronounced "Lick-ert.")

long-term career goal—eventual professional position or desired career path, frequently described in a 10-year plan or similar long view.

M

mastery approach—educational consideration of a student's learning based on what the student knows or what the student can do. This approach does not compare the student's performance to other students' performance.

mentor—experienced professional who serves as guide, advocate, and facilitator for a new professional in the workplace.

mentor—model, supervising professional, guide, advisor, facilitator, friend, experienced worker, manager, teacher. (Terms may be field-specific.)

middle majority—the largest number of group members who accept change and adopt new standards or products.

N

nature versus nurture—the scholarly debate of the relative influence of nature (genetics) and nurture (social environment) on human development, including personality development. Most scholars today maintain that the debate is not *versus,* meaning nature *or* nurture, but a combination approach that incorporates nature *and* nurture; however, the proportion of those elements and, potentially, other elements continues to be debated.

needs assessment—analysis of initial conditions to determine the need, scope, and feasibility of a program. OR analysis of the state of current conditions or services (or lack of) in the community and/or survey of needs for a specific population. Common outcomes of such assessments are identification of program topics or goals, grant applications, and strategies for recruiting program participants and volunteers.

nonzero-sum conflict—the end of the conflict is not represented by the parties "canceling out" each other's position. Thus, resolution could be that both parties lose (lose-lose) or both parties win (win-win).

norm—usual score or value, typically determined by national testing; also called a *standard score.*

normalized—event or process changed to conform to an accepted standard or norm, sometimes by reducing stigma attached to it.

normative events—typical events or transitions experienced in human development or in family life.

O

operational definition—explanation or definition of how a word is used in the current context. For example, in a rubric for scoring a preservice teacher's performance, "unable to articulate rationale for choice of literacy materials" may be the explanatory text for the rating label of "Novice."

outcomes—measurable results of a process.

P

paraprofessional—person in an assisting or support role.

pay grade—job level that typically restricts pay to a specific dollar range, based on experience, training, years of service. Many government entities use standard categories of pay grades, 1 through 15. These are further delineated by numbered steps within each grade.

pedagogy—study of learning by children; also frequently used to refer to learning, teaching, or art of instruction without specifying the age of learners.

personal agency—an individual's self-efficacy, or ability to care for self and advocate for one's own needs.

personality—the collective qualities, traits, and behaviors that are unique to an individual person.

personality disorder—expression of one or more personality traits that interferes with a person's long-term functioning in addition to daily functioning. Diagnosis of a disorder is made by a trained counselor, therapist, or doctor.

plagiarism—using someone else's ideas, words, program, or information without proper acknowledgment and credit.

POV—point of view; perspective or choice of context for opinions or beliefs.

pragmatic—concerned with practical matters; approaching a problem or situation with practical experience or observation, rather than with theory or ideology.

praxis—the integration of ideas and practice; typically, the application of theory or knowledge such as in a field experience. Also a commercial test series.

prepracticum—the preparatory work prior to a practicum placement that facilitates exploring sites and placement options. In some academic programs, prepracticum is a semester course.

prevention program—research-based and goal-focused program incorporating family support measures through which professionals assist groups, families, or individuals.

professionalism—possessing special knowledge and skillfulness.

proprietary information—material that is owned or controlled.

public policy—laws and regulations by which the government allocates resources and sets priorities for action and funding.

Q

qualitative data—information in the form of words, such as written answers to open-ended questions on surveys or oral answers to interview questions.

qualitative methodology—nonnumerical data collection. Research procedures that seek to study through observation, interview, etc.

quantitative data—information in the form of numbers, such as test scores and responses to close-ended questions on surveys.

R

reflexivity—self-analysis that creates change in self simply by virtue of the process of analysis.

reliability—a check on the consistency of a measure, meaning that the measure will produce the same score, time after time.

resilience—ability to bounce back from adversity.

rubric—guideline for assessing performance or learning. Sometimes created as a template for reuse in future assessments, a common style is a table with outcomes listed in the left-hand column and values for rating listed on the top row.

S

scale item—statement that can be responded to with a value; typically several items are listed to permit response about a concept; the values of the responses can then be summed and averaged.

selectivity—commonly a ratio or formula by which the applicant pool is compared to the number of selected interns. A program with a small number of interns selected from a large number of applicants would be referred to as highly selective.

self-monitoring—conscious evaluation of one's own communication and language, including body language.

self-report instrument—measurement tool that the person fills out or answers without assistance. Common self-report instruments are print and on-line surveys.

sociohistorical—view that takes into account the larger social setting as well as the historical era.

solution-focused—short-term intervention or strategy emphasizing desired outcomes.

specs—shorthand for specifications, the details such as size, color, weight of paper.

stakeholders—the people who care about the accountability and effectiveness of a program.

standardized test—assessment or measure that has been used in multiple settings with many test takers to produce a norm or standard score; also called *norm-referenced test*.

standpoint—theoretical assumption that the viewpoint of the person under study has merit and authority, even though it is only one person's (or one group's) interpretation.

subjective definition—the family's or individual's own perception of the situation, including the magnitude of the crisis and the capacity of the family or individual to manage the crisis and emerge from it. Because of subjectivity, this perception may not match an onlooker's assessment.

subsystems—smaller units within a larger unit or system; in a family system, common subsystems are parents, siblings (among children), extended family.

summative evaluation—final assessment of a program's effectiveness and other measures of performance, typically conducted at the end of a program's total life cycle and typically shared with interested parties.

systems thinking—viewing the entirety of the situation, or the big picture. Acknowledges the interconnectedness of parts of a system.

T

TB tine tests—multipuncture skin test for tuberculosis.

teachable moment—time during which a learner is ready to absorb new knowledge about a topic of high relevance.

texting—alphanumeric messaging through cell phone, PDA, and e-mail.

theoretical assumption—statement of a premise that is accepted to be true, on which a theory's rationale is based. For example, social cognitive theory predicts that toddlers learn by observing other people's behaviors; a theoretical assumption is that toddlers have the capacity to observe behaviors. total number of applicants for set number of positions in a program with a known deadline or start date.

triangulation—use of multiple methods and data sources to form conclusions.

U

unidimensional scale—measurement in terms of just one aspect, such as "ranging from heavy to light," without assessing any other characteristic.

V

validity—a check on whether an assessment is measuring what it is intended to measure.

values—beliefs that are held as true and important; can be defined by the individual or by a group or a larger entity such as a business or government.

W

work ethic—a person's attitude toward work exemplified by pragmatics such as attendance and meeting deadlines as well as intrinsic characteristics such as loyalty and commitment.

Z

Zeitgeist—spirit of the time. The German word is pronounced "zite-guyst."

Index